Getting married is one of the most tance and necessity of preparing well for marriage cannot be over-stated—especially when the aisles of the average church are littered with both weak and broken marriages.

Over the past several years, John Henderson's *Catching Foxes* has been one of our go-to resources in all our pre-marriage counseling. John helps engaged couples to truly understand their new covenant together and the impact of the gospel for daily living. His interactive study guide provides couples with many opportunities to discover each other, learn relevant biblical truth, and build a rich foundation for their new life together.

> —**Kevin Carson**, Pastor, Sonrise Baptist Church, Ozark,
> Missouri

Our church has been using this book for years to help couples, young and old, work through a gospel-centered view of marriage. I've yet to find another book that is as biblical and as helpful at engaging the heart when it comes to this topic.

> —**Matt Chandler**, Lead Teaching Pastor, The Village
> Church, Flower Mound, Texas

Finally a premarital book that cuts the fluff and delivers biblically sound preparation that paves the way toward a Christ-centered marriage. Brilliantly laid out, *Catching Foxes* provides couples the opportunity to engage with each other and mentors in honest conversation about vital topics. Faithful to Scripture, each page is packed with solid direction that will both challenge and excite couples to build their marriage according to God's plan. I consider this book an outstanding road map to a God-honoring marriage.

> —**Eliza Huie**, Counselor, Life Counseling Center

Self-centered views of compatibility, relational chemistry, and personal needs are too often the focus of preparation and counseling for marriage. *Catching Foxes* provides a Christ-focused, gospel-saturated alternative. Couples need to see that marriage has been given by God to provide a beautiful picture of Christ and the church. He has given marriage to fulfill and illustrate His mission in the world. They need to see how the gospel connects to their everyday married life. This book can help them make the connection.

—**Lee Lewis**, Pastor of Biblical Soul Care, Radiant Church, Austin, Texas

I am grateful to the Lord for John's work in helping couples who are entering into marriage. John, with his many years of pastoral and counseling experience, prepares couples for the covenant they are entering into by continually pointing them back to the reason for marriage: the glory of God. He provides practical questions, but more importantly he focuses on how each individual heart is corrupted by its own desires and how the gospel of Jesus Christ redeems couples and helps them to move from overly focusing on each other to savoring Christ. I am thankful for his work and how it has aided many of our couples in our premarital ministry at The Village Church.

—**Rachael Rosser**, Counselor, North Texas Christian Counseling

CATCHING FOXES

A GOSPEL-GUIDED
JOURNEY TO MARRIAGE

Marriage is about saying "I do" everyday after your wedding day!

JOHN HENDERSON

*Love,
Jim & Lisa
6/1/2021*

P&R
PUBLISHING

P.O. BOX 817 • PHILLIPSBURG • NEW JERSEY 08865-0817

First published by John Henderson in 2011
P&R edition 2018

Printed in the United States of America

Library of Congress Cataloging-in-Publication Data

Names: Henderson, John, 1974- author.
Title: Catching foxes : a gospel-guided journey to marriage / John Henderson.
Description: Phillipsburg : P&R Publishing, 2018.
Identifiers: LCCN 2017049699| ISBN 9781629953878 (pbk.) | ISBN 9781629953885 (epub) | ISBN 9781629953892 (mobi)
Subjects: LCSH: Marriage--Religious aspects--Christianity. | Marriage--Biblical teaching.
Classification: LCC BV835 .H4567 2018 | DDC 248.8/44--dc23
LC record available at https://lccn.loc.gov/2017049699

To Ruth,
my wife and faithful partner in
pursuing the delight of God in all things.

Thank you for your encouragement and steadfast prayer!

To Gabriel, Faith, Judah, Eliana, and Nathaniel,
our children and constant reminders of the goodness of God.
Thank you for your enthusiasm and endurance!

Catch the foxes for us,
The little foxes that are ruining the vineyards,
While our vineyards are in blossom.
(Song 2:15)

Contents

A leader's guide is available to download
from the *Catching Foxes* page on
P&R's website, www.prpbooks.com.

Acknowledgments

I am thankful to the Lord for all the people He has used in order to bring this book to fruition. In no way could this work have been completed without the help of friends, family, and a host of other authors. I have used very few direct quotations from sources external to Scripture, but many people have still influenced this writing.

My wife, Ruth, and I have been in regular conversation about the contents of this book and the never-ending implications of the gospel for marriage. Ruth has often expressed, in one form or another, that any decent preparation for marriage must include a growing grasp of the grace of God. Ever since Ruth and I concluded that a book for premarital counseling was needed in our church and in surrounding churches, she has been in constant prayer about it.

My friend John Brown has been a source of ongoing wisdom and meaningful conversation that has helped me along the way. The title of this book was his idea.

Jerry Clark, who oversees the premarital counseling ministry at Denton Bible Church, as well as Dennis and Linda Sha, who train couples to provide the counseling, have offered encouragement and direction at various stages in my writing. Eric and Cassie Bryant and Lee Lewis have each provided valuable insight.

There have been several men who contributed indirectly. John Piper, whose preaching serves to remind my soul of the surpassing worth of Jesus Christ and the glory of God as the ultimate reason for everything, has been instrumental in shaping my understanding of marriage according to Scripture. His book *This Momentary Marriage* offers a basic and profound framework for developing a biblical view of marriage.

Paul Tripp and his work have been invaluable. His voice refuses to let me forget the transforming power of the gospel and our constant need of it. His teaching series on marriage, "What Did You Expect?," has been convicting and refining. David Powlison's gracious manner and honest writing have made the living Word more living and the personal God even more personal to my soul. The way he understands, applies, and enjoys Christ and His Word has been deeply instructive and helpful.

From Tom Nelson I have learned the importance of relentless scriptural study. During the past fifteen years, he has helped me to see the endless riches and wisdom of God's Word. While numerous people and their writings have helped me in beautiful ways, Tom has always reminded me to rest on the matchless truth and power of Scripture.

I wanted to acknowledge these individuals because they have influenced this writing in both small and large ways. While I do not quote them directly, their words and work, by the grace of God, have helped to shape my understanding of the Scripture, marriage, and human life.

Introduction

Go forth, O daughters of Zion,
And gaze on King Solomon with the crown
With which his mother has crowned him
On the day of his wedding,
And on the day of his gladness of heart.
(Song 3:11)

There should be no doubt in our minds that Solomon was prepared for his wedding day. The hour of his marriage did not sneak up on him. He was ready. His bride was ready. "How beautiful you are, my darling, how beautiful you are! Your eyes are like doves behind your veil; your hair is like a flock of goats that have descended from Mount Gilead" (Song 4:1).

The parade, the carriage, the columns of smoke, and the vast array of armed attendants signaled a day of triumph and celebration. This wedding had been planned for a while. Indeed, it was "the day of his gladness of heart" (3:11).

We cannot believe, however, that the only preparations for such a day were material or external. After all, the trumpet sounds and smells of perfume would soon fade, and a lifetime of sacrifice, service, and covenantal love would remain. The flowers would wither, and the clothing would wear out, but the marriage covenant was to flourish and strengthen until the end. External adornment was only part of the picture.

"Catch the foxes for us, the little foxes that are ruining the vine-yards, while our vineyards are in blossom" (Song 2:15). Foxes can destroy a vineyard. They love to dig holes and trample vines in search of their prey. They have no regard for the vulnerability of vines and grapes; they care only for their selfish appetites.

With these words in 2:15, Solomon pointed to a critical work that is needed before marriage: finding, capturing, and (if need be) destroy-ing any serious threats to the marriage relationship.

The "vineyard" of any loving relationship and marriage union can be ruined by any number of "little foxes." Pride can reduce the vines of marriage to stubble. Selfish appetites, if left alone, can destroy the sweetness of true fellowship. Extended family members and former lovers can invade the vineyard of marital love with toxins of conten-tion and division. The idols of our hearts have no real concern for our marriage fruitfulness; they only nurture their own personal interests and serve themselves. We all need to know this.

Solomon, inspired by the Holy Spirit, knew that selfish appetites and false idols at work in his heart and the heart of his bride had to be identified and driven away in order for their marital love and affection to grow and blossom. Enemies to a God-honoring union had to be ush-ered out. If the grapes of their vineyard were to fully ripen into marital fruitfulness, then dangers had to be cornered and fenced off.

Surely Solomon was speaking to the condition of their souls and not to actual physical land. He pointed to potential dangers in their relationship, not to the quality of their wedding decor.

God called Solomon and his bride to address matters of the heart before Him and before each other. The critical labor for which He called was not external and physical but internal and spiritual.

This remains true for us today. The most vital preparation for mar-riage is internal. Our hearts must be awakened, matured, and strength-ened in Jesus Christ. We must learn to appreciate the covenant of marriage as God appreciates it. Our hearts must be focused on Him. We must be filled with His grace and learn to follow His Word. After all, a marriage between a husband and wife is primarily, and above all else, about the glory of God and the exaltation of Jesus (see Eph. 5:22–33;

Col. 1:17–18). It is about learning to love another person with the strength that His Spirit provides.

Every generation of God's people lives in constant danger of missing the beauty and seriousness of marriage and, as a result, experiences a shallow and miserable version of the real thing. Whenever we miss its beauty and seriousness, we offer the world and future generations a warped and empty picture of marriage. We then offer them a warped and murky picture of Christ and the church. We all need ongoing, supernatural help in order to notice, enjoy, and project the glory of God in marriage.

The world surrounding every generation of God's people will supply its unique legion of foxes to bring destruction on the vineyard of biblical marriage.

The Word of God offers constant and sure defenses. It offers constant streams of strength and courage to help us along the way. The words of Christ provide a beautiful reminder of what life and marriage are really about, for our sake and the sake of His precious name.

> And He answered and said, "Have you not read that He who created them from the beginning made them male and female, and said, 'For this reason a man shall leave his father and mother and be joined to his wife, and the two shall become one flesh'? So they are no longer two, but one flesh. What therefore God has joined together, let no man separate." (Matt. 19:4–6)

What Jesus declared about marriage—"So they are no longer two, but one flesh. What therefore God has joined together, let no man separate" (Mark 10:8–9)—was something very radical and profound to His hearers at that time. This message was not a new decree from God, because the Old Testament provides this picture of marriage multiple times and in multiple ways (see, for example, Deut. 24:1–4; Mal. 2:13–16); however, this truth was easily neglected. Jesus used strong words to explain an age-old reality. He explained that marriage has always belonged to God. And He was saying that marriage has always been a miracle. Jesus talked about marriage as a miraculous gift from

God—a precious possession that deserves our careful attention and protection. The people of Jesus' day either forgot or failed to notice the splendor and seriousness of the gift. We tend to forget and fail in the same way.

Despite all the wonderful resources and hard efforts that we pour into wedding ceremonies these days, we easily miss the amazing meaning behind the whole show. Behind the beautiful ceremonies, colorful decorations, and snappy outfits, a far more beautiful event—a miraculous event—exists. When an ordinary man and an ordinary woman come together before God and the world to become husband and wife, something extraordinary begins to happen. God joins them together. For this lifetime, at least, He makes them one.

So often we neglect and forget the significance of this union.

At the same time, every generation of God's people may face another (albeit less common) temptation to deify marriage itself, making *it* the primary object of our obsessions and desires. We can worship marriage falsely. As bizarre as it may sound, we can exalt marriage above the Lord Jesus Christ. And when we do, we quickly overlook the central point of marriage: to display God's glory, not our own, and to make much of Christ's eternal union with the church, not our temporary desires. Indeed, constant yammering about the latest strategies for marital romance, new ways to meet spousal needs, and better methods for balancing the household budget can actually, if we are not careful, drown out the majesty of Christ in marriage and thus short-circuit the splendid purposes that God intends marriage to serve.

When we deify marriage, we also miss how God displays His glory and builds His kingdom through a variety of other means and gifts in creation besides marriage. It may seem strange to you, but any one of us can become so preoccupied with celebrating marriage that we fail to behold and celebrate the purposes of God in singleness—to enjoy how those who are not married might contribute to the body of Christ as a whole. Married people may easily become separated from unmarried people, and those with children living at home from those without, who are then separated from the aging, who might as well be separated from people who have dogs or cats or goldfish. Using demographic data as the primary reason for separation in the body of Christ tends to erect walls that the gospel has always sought to demolish.[1]

Hopefully you can see a few reasons to prepare for your marriage prayerfully and thoughtfully. Such preparation can help you to grow your appreciation and respect for the covenant of marriage without making an idol of the institution. This book intends, by the grace of God, to help you understand the miracle and gift of marriage and, through such understanding, to prepare your hearts and lives for the journey you are about to begin. Our goal will be to raise our sights so high, bring our pride so low, and shape our view of marriage so strongly by the gospel that our hearts may be compelled by the Spirit of God to walk every step of the journey in His grace.

So if you are a couple preparing to marry, let me begin by saying, *congratulations!* You have reason to rejoice and be glad. You have chosen to partake in a wonderful miracle. Let me follow by saying this: *Be sober and get ready!* You have chosen to enjoy one of the finest gifts that our God has ever given for life on earth. Marriage comes from God. He designed it in His own mind. He formed it and blessed the union. He owns it. He has attached the glory of Christ and the church to the relationship between a husband and wife. This is what you are getting into—and much more.

Hopefully you have already found an older, wiser, Christ-loving couple to help you along the road. If so, they will be reading this book and learning along with you (and none of us will ever finish learning and growing in marriage on this side of the grave). Yet the real target audience of this study will be you—the man and woman preparing to be joined as one, called to partake of the marriage covenant together, called to worship and enjoy God together, called to reflect Christ and the church together.

---

1. Please read Ephesians 2:11–22—a beautiful passage that addresses this concern.

How to Use This Book

Basic Overview

Catching Foxes has been written to help engaged or betrothed couples prepare for marriage. Written in a semi-interactive workbook format, it guides couples toward a Christ-centered and Christ-exalting paradigm for marriage. It attempts to lay a biblical foundation for marriage and to help couples better understand what God desires for them and from them in marriage.

Although it is possible for engaged couples to complete the book on their own, *Catching Foxes* will be most effective if an older, godly, married couple provides ongoing counsel and direction through this material during the weeks leading up to the wedding ceremony. The material will also be most effective if the discipling or guiding couple can provide ongoing counsel during the months following the wedding.

Catching Foxes can also be used in a small group or large group format. Such an arrangement would allow for teaching and oversight by a pastor or counselor as well as rich small group discussion and interaction.

How the Book Works

Catching Foxes is a fifteen-chapter book containing interactive questions for personal response and discussion. Each chapter includes text to read and Scripture verses to study. Spaces are provided throughout the workbook for readers to use in their responses to questions and exercises. The material from each chapter should stimulate meaningful conversation and prayer between the man and woman who are preparing to marry. This material should also form a framework to be used by the couple who is guiding them along the way.

The first twelve chapters are to be completed before the wedding ceremony. The final three chapters are to be completed in the weeks and months after the wedding ceremony.

Each man and woman preparing to marry should have a copy of the book. Couples are free to complete each chapter individually and then come together for discussion. Or couples can work on the chapters together while answering the chapter questions in their individual books.

No specific timeline is given, so couples will need to establish their own. A couple could complete two chapters a week and finish the pre-marriage chapters in six weeks. The chapters range in length between eleven and twenty-one pages, so two chapters a week could be quite intensive. A couple can complete one chapter a week, or one every two weeks, thus taking twelve to twenty-four weeks for the premarital counseling process. The author definitely recommends taking it slowly and carefully. Walking through a chapter every one or two weeks is probably ideal, but exceptions are certainly expected.

Finding a Couple to Guide You

From my point of view, finding an older, wise, and Christ-loving couple to guide you through the premarital process is essential. Such a couple does not need to look perfect in their own marriage, but they should be striving toward Christ and depending on Him in their daily life and relationship. Your church may provide this couple, or you may need to seek them out on your own. There may be extremely rare cases in which no one is available to help. I pray that the Lord provides an older couple for you. Please take this part seriously.

Once a discipling or guiding couple is assigned or found, you will need to establish when to meet and how many chapters to cover during your meetings together. A *Catching Foxes Leader's Guide* is available on the publisher's website to help the discipling couple guide the premarital counseling process. The leader's guide offers a flexible structure for your meetings together.

Finding a Premarital Counseling Group

The church or ministry community of which you are a part may provide premarital counseling in a small or large group format. If this is the case, then you may not need to find a discipling or mentoring couple. The small or large group environment will offer you the context and structure for the *Catching Foxes* material.

If you cannot find a mentoring couple or premarriage group from your immediate church community, then please know there are various ministries with networks of trained counselors who are available to serve you. The websites of the following ministries provide the names and locations of trained biblical counselors who might be able to help you prepare for marriage well.

- The Association of Biblical Counselors: http://www .christiancounseling.com
- The Association of Certified Biblical Counselors: http:// www.biblicalcounseling.com
- The Biblical Counseling Coalition: http://www.biblical counselingcoalition.org
- The Christian Counseling and Educational Foundation: http://www.ccef.org

Post-Wedding Follow-Up

From my point of view, completing the post-wedding chapters of this book can be extraordinarily helpful. Following up with your discipling couple in order to talk through those chapters and your marriage in the weeks after the wedding will be equally helpful. While a great many couples get through the early weeks of marriage smoothly, another great many couples do not. Ongoing prayer, counsel, and biblical community can help you address any difficulties or questions that may arise.

PART 1

Before the Wedding

1

Telling Your Story

Your faithfulness continues throughout all generations;
You established the earth, and it stands. (Ps. 119:90)

The image of Drew and Rachel sitting on a couch outside my study, waiting to begin our first premarital counseling meeting together, will probably never leave my memory. They looked like they were fourteen years old—as jittery as could be. I came to find out they were a little closer to twenty-two each, but goodness, did they look young.

They didn't have a clue what they were getting into. Neither seemed to care. All they knew was that something really exciting lay ahead and, whatever it was, they were facing it together. Their eyes were wide and bright with equal portions of wonder, excitement, and terror.

A few weeks earlier, someone had told them to get some counsel before jumping into marriage. So here they were.

They had met in a park about eighteen months beforehand. Rachel was jogging with her dog, and Drew was throwing a Frisbee with some buddies. The whole scene unfolded, from the perspective of Drew's friends, in a slow, uncomfortable, even nightmarish fashion. They remember seeing Drew running full speed from the right, looking back over his left shoulder at the Frisbee in flight. They remember seeing Rachel jogging from the left, looking down at the path in front of her. They recall Drew attempting a very impressive Frisbee maneuver in which he kicked his left foot high into the air, letting the flying disc pass under his body and between his legs so that he could catch it with his right hand on the opposite side of his torso. It was a technique Drew had mastered and accomplished many times before. And if Rachel's face had not gotten in the way, according to Drew's friends, it would have been a spectacular grab.

Of course, her face did get in the way. Apparently the sole of Drew's left running shoe hit Rachel's forehead so cleanly and firmly that her entire body went parallel to the ground before she actually landed. Even her dog turned upside down from the abrupt force of the leather leash pulling backward. Drew felt totally horrified. If Rachel had been conscious, she would have heard him crying out apology after apology. By the grace of God, she was out for only a few seconds. She came to consciousness in his arms. The first thing she saw was Drew's face looking into hers with a sense of tragedy and death in his eyes. From her point of view, it was very romantic.

Drew felt compelled to make sure Rachel got home safely that day and received whatever medical attention she needed. He then felt compelled to take her to dinner in order to make reparations. Then he thought it was important and delightful to spend a lot of time with her in the months to follow.

And then he asked her to marry him. He drove her and her dog to the park where they met. They threw a Frisbee around before having a picnic. At sunset, he asked her to marry him; she, without any hesitation, said yes.

They had a great story.

Neither Drew nor Rachel grew up in Christian homes. Drew's parents divorced and remarried when he was young, as did Rachel's. They were drawn to Christ in similar ways. Friends witnessed to them at school and invited them to their respective churches, where they heard the gospel for the first time, repented from their sins, and placed their faith in Jesus Christ for salvation. Their developmental years had been difficult, but the Spirit of God gave them strength to endure. The gospel opened their eyes to Christ and the many benefits of salvation in His name.

Though they weren't entirely sure where the Lord was taking them next, they were thankful for all He had done. They wanted to serve

Him together, but they didn't know what that meant. Almost everyone in their lives believed they were too young to marry, but they didn't really listen. They knew they were young. They didn't know what their future would hold. They knew that Jesus Christ would be with them and for them.

Hopefully you are entering into your preparation for marriage with a good story to tell. Perhaps you are not. Either way, this chapter intends to help you tell that story and to get you further down the road toward marriage.

Certainly the story of Drew and Rachel is not the standard for stories. You will have your own. There will likely be as many stories as there are couples. It is part of what makes premarital counseling so exciting and delightful. No two couples are the same. No two stories are the same. The ways in which the Lord works, moves, and gives grace can never be exhausted. There is always room for another story of God's love and faithfulness in the lives of His people.

Understanding Where We Came From

Personal histories are helpful. They give us a sense of trajectory in our lives. When we are able to see the course of our lives over years past, it can give us a glimpse forward to where we are going in the days ahead and to what needs to change.

If my personal history is full of rage, bitterness, and broken relationships without real heart change, then, if I am honest, I should know that the days ahead will include more of the same. If my personal history is riddled with immorality and drug abuse, but God has brought repentance in my heart and reconciliation in my relationships, then I may walk forward with a sense that God will continue to bring repentance and reconciliation in my life when I am honest about personal sin and cling to His grace.

If I have a track record of dealing with pain by running to Christ, crying out in desperate prayer, and submitting myself to His comfort and instruction, then I can expect that the Lord will remain faithful in these ways down the road. If I have a history of lying, cheating, and avoiding in order to win the approval and praise of people, then I should probably be aware of this and pray for the Lord to alter my course.

Some of us grew up in loving, peaceful homes. Some of us grew up in harsh, abusive homes. Most of us grew up in a home that fell somewhere in the middle. Perhaps your parents left you to navigate life on your own. They were hands off. Or perhaps they examined and critiqued your every move. Your parents may have divorced when you were young, so that you rarely saw your father or your mother. Perhaps relationships with your siblings were a source of joy for you, or perhaps they were a source of pain. Either way, we need to realize that family experiences influence us today. They often matter in ways we do not see, provide a context for understanding our lives, and exert a degree of influence upon our marriages.

Our Personal Histories and the Promises of the Gospel

By the grace of God, our histories do not determine who we are or where we are going—the gospel promises this truth. The gospel is "the power of God for salvation to everyone who believes" (Rom. 1:16).

Even though we all were enslaved to sin and hostile to God from birth, God rescued our souls and made us His children. He accomplished this through His Son, Jesus Christ. Because of our sin, we deserved His judgment forever. Yet God sent His Son to die in our place. Jesus Christ lived a perfectly righteous life. He was crucified as a payment for our sins in order to reconcile us back to God the Father. We are saved because He saved us. We don't earn or deserve it. We receive it as a gift by trusting the Giver and His work on our behalf. We are reborn by the Holy Spirit. When He enters our hearts, we become God's adopted and secure children forever. The trajectory of our lives has changed.

The gospel brings about real transformation. God uses His Word to wash, renew, and mature us over time. The Spirit of God and the Word of God work through and within our life experiences to conform us to the image of Christ, among other things.

Scripture does not minimize our personal histories. It does, however, help us to interpret those histories truthfully, respond to them triumphantly, and behold the glory of Jesus Christ shining through them along the way.

The gospel assures us that our hearts can be filled with (and therefore ruled by) the Holy Spirit. Past experiences, good or bad, assume whatever level of control in our lives the Lord allows them to. Under His loving hand, they assume whatever level of control we allow them to, as well. The sufferings and successes of our past can be seen and understood from God's point of view. Since He uses all our experiences to bring about our true good, then those experiences do not have control of our lives. God does.

The love of Christ should now control us. Second Corinthians 5:14–15 says,

> For the love of Christ controls us, having concluded this, that one died for all, therefore all died; and He died for all, so that they who live might no longer live for themselves, but for Him who died and rose again on their behalf.

If we have been saved by His grace, then we belong to Him now. His Spirit controls our path into eternity. Our lives will follow His perfect design. Will we cooperate or resist Him? Will we stand in awe or stand in protest? Will we walk in the flesh or in the Spirit? Our answers to these questions will govern how much we enjoy the journey.

> Now those who belong to Christ Jesus have crucified the flesh with its passions and desires. If we live by the Spirit, let us also walk by the Spirit. (Gal. 5:24–25)

If we have been redeemed through Jesus Christ, then He determines who we are. We are now "in Him" (see Eph. 1:4–14). In fact, God the Father "chose us in Him before the foundation of the world, that we would be holy and blameless before Him" (v. 4). In Christ, we are new creations: "Therefore if anyone is in Christ, he is a new

creature; the old things passed away; behold, new things have come"
(2 Cor. 5:17). The gospel has delivered deep, lasting, and transforming
grace into our hearts. This changes everything!

Why am I saying all this? So that we will look at our personal histories with honesty and seriousness and will do so without feeling
determined or trapped by these histories. I say it so that you will deal
humbly with who you are and where you have been—and deal humbly
with your fiancé and where he or she has been—in order to apply the
gospel where it needs to be applied and to give no more power to the
past than the Lord allows.

Here is what I would ask of you in beginning this chapter. Please
start with humble prayer. Please thank the Lord for all that He has
brought you through to this point and for the grace that He has poured
on your soul. Then ask Him for wisdom as you respond to the questions and requests throughout this chapter.

The Story of Your Family

Each of us grew up in a family. Perhaps we had a father and a
mother present in our home growing up. Perhaps we had siblings
around. Perhaps we grew up in an orphanage or bounced from home
to home without exactly feeling like we were part of any family at all.
Some of us enjoyed our families as children. Some of us did not.

No matter what your experiences have been throughout your life,
they are important. They do not *determine* you, nor do those experiences compose who you are, but they have *influenced* the way that you
think, feel, and live. They have not *caused* your view of marriage, family,
and life, but they have *impacted* your view. They are worth some consideration at this point of your preparation for marriage.

Now is the time to be honest. Hiding from people now will only
make it more difficult to expose and face truth later. If you have a relevant sexual history, then please share enough of your history to bring
into the light the sins and struggles that should be in the light. If you
were physically abused as a child, please pray for the courage, if need
be, to share about those experiences. If your extended family is marked

by chronic divorce, domestic violence, drunkenness, or anything else noteworthy, then please be open. How have you experienced anger, or hurt, or forgiveness? How have you expressed anger, hurt, and forgiveness?

In the same way, please be honest about the joys, delights, and blessings of your history. If you were reared in a home in which Christ was cherished, the gospel proclaimed, and marriage treated with reverence and wonder, then please don't hold back. If you are overwhelmed by the peace and harmony you have enjoyed in your relationships, feel free to rejoice. Now is the time to start placing any important stuff from your past onto the table.

1. Please share about your life growing up in your home. What were some defining events, whether good or bad?

2. What family experiences do you believe were most profound in shaping who you are today? How do you think they have shaped your expectations for marriage?

3. Share any areas of bitterness, resentment, and shame that remain in your heart concerning your childhood and adolescence.

4. How has marriage been viewed, talked about, and treated in your family?

5. What particular "foxes" might your family bring to your "vineyard"? What particular foxes have you brought from your family into your engagement?

The Story of Your Salvation

From my point of view, this aspect of your story is the most significant and powerful. The supernatural and gracious intervention of God in our lives through Jesus Christ has changed everything—and forever. We should never stop thinking about this and worshiping God for who He is and all He has accomplished for His people. "Praise the LORD! Sing to the LORD a new song, and His praise in the congregation of the godly ones" (Ps. 149:1).

Life may well have been a long series of disasters before we were introduced to Christ, yet all has been made new in Him. Our sins have been forgiven in Jesus Christ. His righteousness has been imputed to us (conferred on us or reckoned to us). Life may be a continual battle with sin and suffering, but we now fight the battle as reconciled children of God rather than enemies of God.

Our lives as followers of Christ could be riddled with sinful escapades and explosions of pride, but He continues to wash us anew.

My little children, I am writing these things to you so that you may not sin. And if anyone sins, we have an Advocate with the Father, Jesus Christ the righteous; and He Himself is the propitiation for our sins; and not for ours only, but also for those of the whole world. (1 John 2:1–2)

Now that we are beloved children of God, our life trajectories have changed forever. The rest of our time on earth can and should be a grateful preparation for eternity, a constant mission to call the whole world to faith in Jesus Christ, and a daily remembrance of His goodness and grace in our souls. We will all stumble along the way, but our course and destination have been charted for us by the sovereign will and love of God.

6. Is your faith in Jesus Christ for your salvation? Please explain your answer.

7. Briefly share how you were drawn to Jesus Christ.

8. Who were the people God used to bring about your initial faith in Jesus Christ?

9. How have you seen the Holy Spirit growing you in Christ over time?

10. Share the areas of life in which you continue to need serious transformation.

11. What does life with Christ look like for you, hour by hour and day by day? Describe your relationship with Him.

The Story of Your Relationship

The way you met your fiancé and the reasons you have pursued each other toward marriage will impact the days to come. If you met your fiancée at a nightclub and want to marry her because you want sex, then you should rethink your motivations for marriage. If you are marrying the man next to you because all your friends are married and you believe this may be your last chance for a husband, then you may want to step back for a moment and consider your intentions. If your relationship has been full of disputes, anger, and fears, with few seasons of selfless, peaceful love, then you have something really important to address before you move further toward marriage.

It may be that you were drawn to each other because of a mutual love for Jesus Christ. It may be that your relationship has been full of peace and humble service. It may be that you share a deep affection for each other and can't really explain it. God may have brought your relationship about miraculously. The relationship may be a mixed bag of selflessness and selfishness, patience and impatience, fear and rest, depending on the condition of your soul in the moment. The spaces below give you an opportunity to present the relevant pieces of your relationship up to this point in time.

12. Briefly share how you came to meet the man or woman you are preparing to marry.

13. How did you get to know your fiancé? How did you come to know that this was the person you wanted to marry?

14. What do you enjoy about your fiancé? What have been the greatest delights of your relationship?

15. Share how you have handled pain and difficulties as a couple.

The Story of Your Engagement

You may have been asked a hundred times before to tell the story of your engagement. This will be another opportunity. Please share the story of how you came to be engaged.

The Story of Your Future

Two people can meet at a moment in time and get along very well while heading in two completely different life directions. A man with dreams of missionary work in Africa and a woman with dreams to be a surgeon in Florida can meet, enjoy each other, and fall in love while spending the summer in Spain. While they are in the same place for a single season of life, they are going in opposite directions. If they are going to spend their lives together as husband and wife, then either one or both of them have to drastically change their life direction.

I hope and pray this is not the case for you and your fiancé. I hope you are not simply crossing paths on your way to separate destinations. If you are, then you definitely need to be aware that you are walking different roads and planning different futures. Even more, someone in your relationship (and perhaps both of you) will need to change course in order for you to spend your lives together. Even if you are headed in the same direction, you still need to talk about your desires for the future and to hear the desires of your fiancé.

16. What are your dreams for your marriage? What do you expect your marriage to be like?

17. Where do you see your life going? Share what you expect of yourself in the future. Share what you expect of your fiancé.

18. What dreams might you need to give up in order to honor God's purposes for marriage and your future mate?

19. What fears do you bring to your relationship? What terrifies you? Share how you intend to respond to these anxieties.

20. How has God gifted you for marriage? How has He gifted your fiancée?

There may be much more that can be said and discussed. The chapter was meant not to be exhaustive but to get you started in thoughtful discussion and prayer. I hope you are able to look back on your life and see the patience and grace of God at work. In the days ahead, I pray that you can more clearly see your experiences and personal story as small pieces of His eternal story.

Please take time in the hours and days ahead to thank God for all He has done. Thank Him for His patience and faithfulness. Ask Him to strengthen you,

> with power through His Spirit in the inner man, so that Christ may dwell in your hearts through faith; and that you, being rooted and grounded in love, may be able to comprehend with all the saints what is the breadth and length and height and depth, and to know the love of Christ which surpasses knowledge, that you may be filled up to all the fullness of God. (Eph. 3:16–19)

2

The Reason for Everything, Even Marriage

*For by Him all things were created, both in the heavens
and on earth, visible and invisible, whether thrones or dominions or
rulers or authorities—all things have been created
through Him and for Him. (Col. 1:16)*

Rick and Pamela sat across from me dejected and angry. All eighteen years of marriage, from their point of view, had been a disappointment. The romantic feelings, the excitement of spending time together, and all the glories of youthful passion had faded long ago. When she talked, he cringed. When he talked, she rolled her eyes and sighed.

His career was difficult, his friends were gone, and his wife was "never happy, always complaining, and more of a burden than a helper." Life as a mom was strenuous for Pamela. She felt trapped at home. "Worst of all," she said, "I don't have a husband who cares or knows how to meet my needs."

Since they were Christians, they felt obligated to stay together. They didn't really understand why. Something about how "God disapproves of divorce." It was wrong to quit, they believed, but hopeless to continue. They were at the end of their rope and didn't know what to do.

They saw only two options: be miserably married or get divorced. They selected the "noble option"—be miserably married—yet God offered them a third and far more glorious way. And the glorious way began with dwelling on Him, not on marriage.

Even though they wanted to talk about marriage right out of the gate, we didn't. They needed to talk and hear about bigger, more critical ideas. Namely, they needed to understand the God of creation and His reasons for creation. So we conversed about the reason for everything in existence. We began looking into the Word of God in order to understand the reason God had created the world, and them, and marriage.

And they were caught a little off guard. After all, no one had ever told them that life and marriage do not exist, first or foremost, for them. No one had ever told them that they are not actually the main reason for their own existence. They had never heard that marriage did not exist to be a delivery vehicle for their appetites, dreams, and personal needs.

Most of us, I would guess, began dreaming of marriage not as a way to sacrifice our desires and wants, but as a way to fulfill them. I know this was the case for me. It was certainly the case for Rick and Pamela. Their marriage was a small piece of a much bigger story. We had to begin there. All of us have to begin there.

A Vision for Marriage Bigger Than Marriage

We cannot really understand marriage unless we understand far bigger and graver truths. Human life with God is bigger than marriage. Eternal life is longer than earthly marriage. God is far grander and far more ultimate than everything else, including marriage. Marriage serves a finer purpose and expresses a relationship that is far more wonderful and eternal than itself.

This may be hard to understand right now. After all, you are excited about getting married. You want to talk about getting married. Why delay the conversation? Because we need a God-centered, Christ-exalting, and Spirit-dependent framework for seeing and talking about marriage. We need more insight into the Person behind marriage and what He is bringing about in this world. A foundation needs to be formed so that future chapters can build on it.

Imagine this. An impressive-looking stranger offers you a curi-ous-looking, complex, and beautiful device, and then says to you, "This treasure is yours to accept or reject. It is designed to be a wonderful blessing to human life. Of course, if you accept it, you are responsible for it. You have to apply and enjoy it properly. Oh, by the way, the treasure explodes when mishandled!" Think about it a minute. Would you accept or reject the treasure? If you were to accept the treasure, what critical questions would you insist on asking before the stranger walked away?

A number of possible questions should race into our minds: What is this thing you just handed me? Who made it? To whom do I answer? What is it meant to do, and how does it work? Is it an independent object, or does it fit into something else? Why are you choosing me? What are you expecting from me? What did you mean by "explodes when mishandled"?

We could probably list more questions, but hopefully the point has been helpful and clear. If we are going to understand marriage in order to prepare for it well, then we must come to know God well in order to gather some sense of what He has been doing with creation, humanity, and marriage, and then to gather some sense of why. We must begin at the beginning.

In the Beginning

God created the heavens and the earth. Everything we see, hear, and smell around us God formed by His spoken word. Genesis 1:3 tells us, "God said, 'Let there be light'; and there was light." The rest of creation followed the same pattern. God decided, designed, and spoke the whole universe into existence.

Now, the ultimate reason that God created the universe was to display and share His glory (see Ps. 19:1–6; Col. 1:16–17). Creation exists to show His power and majesty so that all who behold cre-ation will worship and enjoy Him. "The heavens are telling of the glory of God; and their expanse is declaring the work of His hands" (Ps. 19:1). Since God loves to give Himself and share Himself, He created a universe where He may be experienced and enjoyed by His creatures.

Humanity was the crowning act of His creation. Mankind was made in the very image of God in order to worship, serve, and cherish Him in special ways. "Then God said, 'Let Us make man in Our image, according to Our likeness'" (Gen. 1:26). Though God was eternally happy and content, He formed mankind in order to share His glory with others. His creative acts were not from boredom or loneliness but from the overflow of His loving nature. He decided to make people as a special reflection of His image, as a picture of the loving community that He had enjoyed from eternity (see John 17:20–26).

So, then, we exist first and primarily to glorify and enjoy our God. First Corinthians 10:31 says, "Whether, then, you eat or drink or whatever you do, do all to the glory of God." The reason we live is to reflect our God and enjoy our God. He is the ultimate reason for everything. His perfect and eternal purposes are the reasons that the creation exists and functions as it does.

Often John Calvin, a sixteenth-century French theologian, referred to the created world as a "Theatrum" or "Theatre," in which God's glory is displayed and the glory of His grace represents the main theme.[1] What a beautiful truth! Creation was God's forming and arranging of His grand stage. It exists to provide an organic portrait through which He may display Himself—a kind of living environment in which He could fulfill His eternal mission.

In the theater of God we find a cast of characters, including God the Father, God the Son, and God the Holy Spirit, who exist above and outside the theater while being intimately engaged throughout the whole program. There are angels and demons, people of all shapes and sizes, as well as heroes and villains.

There are settings and stages, plots and themes, mysteries and revelations. Battles, romances, nations, kings, citizens, marriages, families, friends, and enemies all find a place in the show. There are tragedies

---

1. See John Calvin, *Institutes of the Christian Religion*, ed. John T. McNeill, trans. Ford Lewis Battles (Philadelphia: Westminster Press, 1960), 1.5.8, 1.6.2, 1.14.20.

and celebrations. There are victories and defeats, songs and poems, blessing and cursing.

The revealed Word of God describes and explains God's story and purposes. A dominating climax occurs at the cross of Jesus Christ, where all of human history gathers in a heap. The climax continues to the empty tomb, where ultimate victory over sin and death is proclaimed. The plan of God will be fulfilled by story's end, followed by an eternity of wrath and mercy, damnation and jubilation, hell and heaven. The destiny of every character is dependent on the divine Author of the whole show.

We have all been given parts to play in this grand production. We have received His love and mercy. We have been given the privilege of honoring and delighting in God forever. Marriage plays a part in the whole program, as does singleness. Whether we are single or married, our lives are unfolding according to His perfect will and design, and always for our ultimate good. We cannot try to make sense of our lives in isolation, nor can we try to make sense of marriage in isolation from God and His design. Our personal stories and experiences are all part of the bigger picture.

Rick and Pamela, while caught off guard by these truths, found them comforting and convicting to their souls. Their lives and marriage play a part in a grander story about God and His glory—and this realization brought excitement and hope into their previously self-absorbed, despairing way of being married. It moved them away from a need-driven, me orientation toward a grace-filled, God orientation. It helped them slide out from beneath the weight of their individual disappointments. It drove them to greater dependence on God and greater passion in their hearts for His kingdom purposes.

It also provided a way to talk about God's love for them. Their marriage was not an accident. It was a gift from God. They were not the victims of a bad marriage joke. They were recipients of God's good for them. Their marriage had been hard, but God's grace had sustained them and would continue to sustain them until the very end.

The Display and Praise of the Glory of His Grace

> Just as He chose us in Him before the foundation of the world, that
> we would be holy and blameless before Him. In love He predestined
> us to adoption as sons through Jesus Christ to Himself, according
> to the kind intention of His will, *to the praise of the glory of His grace*,
> which He freely bestowed on us in the Beloved. (Eph. 1:4–6)

Perhaps the most ultimate point that Paul makes in Ephesians 1 can
be found three times in the first fourteen verses. Namely, God enacted
His plan of salvation before the foundation of the world to display the
glory of His grace in order to bring about "the praise of the glory of His
grace" (v. 6; see also vv. 12, 14).

If we are God's children, then we have been saved by His grace.
We are saved as a gift from God. We were chosen in Christ, before the
world was formed, because of His grace. The fall of the human race into
sinful, condemned misery was ordained by God before the foundation
of the world so that God would display the immeasurable riches of His
kindness toward us in Jesus Christ. In redeeming rebellious and hostile
people by sacrificing His Son in their place, God shows the size and
splendor of His grace. He shows Himself in all the glory of His grace
so that those redeemed by His grace would praise and enjoy Him forever. The apostle Paul captures this idea quite beautifully in his letter
to Timothy.

> It is a trustworthy statement, deserving full acceptance, that Christ
> Jesus came into the world to save sinners, among whom I am fore-
> most of all. Yet for this reason I found mercy, so that in me as the
> foremost, Jesus Christ might demonstrate His perfect patience as an
> example for those who would believe in Him for eternal life. Now
> to the King eternal, immortal, invisible, the only God, be honor and
> glory forever and ever. Amen. (1 Tim. 1:15–17)

God saved Paul (showed him "mercy") in order to demonstrate the
greatness of His patience as an example to everyone who would believe

in Him. Paul was saved not primarily for his own sake, but for the sake of God's glory and eternal purposes. God reconciled Paul to Himself because He loved Paul and wanted the rest of His people to behold His love for "the foremost" sinner of all.

The realities of the gospel should lead us to worship and adore our Savior. Our salvation was not for its own sake. It gives testimony to the redeeming love of God. This testimony is meant to provoke heartfelt worship.

What was the chief reason that Christ was crucified in our place, His righteousness given to us, His promises attached to us, and His inheritance placed on us? So that God could reconcile His people back to Himself and show the whole universe the splendor of His grace. He has brought about salvation so that He can dwell with His people forever and be rightly known, worshiped, and enjoyed forever. Paul led us through this exact sequence in the verses to Timothy above.

Seeking God above All Else

> The God who made the world and all things in it, since He is Lord of heaven and earth, does not dwell in temples made with hands; nor is He served by human hands, as though He needed anything, since He Himself gives to all people life and breath and all things; and He made from one man every nation of mankind to live on all the face of the earth, having determined their appointed times and the boundaries of their habitation, that they would seek God, if perhaps they might grope for Him and find Him, though He is not far from each one of us; for in Him we live and move and exist. (Acts 17:24–28)

The point of everything, therefore, is God. All that God has created was actually created in order to point to Him. It helps lead us to Him so that we may worship and enjoy Him. He intends for us to seek Him passionately and wholeheartedly, not because He needs us but because He loves us. He has chosen to redeem a people for Himself in order to dwell with them in holy fellowship forever. His joy does not depend on us, but He takes pleasure in us as His children. In no way is God dependent on us for anything, but He delights in sharing Himself with us and saving us to reflect His beauty, majesty, and redeeming love.

These ideas are vitally important in building toward a discussion of marriage. The reason for our lives is, first, God. Whether in singleness, marriage, work, or leisure, we are created to enjoy and worship God. When eating food or teaching children or playing a sport, we are called to partake in these activities with gratitude toward God. First Corinthians 8:6 teaches, "Yet for us there is but one God, the Father, from whom are all things and we exist for Him; and one Lord, Jesus Christ, by whom are all things, and we exist through Him."

Rick and Pamela had spent the first eighteen years of marriage seeking treasures of the world above all else. They cherished praise, honor, esteem, sex, pleasure, money, and a spouse who would help to deliver these goods. They worshiped these aspects of creation daily. Transformation of their marriage first required a transformation of the desires and treasures of their souls.

Once they began seeking Christ, enjoying Christ, and finding deeper satisfaction in Christ every day, they could begin to realize just how blessed and full their lives actually were. Marriage could then assume the right place in their hearts. It was a means to see, enjoy, and serve Christ, not a means to feed their lusts. Each one's mate could also assume the right place in their heart, as a person to love and serve through the grace that God had poured into their souls, not a God-given servant of their selfish appetites.

Here we find one of the most vital preparations you could ever make for marriage: Learn to seek God above all else. Learn to be satisfied in Jesus Christ. Learn to appreciate the infinite riches you have been granted in Him so that marriage assumes the proper place in your heart and life.

1. *Who* are you seeking most passionately? Be honest! Do you seek God, your soon-to-be husband or wife, yourself, or someone else?

2. *What* do you seek most passionately? Again, be honest! Do you seek earthly treasures or eternal treasures—Christ's kingdom or your own?

3. What riches have you been granted in Christ? How can you grow more content in Christ and in what He has for you?

4. What do you think it means to seek Christ and His kingdom in your marriage?

5. How do you foresee yourself misusing the gift of marriage by using it as a vehicle for your own desires and interests?

Taking the Point to Heart

The greatest preparation for marriage is your heart's response to God. He created you to glorify and enjoy Him forever. Through your life He intends to display the glory of His grace so that the whole universe can join in praising the glory of His grace. This is why He sent His Son to die in your place, to reconcile you to Himself, to fill you with His Spirit, and to make you a living example of His eternal love. The ultimate gift of the gospel is God Himself. Christ has brought you back to the Father. The Father has given His Son to you and you to His Son. You have received His Spirit to fill your heart forever.

Do you cherish these truths? Do you treasure Christ? Is He first place in your heart, or is someone else ruling there? As you approach marriage, are you seeking first His kingdom and His righteousness? Do you long for the furtherance of the gospel above all other ambitions on earth?

If you are not seeking God above all else, then marriage will bring frustration, bitterness, and disappointment. Your mate is not God—cannot be God. If you try to worship him or her rather than God, pain will be the result.

None of us enter into marriage with pure motives and desires. Please don't feel the pressure to have your answers perfectly formed or lived out quite yet. What will be important is that you become increasingly aware of God's intention for your marriage and the many ways that your ambitions for marriage collide with His. Ask Him to constantly reform who you worship, redirect what you seek, and reshape the desires of your heart for marriage.

3

Understanding Who You Are

Your eyes have seen my unformed substance;
And in Your book were all written
The days that were ordained for me,
When as yet there was not one of them.
(Ps. 139:16)

A healthy preparation for marriage begins with a growing understanding of God and the reasons He created everything, including marriage. God did not create marriage to exist in a vacuum. It fits into His eternal plan and serves His particular purposes. Our hearts must be prepared by His Word and Spirit to receive and handle the gift of marriage rightly. The previous chapter sought to increase our awareness in this regard.

Another step in a healthy preparation for marriage involves a growing understanding of yourself and other people. It helps to know where you have came from, who you are in Jesus Christ, and where you are going. Since you do not exist in a vacuum either, but fit somewhere into God's eternal plan, your heart must be prepared by His Word and Spirit to see yourself more clearly and biblically. This will help you to approach marriage more clearly and biblically.

Our Beginning

Then God said, "Let Us make man in Our image, according to Our likeness; and let them rule over the fish of the sea and over the birds of the sky and over the cattle and over all the earth, and over every creeping thing that creeps on the earth." God created man in His own image, in the image of God He created him; male and female He created them. . . . God saw all that He had made, and behold, it was very good. (Gen. 1:26–27, 31)

A great many truths about our origin as human beings may be learned from the Genesis story. We will identify three, in particular, from the verses above. First, we were *purposed* by God to exist (v. 26). He decided in His own mind to form the world and everything in it. Second to this, God *created* us in His image (v. 27). The human race was a unique and special part of the creation account and purpose. Third, God *declared good* His creation of humanity (v. 31). That is, God was pleased with His creation of man—with who he was and how he was created.

Every person in the world, therefore, has God-bestowed dignity and beauty. Every person in the world reflects the image of God in a general sense.

Redeemed people reflect God in additional and unique ways. We who are redeemed are slowly being conformed to His nature and glory over time. In us, the Father displays His redeeming love. With us, He forms a bride for His Son. The Father willed to create us through Christ and for Christ so that Christ would have first place in all things (see Col. 1:16–18).

Our Fallen Nature

Even though we were made through Christ and for Christ so that He would have first place in our hearts and lives, we revolted. We rebelled. Though we were created dependent on God—to love, worship, and enjoy God—through Adam we grasped for our own glory and independence.

When the woman saw that the tree was good for food, and that it was a delight to the eyes, and that the tree was desirable to make one wise, she took from its fruit and ate; and she gave also to her husband with her, and he ate. Then the eyes of both of them were opened, and they knew that they were naked; and they sewed fig leaves together and made themselves loin coverings. (Gen. 3:6–7)

From that moment onward, humanity died. We died spiritually and began to die physically. We began running from God rather than to God. We began seeking our own righteousness rather than His righteousness alone. We started hiding from God and covering up before one another. Our eyes became open to a world of sin and shame, and we didn't have a clue what to do about it. Every human being born thereafter would be conceived in iniquity and brought forth in sin (see Ps. 51:5).

And to say we are conceived in iniquity and born in sin is not simply to say that we do bad things. It means *we have adopted an entire way of life that devalues God and exalts Self at the very core.* It is not merely that we have failed to attain the good behavior God asks for, but that *we have, in the depths of our hearts, cast Him from the throne of our universe, trodden Him underfoot as worthless, and placed ourselves as the rulers and saviors of our own lives.* What we love, hate, cherish, think, feel, do, and long for has been basically and completely twisted. Overt sinful behavior, therefore, is simply a symptom of a much deeper, hidden revolt against God.

1. Take a few minutes to read Romans 7:21–25. When you read this passage, what sinful attitudes and ways of living do you see in your own life?

2. Do you believe that you see yourself clearly and truthfully? Do you believe you see others clearly and truthfully? Please explain.

3. Who helps you to clear your vision? Who loves you enough to tell you when you're walking against Christ?

Our Corrupted Desires

Since our fallen nature is corrupted and sinful, our desires in daily life are corrupted and sinful. What we want, as well as why we want it, is misplaced and misshapen. This can be seen most clearly through our constant battle with lust and fear.

Lust

Lust is one expression of the pride and idolatry that rule our hearts. When my mission in life is "My kingdom come, my will be done," then my heart will be ruled by selfish desires. Lust is simply one expression of selfish desire. Although the term often refers to sexual sin, lust can refer to a selfish desire for anything that I do not have but desperately want. Lust expresses cravings to please and promote the self. It is instinctive to the sinful flesh: "What is the source of quarrels and conflicts among you? Is not the source your pleasures that wage war in your members? You lust and do not have; so you commit murder. You are envious and cannot obtain; so you fight and quarrel" (James 4:1–2).

Now, most of the objects that we lust for are not evil in and of themselves. Money and health are good gifts of God. Alcohol may be used as a gift from God for our enjoyment of Him and one another. God gave sex to husbands and wives as a gift in marriage. The objects themselves are not the main problem. Pride and idolatry ruling our hearts is the problem. What our sinful hearts do with these objects is the real concern.

In the list below, circle the lusts with which you most struggle.

Approval	Health
Acceptance	Body image
Success	Food
Money	Drugs/alcohol
Sexual pleasure	Personal holiness
Honor	Cleanliness
Emotional pleasure	Order
Entertainment	Peace/quiet
Marriage	Comfort
Children	Ease
A good marriage	Power
Good children	Sleep
Good employment	Other examples:
Possessions	_____
Sport	_____

Fear

Alongside lust, another expression of pride and idolatry ruling our hearts is unholy fear. Fear is always an expression of worship and deep reverence. This is one reason the Scripture calls us to fear God alone. Only God deserves our worship and deep reverence. Only He deserves our fear. Yet we enter the world fearing almost everyone and everything besides Him.

Lust and fear go hand in hand. They are two sides of the same coin. They are two sides of selfish desire. They are two forms of spiritual idolatry. If I crave approval, then I will, by nature, fear disapproval (see Luke 18:18–23). If I long for financial security and wealth, then I will fear poverty or a job loss or anything else that threatens my financial livelihood (see Heb. 13:5–6). When I long to preserve and protect myself above all things, then I will fear almost everything except God. Sometimes our fears can help us identify our lusts. Our fears point to who and what we worship.

In the list below, circle the fears with which you most struggle.

Disapproval	Sickness
Rejection	Being overweight
Failure	Public embarrassment
Death	Discomfort
Sexual frustration	Sinful failures
Dishonor	Messiness/dirt
Pain	Disorder
Boredom	Hunger
Lifelong singleness	Weakness
A hard marriage	Divorce
Childlessness	Abuse
Dishonorable children	Adultery
Bad employment	Other examples:
Poverty	
Physical hardship	_____
	_____

Our human nature is fallen, and all our desires, passions, and activities are selfish and distorted as a result. We cannot please God. Without His help, we cannot love and obey Him from our hearts. Without His Spirit, our hearts refuse to worship Him and prefer to worship the creation. Nothing in ourselves or of ourselves can save us and reconcile us back to God.

Our Inability to Reconcile Ourselves to God

Scripture says that we cannot appease God by works, no matter how sincere these works may be. He is holy. There is no sacrifice we could ever offer that is worthy enough to pay the penalty for our sin. Only a perfect sacrifice will do.

> With what shall I come to the LORD
> And bow myself before the God on high?
> Shall I come to Him with burnt offerings,
> With yearling calves?
> Does the LORD take delight in thousands of rams,
> In ten thousand rivers of oil?
> Shall I present my firstborn for my rebellious acts,
> The fruit of my body for the sin of my soul? (Mic. 6:6–7)

> For all of us have become like one who is unclean,
> And all our righteous deeds are like a filthy garment;
> And all of us wither like a leaf,
> And our iniquities, like the wind, take us away. (Isa. 64:6)

We cannot be reconciled to God by our own efforts. There is no sacrifice we could offer Him, nor any punishment we could endure from Him, that would gain us right standing before Him. We cannot change who God is (absolutely holy and righteous) or what God is about (displaying His glory by taking a people for His own possession who are holy and righteous before Him). We cannot change who we are (unholy and unrighteous) or what we are about (living for our own glory). Apart from Christ, we are trapped at odds with God—there is nothing we can do about it.

Our Futile Attempts to Achieve
Our Own Righteousness

Even though we cannot do anything to pay for our sins and achieve right standing before God, we all like to try. In our pride, we try to atone for our sins and achieve a righteousness of our own. Self-righteousness comes to us naturally. We prefer to pay our own way. Our sinful flesh has no desire for grace. It wants to justify itself. Watch the natural and immediate response of Adam and Eve when they realized their sinful estate:

> Then the eyes of both of them were opened, and they knew that they were naked; and they sewed fig leaves together and made themselves loin coverings. They heard the sound of the LORD God walking in the garden in the cool of the day, and the man and his wife hid themselves from the presence of the LORD God among the trees of the garden. (Gen. 3:7–8)

By grasping and eating the fruit, Adam and Eve were grasping independence from God. They were seeking their own glory. From this position, their natural response to their sinfulness was to fix it themselves. They covered themselves with garments of their own design and making.

At the same time, they had never encountered the wrath and grace of God before this point. They had no clear idea how God would respond to their new and fallen estate. They didn't want to find out.

After falling to temptation, they attempted to cover their sin with garments of their own self-righteousness. When they heard God approaching, they fled and hid from Him. And when God confronted their transgression, they blamed others. Adam and Eve refused to face God as sinners. Once they faced Him, they tried to shift responsibility onto someone else. These are natural human responses to sinfulness.

4. Share ways that you try to earn God's favor and establish a righteousness of your own, whether through job performance, moral performance, knowledge performance, or anything else.

5. Share areas of your life in which you try to appear or feel more righteous than others are.

6. Think of a recent time that you sinned. Whom did you blame? What "garment" did you make to cover yourself? In other words, how did you justify your sin and avoid confession?

7. What do you tend to run after for comfort, refuge, and deliverance? Do you run to sports, food, career, isolation, or something else?

Our Redemption

The gospel denounces our attempts to earn right standing before God. The Lord refused to accept Adam and Eve's attempts to cover their sin and avoid Him.

What He did do, however, was to lovingly and perfectly provide a way of salvation for them to receive by faith. In His words to the Serpent, God promised Adam and Eve a future deliverance: "And I will put enmity between you and the woman, and between your seed and her seed; He shall bruise you on the head, and you shall bruise him on the heel" (Gen. 3:15). The promise of ultimate victory was a foreshadowing of Jesus Christ. He is the seed of woman who would crush the Serpent's head.

God also provided a temporary deliverance through a remarkable act of atonement and forgiveness: "The LORD God made garments of skin for Adam and his wife, and clothed them" (Gen. 3:21). God stripped Adam and Eve of their self-righteous garments and covered them with garments of His provision and design. Blood was shed that day—just not Adam's or Eve's. Atonement was made. God accepted a sacrifice—the slain body and shed blood of an animal—in their place. God used the skin of that animal to clothe His children. This offers another beautiful foreshadowing of the coming "Lamb of God who takes away the sin of the world" (John 1:29).

This ultimate Lamb of God (Jesus Christ) would live the perfectly righteous life we could not and then would die in our place, crucified at the hands of sinful people, all according to the preconceived plan of God to satisfy His wrath, display His grace, and provide a way of salvation for His children (see Acts 2:22–24). This way of salvation is walked by faith. It comes to us as a gift from God; we receive it as a gift from God.

The Righteousness of God through Faith

"But now apart from the Law the righteousness of God has been manifested . . . even the righteousness of God through faith in Jesus Christ for all those who believe" (Rom. 3:21–22). Salvation comes to us apart from law—that is, apart from our ability to keep the law by our works. Praise the Lord! We are declared righteous before God, freed from sin's power, and reconciled to God the Father through the perfect work and the perfect sacrifice of the Son of God in our place.

All His righteousness is imputed or assigned or accredited to us as a gift of God's grace, and we receive this gift by faith alone. We renounce any claim to our own righteousness and appeal to His righteousness. In that moment of faith, the Holy Spirit unites us to Jesus and our standing before God becomes secure.

We are also redeemed by God's grace, not our efforts. That is, we are freed from sin and death in order to serve the living God. Our bondage to sin was hopeless, but God set us free in Christ. The debt that we owed God was too great to fathom. That debt was paid by the blood of Jesus Christ. Only the payment that Jesus offered could ever be enough.

Of course, our salvation includes far more than simply being freed from sin and death. In Christ we received a new and peaceful relationship with God Himself. We have been brought back to right relationship with the Father through Jesus Christ, not through our efforts. We were at war with God, hostile to His nature and word. Through Jesus Christ we have been reconciled to God and enjoy peace with God (see Rom. 5:1–2).

Through the grace of God we have received these gifts and much more. A deep grasp of this grace is one of the sweetest qualities you can ever bring into your marriage. The more you comprehend and marvel at the fact that you "have been chosen of God, holy and beloved," the more eagerly and cheerfully you will "put on a heart of compassion, kindness, humility, gentleness and patience; bearing with one another, and forgiving each other, whoever has a complaint against anyone; just as the Lord forgave you, so also should you" (Col. 3:12–13).

The New Person

Once we have been reconciled to God the Father, our life should begin to change. Rather than being under the control of sin and Satan, we start living under God's control.

> For the love of Christ controls us, having concluded this, that one died for all, therefore all died; and He died for all, so that they who live might no longer live for themselves, but for Him who died and rose again on their behalf. (2 Cor. 5:14–15)

We are no longer to live for ourselves, because Jesus Christ gave His body and blood as an atonement for our sins. He purchased us. And when He died, we died with Him. When He was raised in new life, we were raised in new life with Him. The Holy Spirit joined us to Him and initiated a process of complete life transformation, granting us the very life of God.

In 2 Corinthians 5, Paul goes on to say, "Therefore if anyone is in Christ, he is a new creature; the old things passed away; behold, new things have come" (v. 17). Being "in Christ" makes us new people. Old ways of thinking begin to die away. Old patterns of living start to fade. Our affections, thoughts, and behaviors begin to resemble those of Christ Himself.

As new creations in Christ, we are called to live in a new way. We should see God, ourselves, others, and our world with a new perspective—with a renewed, eternal point of view. In our souls there has been an awakening to God, man, sin, heaven, hell, and just about everything else. We to live no longer for ourselves, but for the glory of Christ and His kingdom. We have a whole new mission in life.

The Maturing Person

Healthy little children grow. If a three-year-old girl receives the right nutrition and care, her body will develop and mature with each passing day. The same can be said of newborn children of God. Paul said to the Ephesians, "We are no longer to be children, tossed here and there by waves and carried about by every wind of doctrine, by the trickery of men, by craftiness in deceitful scheming; but speaking the truth in love, we are to grow up in all aspects into Him who is the head, even Christ" (Eph. 4:14–15).

When we are growing up in Christ, we will be less and less carried away and deceived by worldliness and false teaching. We will be learning to speak the truth in love with one another. Over the course of time, we will grow in the likeness of Jesus Christ across every area of life. By definition, we are growing in unity with the body of Christ, growing in knowledge of God, and constantly being "renewed in the spirit of our minds" (see Eph. 4:23).

Since we have not yet been made perfect, each day we cry out to God to help us put on a new self that abounds in righteousness and truth. With the strength He supplies, we are maturing in active service in the body of Christ. In fact, our self-image should now be defined partly by service to others (see Rom. 12:1–13).

As maturing followers of Christ, we are (by definition) maturing in why, what, and how we worship. The reason for all that we think, feel, and do is driven more by "glory of Christ" and less by "glory of self." The object of all that we think, feel, and do is more "Christ" and less "self or selfish idols." With each passing day, Jesus becomes more firmly established as our Master, His kingdom becomes more firmly established as our mission, and eternal glory (namely, God Himself and eternal life with Him) becomes more firmly established as the treasure of our hearts. With each passing hour, the gospel more radically shapes our view of life, people, conflict, food, marriage, money, and every other detail of our existence.

Our Ultimate Fate

Eternal death and eternal life are the only and final destinations available to human beings. There are two roads being walked, by two groups of people, toward two fates. On which road do we walk? To which group of people do we belong? To which fate do we journey?

I suppose the more pressing question is, with whom do we walk? The road to glory seems not so much a combination of proper choices, or of personal achievements in spiritual disciplines, as it does devotion to a specific Person. Life comes not to those who figure it all out or arrive at some pinnacle of enlightenment, but to those who attach themselves by faith to a very particular Savior. From that attachment flows an entire way of being before God and fellow men that, by consequence, marches straight through heaven's gates.

The reality of eternal life, when we consider it truthfully and often enough, controls the way that we live in this present life. There will be a resurrection. The trajectory of our souls will continue onward forever.

Eternal Death

Take a minute to read Revelation 20:11–15. John offers a terrifying and sobering picture of eternity under the wrath of God. It is a second death. It is an eternal death. It is a death in which no one actually stops existing. Eternal death is the final destination of those who perish without Christ as their Savior. They will spend it separated from God in the abyss of hell, where "their worm will not die and their fire will not be quenched" (Isa. 66:24; cf. Mark 9:44, 46, 48).

The reality of eternal death should sober us and then stir us to share the gospel of Jesus Christ with all people who are willing to hear. The truth should also sober our approach to marriage and stir us to lifelong gospel ministry as husbands and wives who are committed to seeing all peoples from all countries hear and believe the message of Jesus Christ.

Eternal Life

Now read Revelation 22:1–5. The apostle John foresaw a delightful and awesome picture of eternity in the very presence of God. Those who die as Christians will spend eternity in the presence of an infinitely wonderful Father in heaven—in perfect fellowship with God and one another, singing praises and enjoying all that is meant to be enjoyed forever.

These promises and images can invigorate our prayers, thanksgivings, and efforts to proclaim the good news of salvation to all who do not know God. They can invigorate our encouragements to one another in this life. They can challenge us to live eternally minded and to look toward a better country with a better citizenship and a better reward (see Heb. 11:24–27, 39–40).

Receiving the gift of marriage will bring with it a great number of temptations. One temptation will be to live more attached to this present world rather than anticipating the age to come. Houses, cars, children, financial securities, and other details of human life on earth, while good and helpful, can become so consuming to our hearts that they squash or numb all zeal for our eternal God and His eternal kingdom. We must pray for the Lord to keep our spiritual senses alive. We must ask His Spirit to renew our affections for Him each day and to keep our marriages brimming with desire for the advancement of His name and renown.

8. Have you been maturing in Jesus Christ? In what ways has God transformed your way of thinking, feeling, and acting from day to day?

9. Do you and your fiancé carry a zeal for the eternal purposes of God? Share some ways you could encourage each other to live more eternally minded.

10. How could marriage and family tempt you to become preoccupied with houses, cars, schools, bank accounts, and other temporal things? How do you plan to face this temptation?

Understanding Who You Are 65

Taking the Point to Heart

Marriage has always been a wonderful gift from God. It is now being offered to you. Praise God!

Remember, however, that you are a sinner. You plan to marry a sinner. And you cannot possibly enter marriage on stable ground if you do not understand the implications of human sinfulness—especially your own. Both you and your fellow sinner / mate-to-be have been created to glorify and enjoy God. Yet you are fallen, and your flesh lives for nothing more than its own desires. You cannot fix this. You cannot fix your fiancé. Thank God you don't have to!

Salvation has come to you through Jesus Christ. Like marriage, it is a gift of God's grace. Unlike marriage, it is eternal. Your marriage to Jesus lasts forever. It costs you nothing. It cost Jesus His life. Now your life belongs to Him. Now you are filled with His Spirit. In Christ you were made new, and God has been conforming you to the image of His beloved Son ever since.

Temptations will come to you every day. Your flesh will crave, worry, burn, and fight every day. It will be a daily, humbling battle to grow in love and grace with your mate.

The ability to grow and the strength to persevere will come not from you but from Christ in you. Philippians 2:12–13 reminds us,

So then, my beloved, just as you have always obeyed, not as in my presence only, but now much more in my absence, work out your salvation with fear and trembling; for it is God who is at work in you, both to will and to work for His good pleasure.

Suffering will come to your life. Sometime after your wedding ceremony, pain will happen in your marriage. This is ultimately a gift from God too. The molding of your heart requires intense heat. Suffering, by the grace of God, can refine your faith, like gold smelted in a furnace.

In this you greatly rejoice, even though now for a little while, if necessary, you have been distressed by various trials, so that the proof of your faith, being more precious than gold which is perishable, even though tested by fire, may be found to result in praise and glory and honor at the revelation of Jesus Christ. (1 Peter 1:6–7)

So please take time to prayerfully consider yourself and all that God has brought about in your heart and life. Be honest about who you are apart from Christ. Know who you are in Christ. Get ready to trust Him in every corner of your marriage. He will accept nothing less. He will be infinitely patient with you, but He insists on changing you. He loves you too much to let you go through life believing that you don't depend on Him for breath, let alone everything else. He loves you so deeply that He will force Himself into the very middle of your heart and marriage. May we all be grateful for His persistent love!

4

Understanding What Marriage Is Really About

For this reason a man shall leave his father and mother
and shall be joined to his wife, and the two shall become one flesh.
This mystery is great; but I am speaking with reference
to Christ and the church. (Eph. 5:31–32)

It began as one of the most troubling and difficult marriages I had ever observed or counseled. Their names were Sam and Grace, and they'd been married for only sixteen months when we first met. They had twin girls who were three months old. Sam had admitted not really loving Grace anymore and wished he had married someone else. Grace, devastated and confused, filed for divorce. Her parents were helping her to get through the divorce process quickly—even funding it. They felt it was their role to protect their daughter and their granddaughters. Sam didn't seem to care. Going to counseling was "a last ditch effort" to salvage their relationship and family.

The more they talked in our first meeting, the more obvious their *misunderstanding* of marriage became. They spoke of it very lightly. It was not something sacred to them, but something casual and disposable. They spoke of marriage as one would speak of an old pair of jeans—something to pull on and off based on your mood and the need of the moment. If it doesn't fit anymore, throw it away—just like an old pair of jeans.

The Spirit and Word of God met them right where they stood. By the grace of Jesus Christ, their hearts and marriage began to unravel and then to heal, in ways they could never have imagined. The work of Christ spoke strong and merciful words to their souls.

It all started when they began to understand that marriage was not something that belonged to them. It was not a plaything or an invention of people for the amusement of people but a possession of God. It was not an old pair of jeans but a priceless creation. And the more Sam and Grace embraced what marriage was really about, the more God transformed their attitudes and actions toward one another.

The Origin of Marriage

How we understand the origin of marriage will probably determine where we go and to whom we go for truth about marriage. This understanding will also define the entire course and goal of our lives as husbands and wives.

If we are to seize and enjoy marriage as God intends, then knowing who made it and why He made it are essential. Consider this primary text from Genesis 2:

> Then the LORD God said, "It is not good for the man to be alone; I will make him a helper suitable for him." Out of the ground the LORD God formed every beast of the field and every bird of the sky, and brought them to the man to see what he would call them; and whatever the man called a living creature, that was its name. The man gave names to all the cattle, and to the birds of the sky, and to every beast of the field, but for Adam there was not found a helper suitable for him. So the LORD God caused a deep sleep to fall upon the man, and he slept; then He took one of his ribs and closed up the flesh at that place. The LORD God fashioned into a woman the rib which He had taken from the man, and brought her to the man. The man said,
>
> > "This is now bone of my bones,
> > And flesh of my flesh;

> She shall be called Woman,
> Because she was taken out of Man."

For this reason a man shall leave his father and his mother, and be joined to his wife; and they shall become one flesh. And the man and his wife were both naked and were not ashamed. (vv. 18–25)

God Conceived Marriage in His Mind

The Genesis 2 passage shows us that *the concept of marriage originated in the mind of God.* Marriage was conceived in the mind of God when He made two primary conclusions: (1) it was not good for man to be alone (v. 18), and (2) a suitable helper was not found (v. 20).

What prompted God to reach these two conclusions?

In order to answer this question, it may be wise for us to review the reason that everything has been created and then to bring that reason to bear on the answer. As we have said before, every created thing exists to display the glory of our God. The first two chapters of Genesis record God creating the world like a designer and builder of a theater, arranging His stage and outfitting all His characters. The stage and characters would then provide the showcase for the glory and splendor of their Maker.

The crowning act of creation came when God made man in His image. This particular creature (man) was unique because he, in particular, was to reflect the very image of God. He was created to know, enjoy, and worship God in special ways—ways that everything else doesn't and can't.

We know from other places in Scripture that God has existed eternally in three persons: Father, Son, and Holy Spirit (see Matt. 3:16–17; 28:19). Even in the creation narrative we are given a hint of the three-in-oneness of God when He says, "Let Us make man in Our image, according to Our likeness" (Gen. 1:26). We know that God has been eternally loving, eternally giving, and eternally oriented to others. Because God exists in three persons, His nature has always been to sacrifice, share, and concern Himself with the welfare of others.

So God made Adam in His image. Then God declared that "it is not good for the man to be alone" (Gen. 2:18). Here is my question: in light of all we just said, why is it not good for the man to be alone? What is God seeing and talking about?

The problem that God identifies, and wants us to see, is that Adam has no one of his nature and substance to think about. He has no one in his likeness to love, serve, and honor. Left alone, his thoughts would be too wrapped around himself. This was a problem. This is what God called "not good." In his alone state, Adam could not reflect the complete image that God wanted him to reflect. He was not as full an image-bearer of God's glory as God desired.

At the same time, Adam in his alone state could not function the way that God wanted him to function. There were tasks God wanted Adam to accomplish in stewarding His creation, but he could not fulfill those tasks alone. He needed a helper in order to reflect what God wanted him to reflect and to work as God wanted him to work.

This is really important to our view of marriage and, therefore, to our preparations for marriage. The problem was *not* that Adam was lonely. He wasn't. Adam had God in three persons. The problem was not that Adam needed sex, or someone to cook for him, or someone to clean his living quarters. He didn't. He *felt* totally complete. Those would be *man-centered* appraisals of the issue. If we had asked Adam about his *needs for service,* he would have been bewildered by our question. At this time in his life, Adam existed in perfect, blissful union with the Lord.

The problem God saw was in Adam's inability to display the image that God wanted him to display because he was alone. He was not able to steward God's creation in a form that God thought best. Adam would be *too preoccupied with himself.* He needed a helper—someone of his own nature and substance to help him to steward the glory of God in creation and over creation. God creates and subdues life. He wanted His image-bearer to create and subdue life. So Adam needed a helper to create and subdue life.

God Created Marriage

The Scripture tells us that *the reality of marriage originated in the hands of God.* Marriage, as an institution, was an act not of society or human will, but of God. God created and prepared the first bride, Eve. Adam was asleep when Eve was formed, so he didn't offer any insights or wisdom in the matter. Adam woke up and responded to all that God had brought about for good. It was God who witnessed and conducted the first wedding ceremony. He created the first human relationship on earth. He created the first marriage on earth.

"The man said, 'This is now bone of my bones, and flesh of my flesh; she shall be called Woman, because she was taken out of Man'" (Gen. 2:23). Eve was formed from Adam's body and thus was composed of his very substance and nature. Adam acknowledged this and accepted her as a provision from God.

Think back to Sam and Grace for a moment. Throughout their young marriage, they had never really accepted that marriage as a gift from God. They didn't see their union as first and foremost about God; they didn't yet see that it existed for His reasons, not their own. The Lord had given them to each other as a gift for this lifetime. He had made them one flesh in order to serve His beautiful purposes. The marriage wasn't to be over until He said it was over.

It was fascinating to see how relieved Sam and Grace felt after learning these truths. A great deal of weight was removed from their shoulders. God was with them, for them, and committed to their marriage. The burden of choosing whether to stay or leave wasn't actually theirs to carry. They were not free to decide whether or not to divorce; her parents were not free to decide whether they should divorce. They were free to repent, forgive, and learn to love each other the way that God loves them.

At the same time, these truths also added a weight to their shoulders: the weight of the privilege and responsibility of holding a precious gift of God in their hands—a weight that was meant to drive them back to God for His mercy and aid. Not only were they free to repent, forgive, and learn to love one another the way that God loves them, but they were also obligated and constrained to do so. The God who loved them also required them to love each other. Ephesians 4:30–32 commands us,

> Do not grieve the Holy Spirit of God, by whom you were sealed for the day of redemption. Let all bitterness and wrath and anger and

clamor and slander be put away from you, along with all malice. Be kind to one another, tender-hearted, forgiving each other, just as God in Christ also has forgiven you.

God Assembled Marriage

In addition to the concept and reality of marriage, God established *the covenant of marriage* (the forming of two as one flesh for earthly life). A covenant is an agreement between two or more parties. It involves a mutual commitment to fulfill whatever obligations and enjoy whatever privileges the covenant states.

From the beginning, God established marriage as first place among all other human relationships. It is more sacred and intimate than all the other relationships of a married person's life and is fiercely guarded by God. Genesis 2 emphasizes this idea: "For this reason a man shall leave his father and his mother, and be joined to his wife; and they shall become one flesh" (v. 24). Jesus later builds on Genesis 2 in order to drive the point home: "So they are no longer two, but one flesh. What therefore God has joined together, let no man separate" (Matt. 19:6).

In the process of becoming married, a son or daughter must separate from his or her parents in order to become one flesh with his or her mate. Cleaving to a wife requires a man to cut any physical, emotional, and spiritual dependencies on his parents. Hopefully that man, before his wedding day, has been learning greater dependency on the Lord and less dependency on his parents. This does not mean that, in some cases, a newly married couple cannot live with parents for a season of time or be employed by parents or otherwise connected to parents. Rather it means that a qualitative change of relationship must happen, by which the marriage union is treated as sacred and more vital than any other human relationship of the bride or groom. Whenever a conflict of interests arises, the other relationships are to suffer and give way, not the marriage.

Cleaving to a husband requires a woman to cut the physical, emotional, and spiritual dependencies that she has on her father and mother. Hopefully a woman, before her wedding day, has been learning deeper dependency on the Lord.

Both husband and wife remain called to honor their father and mother, but in a qualitatively different way from before. Their marriage comes first. The growing of their marriage in Christ comes first. The edification of their marriage comes before the pleasing of their earthly parents.

Once a man leaves his father and mother to become one flesh with his wife, Jesus tells us there is no going back. "Let no man separate" means that only God is free to dissolve the union. A husband and wife are not to part until death. The Lord intends for the covenant of marriage to hold fast until He brings it to an end.

1. Explain what "Let no man separate" really means to you.

2. What difficulties do you foresee in leaving your original family in order to be joined to your husband or wife? Share ways in which you could be too attached to or dependent on your father, mother, or siblings—whether this involves their approval, respect, money, or advice.

3. Write down any threats you anticipate from your extended family to the marriage you are about to enter. In what ways might they impose themselves on your marriage, demand things of your marriage, or otherwise disrupt your relationship with your spouse?

4. What physical, emotional, and spiritual gifts has your family given to you that will be a blessing to your marriage?

The Ultimate Purpose of Marriage

Why marriage? In other words, what is the ultimate purpose or aim of marriage? What is it intended to display and produce?

Explaining a Mystery, to the Glory of God

> So husbands ought also to love their own wives as their own bodies. He who loves his own wife loves himself; for no one ever hated his own flesh, but nourishes and cherishes it, just as Christ also does the church, because we are members of His body. For this reason a man shall leave his father and mother and shall be joined to his wife, and the two shall become one flesh. This mystery is great; but I am speaking with reference to Christ and the church. Nevertheless, each individual among you also is to love his own wife even as himself, and the wife must see to it that she respects her husband. (Eph. 5:28–33)

God sent His only begotten Son, Jesus, to live among people. Jesus loves people. He spent His earthly life serving, teaching, and shepherding people. Then the Father delivered Him to be tortured, crucified, and resurrected in order to redeem and sanctify those who were chosen to be His people. Romans 8:32 tells us, "He who did not spare His own Son, but delivered Him over for us all, how will He not also with Him freely give us all things?"

The church is the bride of Christ. The church has received Christ and been given to Christ in marriage.

According to Paul, a human marriage helps to explain the mystery of Christ and the church. Human marriage brings to light what was hidden in the Scriptures prior to the coming of Jesus Christ. It provides a visible picture of an invisible reality; the physical relationship gives body to a spiritual truth; the temporal covenant points to the eternal covenant. Marriage is a visible, physical, temporal covenant that pictures, embodies, and points to the eternal covenant between Christ and the church.

A husband and wife forsake all other lovers, just as Christ and the church forsake all other lovers. A husband commits his life to the true good of his wife, just as Christ gave His life for the church. The father of the bride gives his daughter to her husband, just as the Father gives the church to His Son (see John 6:37). A husband and wife become one flesh, just as Christ and His bride are one spirit (see 1 Cor. 6:17). A husband and wife are visibly united through sexual union. We are invisibly united to Jesus Christ through the filling of His Spirit.

We could keep going with implications and parallels, but the point remains clear: the unique and significant relationship between a husband and a wife provides an opportunity to showcase the splendor and beauty of God's redeeming love. Christ's union with the church is one eternal reality to which marriage points and speaks.

But here is another side. A marriage between a husband and wife also provides an opportunity to distort and disgrace the picture of Christ and the church. Our marriages can also be used to show what God's redeeming love isn't about. We pray and hope that this will not be the case for our marriages, but sometimes our pride and sinfulness provide a striking contrast to the majesty and holiness of our God, or an unclear and even disturbing image of Christ and His church.

Expanding His Kingdom, to the Glory of God

> God created man in His own image, in the image of God He created him; male and female He created them. God blessed them; and God said to them, "Be fruitful and multiply, and fill the earth, and subdue it; and rule over the fish of the sea and over the birds of the sky and over every living thing that moves on the earth." (Gen. 1:27–28)

Another function of marriage is to populate the earth and, therefore, to expand the people of God by His preordained means. "Be fruitful and multiply" was a command given to Adam and Eve, in order to "fill the earth, and subdue it." Since sexual union is prohibited outside of marriage, the only God-honoring means for this kind of fruitfulness occurs within marriage (see 1 Cor. 6:9; Heb. 13:4).

Now let me say this. Not all believers marry, and not all married believers are able to have children. Thus, the bearing of children is not a marker of spiritual maturity or success, but rather it's one possible means that the Lord uses to expand His kingdom. And this expansion is dependent on spiritual rebirth. God builds His kingdom by spiritual birth. Physical birth must happen first, but rebirth provides the final entrance. Jesus stated this strongly to Nicodemus: "Truly, truly, I say to you, unless one is born again he cannot see the kingdom of God" (John 3:3).

In a way, Jesus placed greater emphasis on spiritual reproduction than on physical reproduction. Matthew 28:19–20 says,

> Go therefore and make disciples of all the nations, baptizing them in the name of the Father and the Son and the Holy Spirit, teaching them to observe all that I commanded you; and lo, I am with you always, even to the end of the age.

Physical reproduction is important, but making disciples of all the nations is even more important. Marriage provides a God-ordained means for producing children and then, by the grace of God, producing followers of Jesus Christ.

5. Share your desires for having children or not having children.

6. Share your fears about having children or not having children.

7. If you already have children, what challenges and joys do you think might lie ahead in your forming of a new family?

8. Up to this point, how have you been involved in making disciples of Jesus Christ? Have you been taught by others to love and follow Jesus Christ? Do you teach others to love and follow Jesus Christ?

Exhorting the Next Generation, to the Glory of God

Hear, O Israel! The LORD is our God, the LORD is one! You shall love the LORD your God with all your heart and with all your soul and with all your might. These words, which I am commanding you today, shall be on your heart. You shall teach them diligently to your sons and shall talk of them when you sit in your house and when you walk by the way and when you lie down and when you rise up.

You shall bind them as a sign on your hand and they shall be as frontals on your forehead. You shall write them on the doorposts of your house and on your gates. (Deut. 6:4–9)

Godly marriage provides a foundation for teaching the next generation how to love God and the people He created in the context of family and community. Marriages are meant to produce offspring who are well informed of God and His ways. We are called to talk about Him in our homes and to display His grace in our daily lives.

Families are called and enabled by the Spirit of God to speak and demonstrate God's love and truth to the next generation. Family meals can be a time to talk about God, His goodness, and His Word. The Christian home can be a place where Christ is exalted and the gospel is spoken. The way we love one another in marriage could invite questions from our children about the peace and hope that are in us. The ways in which we resolve conflict, deal with our sin, and handle mistreatment are all means that God might use to display His grace and power. Younger generations have front-row seats to watch and learn from the marriages of the generations before them.

Endowing a Suitable Companion, to the Glory of God

Another reason that God gave Adam a suitable companion was for his pure enjoyment. Marriage provides a means for us to enjoy God by enjoying our God-given mate. We are supposed to delight in our spouse.

Think about this very interesting charge that God gave newly married men in Israel: "When a man takes a new wife, he shall not go out with the army nor be charged with any duty; he shall be free at home one year and shall give happiness to his wife whom he has taken" (Deut. 24:5). It seems that God wanted husbands and wives to enjoy each other and to begin their marriage on a foundation of service and godly happiness. The charge seems especially important in light of the context in which it was written. The preceding verses of Deuteronomy 24 contained Moses' instructions to the hard-hearted men of Israel who were dead set on divorcing their wives. Men who enjoy their wives (something that God fully intends) won't divorce their wives (something that God fully despises).

There are pleasures in marriage. Although keeping the covenant of marriage joyfully and faithfully can prove difficult, the fault does not fall on the side of marriage itself but on the side of the sinners involved. Jesus is happily married to His bride, despite all her sinfulness and fickleness. He delights in His eternal wife. So we should delight in our earthly wives. "He who finds a wife finds a good thing and obtains favor from the LORD" (Prov. 18:22).

God gives marriage as a gift to humanity. It can be the source of untold delights and wonders. Just as any earthly father wants his children to enjoy and prize the gifts that he gives, God wants us to thoroughly enjoy and appreciate the gift of marriage. There will be many days when marriage is painful and difficult, but this is part of the gift too, and God receives great glory and honor when we receive with thanksgiving all the blessings that He offers in marriage.

Taking the Point to Heart

A healthy preparation for marriage requires you to grow your understanding of what marriage is really about, according to God's design and intention. Marriage originates with God, who determined it, created it, and assembled its essential parts. God formed marriage between a husband and a wife to display His glory—especially the glory of Christ and the church. Marriage offers a visible, living picture of God's redeeming love. In a related way, it provides a means to expand the kingdom of Christ by producing children and training them to love God and further His kingdom purposes. Through marriage, God grants to you a suitable companion for your life on earth—someone to help you become less self-absorbed and more oriented to another, someone for God to use in conforming you to the image of Jesus Christ.

5

The Covenant of Marriage

*So they are no longer two, but one flesh. What therefore God
has joined together, let no man separate. (Matt. 19:6)*

A covenant is an agreement between two or more parties. It involves promises (see Ps. 89:3). It involves pledges. It requires witnesses. Often it involves signs and symbols to help those included in the covenant to remember and celebrate the exchange.

The first mention of the word *covenant* in the Bible occurs in Genesis 6:18, when God said to Noah, "But I will establish My *covenant* with you; and you shall enter the ark—you and your sons and your wife, and your sons' wives with you." The covenant was explained by God in Genesis 9, and a sign was given by which God and all creation would remember it.

> It shall come about, when I bring a cloud over the earth, that the bow will be seen in the cloud, and I will remember My covenant, which is between Me and you and every living creature of all flesh; and never again shall the water become a flood to destroy all flesh. (Gen. 9:14–15)

God promised Noah that He would deliver Noah and his family from worldwide judgment. He covenanted with Noah to never destroy the human race through a flood. He created and displayed a rainbow as a sign of this covenant.

Every time we see a rainbow in the sky, it helps us to remember God's patience toward sinful humanity. It points to His faithfulness in keeping His gracious promises.

God also made a covenant with Abraham to multiply him and make him the father of many nations, and then He gave Abraham and his offspring the sign of circumcision (see Gen. 17:2–11). The nation of Israel was given "the book of the covenant" (Ex. 24:7) composed of the laws and ordinances that God gave through Moses at Mount Sinai, and the people entered into covenant with God to keep His Law and to walk in His ways.

The apostle Paul referred to this covenant as "the old covenant" (2 Cor. 3:14)—a binding agreement and relationship between God and the people of Israel based on the words that God spoke to Moses on Mount Sinai. The people of Israel vowed to honor the covenant, receiving "the blood of the covenant" (Ex. 24:8) as a sign. That is, Moses sprinkled the people with the blood of a sacrifice as a kind of seal on their covenant with God—a symbol of life for those who keep the obligations of the law, and a symbol of death for those who break them. Because of their sin, the people of Israel were never able to keep the old covenant (see Jer. 31:31–32). Of course, none of us are able to keep it either.

The covenant of law displays the holiness of our God and highlights the sinfulness of humanity and our need for a divine Savior. The law proves our need for someone to fulfill and satisfy the old covenant on our behalf, to atone for our sins, and to usher us into a new covenant and reconciled relationship with the Father (see Rom. 7:12–13).

Jeremiah explicitly announced this new covenant—a covenant based on grace, not law, received by faith, not works:

> "But this is the covenant which I will make with the house of Israel after those days," declares the LORD, "I will put My law within them and on their heart I will write it; and I will be their God, and they shall be My people. They will not teach again, each man his neighbor and each man his brother, saying, 'Know the LORD,' for they will all know Me, from the least of them to the greatest of them," declares

the LORD, "for I will forgive their iniquity, and their sin I will remember no more." (Jer. 31:33–34)

The old covenant has been fulfilled by Jesus Christ so that we are no longer under its terms. We do not have to be perfect in order to restore our relationship to God, because Christ was perfect and He restores our relationship to God for us (see 1 Peter 3:18). The righteousness of God, as well as the wrath of God, was satisfied by Jesus in His life and death. Because of Him, we can be offered a new covenant based on Christ's merits, not on our merits.

Now this new covenant promises the forgiveness of sins. It promises a reconciled relationship to God—that we can truly know Him and serve Him with a new heart and a Spirit-filled life. By accepting the body and blood of Jesus Christ in our place as atonement for our sins, and by accepting the righteousness of Jesus Christ in our place as our obedience to the law, God the Father has brought us back to Himself. Because we have been united to Jesus Christ, He covers us. When God the Father looks on us, He sees His beloved Son covering us and hears His Son interceding for us. "For this reason [Jesus] is the mediator of a new covenant, so that, since a death has taken place for the redemption of the transgressions that were committed under the first covenant, those who have been called may receive the promise of the eternal inheritance" (Heb. 9:15).

In other words, the new covenant is a marriage covenant with Jesus Christ. He has taken us to be His bride. We have taken Him to be our husband, forever. The marriage has been accomplished through the sacrifice of His body. It has been sealed through the shedding of His blood. The moment our faith came to rest on Jesus, we were joined to Him by the Holy Spirit. Now, according to the apostle Paul, we are one spirit with Him (see 1 Cor. 6:17). Jesus instituted communion as a sign of this new covenant (see Luke 22:20).

A marriage between a husband and wife is also a covenant. "The LORD has been a witness between you and the wife of your youth, against whom you have dealt treacherously, though she is your companion and *your wife by covenant*" (Mal. 2:14). A wedding ceremony includes the exchanging of covenant promises, or vows, and covenant signs, such as rings, unity candles, and gifts. There are witnesses. There is a mediator, or official, who oversees the ceremony.

Sexual union consummates and seals the covenant. God is present. God is glorified. God joins a husband and wife together. "So they are no longer two, but one flesh. What therefore God has joined together, let no man separate" (Matt. 19:6). Marriage is a beautiful and serious covenant—witnessed, honored, and guarded by God.

At the same time, in almost every culture and society of the world, a marriage also involves a contract. That is, a socially recognized marriage requires legal or societal agreements between the husband and wife. In most states of the United States, there must be a marriage license and an official who signs the marriage license. There are certain legal responsibilities and privileges inherent to marriage. From a Christian point of view, the contract provides a human acknowledgement of the God-wrought covenant.

1. How is marriage a covenant before God and your spouse? How do you believe this should influence your approach to marriage?

2. Do you have a track record for keeping promises—even when keeping them hurts or costs you a great deal? Give an example.

The Suffocating Burden of
Keeping Covenant by Our Works

After considering all that has been said so far in this chapter about the seriousness and beauty of the marriage covenant, we may be tempted to grit our teeth and press into marriage with greater strength and resolve. It is quite important that we do no such thing. The sacredness and awesomeness of the marriage covenant should first and foremost humble our hearts and drive us to God for His merciful aid. It should not act as a motivation for us to pull up our bootstraps and run into the vineyard of marriage armed with personal wisdom and power.

Law Cannot Save, but It Can Awaken Our Need for Christ

We are covenant breakers by our sinful nature. We tend to defect and revolt—perhaps not always in external behavior, but certainly in heart. Our covenant keeping depends on the grace of God, not on our works. We cannot enjoy what God desires for our marriages without God teaching and enabling us to enjoy them. Left to our own strength, we will either collapse under the weight of marital duties or will take the sacred covenant by the horns in self-righteous performance and vanity.

The apostle Paul helps us to guard against all such temptation and to walk the road by faith alone. "It was for freedom that Christ set us free; therefore keep standing firm and do not be subject again to a yoke of slavery" (Gal. 5:1). Living under law is the yoke of slavery to which Paul refers. He applies the phrase in order to express the burdensome effects of trying to perfectly follow the law as a means for salvation and sanctification—or even, we could say, as a means to save or sanctify anything in our lives, including our marriages.

A farmer places a yoke around the necks of animals in order to control and direct their work. A yoke harnesses animals to plows, carts, or anything else that their masters want. The animals are in bondage and cannot escape. Often two animals are yoked together and thus enslaved together.

This image captures what the law brings to our spiritual lives: a yoke of slavery. The image also captures what living under law brings to our marriages: being yoked together in slavery.

Now, the law of God is a beautiful and wonderful provision. "The Law is holy, and the commandment is holy and righteous and good" (Rom. 7:12). The entire collection in the Old Testament of statutes and commandments given by God helps us to *see* and *feel* our slavery to sin and death, as well as our need for a Redeemer. The law expresses the holiness and splendor of God. It helps us get a sense of what it looks like to love God and our neighbors. The law of God also helped us to perceive our condemnation as lawbreakers before compelling us to cry out for our Savior. It cannot save, but it can point us to the Savior.

> But before faith came, we were kept in custody under the law, being shut up to the faith which was later to be revealed. Therefore the Law has become our tutor to lead us to Christ, so that we may be justified by faith. But now that faith has come, we are no longer under a tutor. For you are all sons of God through faith in Christ Jesus. (Gal. 3:23–26)

The law serves as our tutor and our guide to Christ. Once Christ redeems our hearts, our need for a tutor and guide dissolves. Christ fulfills the law on our behalf. He accomplishes in our hearts what the law cannot. Romans 8:3–4 explains,

> For what the Law could not do, weak as it was through the flesh, God did: sending His own Son in the likeness of sinful flesh and as an offering for sin, He condemned sin in the flesh, so that the requirement of the Law might be fulfilled in us, who do not walk according to the flesh but according to the Spirit.

Christ places His Spirit in our hearts to help us live for Him and obey Him, increasing our belief and trust in Him. This happens by His grace, not by our works.

Law Cannot Nurture a Marriage, but It Can Suffocate a Marriage

The law cannot free or cleanse us from the effects of sin—either our own or anyone else's. In response to our sinfulness, our failures, we tend to sit around in guilt and shame rather than walking in Christ-centered repentance, gratitude, and worship. When sinned against by others, we tend to become angry, bitter, and dejected. We will be constantly tempted to teach those who wrong us lessons in the right way to live. Living under law—or *legalistically*, to put it another way—probably looks a little different for each of us, but it carries many of these characteristics.

Living under law in our marriages means we will judge the quality of our marriages by the quality of our performance. Our joy and peace will be sought in keeping rules and commandments (perhaps very good ones). Our marriages are called "good marriages" if we do good deeds and make sure not to do bad ones. At least, not really bad things like "actual adultery" or "actual murder." If we stay out of debt, don't get drunk, attend church together, tithe the right amount, and don't scream too much, then we have "a good marriage." God, therefore, can be happy with us. Every day we will be tempted to compare our marriages to other marriages and to either triumph or despair based on how well we stack up.

Under the law, we will, perhaps unawarely, judge ourselves constantly against the standards of law that we find most important. We will judge our spouses. We will be highly sensitive to how well or how poorly we have been treated. We will enjoy our spouses based on their performance. If they treat us the way we want to be treated, then we will be somewhat pleased and content. If they give us the "right amount" and "right kind" of sexual intimacy, then we will be glad. If they don't, we will be disappointed and angry. Resentment will build over time. If our mates give us the attention, approval, honor, respect, and cooperation that we desire and "deserve," then we will be pleased with marriage and happy with our mates—for a few minutes at least. If they fail, then we will be frustrated and will start finding ways to train our spouses how to serve our needs more effectively—or will start looking for a new spouse altogether.

Law-driven, self-righteous covenant keeping can be deadly to your marriage. We could go on for pages talking about the ways this can play out in human relationships. Of all the foxes that can get loose in your marriage vineyard, this one can wreck the whole thing in very little time.

Living under law and viewing our mates through the law offers one of the best ways for us to make our marriages truly miserable. It makes it impossible to freely enjoy and love our spouses. It brings bitterness, anger, and despair long before it brings love, joy, and peace.

3. Identify ways that you live under law in your life, whether by external performance in order to earn praise, or by sorrow over sin without repentance, or by believing that God loves you based on how morally you live.

4. What "laws" do you hold dear in your relationships?

5. Identify ways that you place others under the law, whether by expecting them to perform up to your standards, or by becoming bitter when they fail or hurt you, or by punishing them in response to their wrongdoings.

A Covenant Sustained by Grace

Come to Me, all who are weary and heavy-laden, and I will give you rest. Take My yoke upon you and learn from Me, for I am gentle and humble in heart, and you will find rest for your souls. For My yoke is easy and My burden is light. (Matt. 11:28–30)

Jesus fulfilled the law on our behalf. He satisfied all its righteous requirements to perfection. Because of this, He could offer Himself as the unblemished, perfect Lamb of God on the cross (see John 1:29; 1 Peter 1:18–19). He completely satisfied God's wrath toward sin and sinners. This is why we find rest for our souls in Jesus Christ. This is why His yoke is easy and His burden is light. All we do is come and receive Him by faith (and we come by the grace of God—see John 6:37–38, 44–45); then we spend the rest of our lives growing in understanding of this grace and celebrating its implications.

God Enjoys and Keeps Covenant with Us by His Grace

Therefore, having been justified by faith, we have peace with God through our Lord Jesus Christ, through whom also we have obtained our introduction by faith into this grace in which we stand; and we exult in hope of the glory of God. (Rom. 5:1–2)

God *entered into covenant with us* through Jesus Christ. We receive full, unhindered fellowship with Him because of His grace. Through faith (an active trust or belief in God and His promises), God introduces us "into this grace in which we stand." Augustine spoke about this grace as "unmerited mercy."[1] Those who receive the grace of God cannot and do not deserve the good they are given. God is not obligated to give it. It arises from His own free will. It flows from His nature to love, give, and redeem.

Jonathan Edwards believed that "special grace" or "saving grace" is "that peculiar kind or degree of operation or influence of God's Spirit, whence saving actions and attainments do arise in the godly, or, which is the same thing, special and saving assistance."[2] Edwards is saying that our salvation arises from God's power, not ours. We received justification, reconciliation, and redemption as a gift from God. All good faith and work that comes from us happens because of His Spirit's work inside our souls. We enter into permanent covenant with God through the "operations" of His Spirit.

God *keeps covenant with us* through His strength. We are sustained by His grace, not by our works. We are renewed, transformed, and glorified as a gift from God. We receive this gift by faith, too. First Peter 1:5 says that we "are protected by the power of God through faith for

1. St. Augustine, "Faith, Hope, and Charity," trans. Bernard M. Peebles, in *Fathers of the Church*, vol. 2, *Writings of St. Augustine: Christian Instruction, Admonition and Grace, The Christian Combat, Faith, Hope and Charity*, ed. Ludwig Schopp (Washington, DC: Catholic University of America Press, 1947), 447.

2. Jonathan Edwards, "Treatise on Grace," in *The Works of Jonathan Edwards*, vol. 21, *Writings on the Trinity, Grace, and Faith*, ed. Sang Hyun Lee (New Haven, CT: Yale, 2003), 154.

a salvation ready to be revealed in the last time." We can never lose our salvation. We have been adopted as sons and daughters of God. This adoption cannot be reversed. Despite our frequent steps down proud and sinful roads, we are forgiven and continually restored by God's grace in Jesus Christ (see 1 John 2:1–2).

We Enjoy and Keep Covenant with One Another by His Grace

A growing understanding of how God keeps covenant with us will help us to keep covenant with others. Since our marriages will be full of sinfulness, they must also be full of genuine repentance and genuine forgiveness. Only grace can accomplish such a feat. Only the wellspring of God's unmerited mercy can provide enough reason and strength for us to repent, forgive, and love in our marriages. If we want to keep our marriage covenants, then we absolutely, positively must learn and grow in the grace of the Lord Jesus Christ. Notice how Paul pulls all this together in Colossians 3.

> So, as those who have been chosen of God, holy and beloved, put on a heart of compassion, kindness, humility, gentleness and patience; bearing with one another, and forgiving each other, whoever has a complaint against anyone; just as the Lord forgave you, so also should you. (Col. 3:12–13)

Right away the apostle asks that we come to terms with who we are in Jesus Christ. First, we have been *chosen of God*. Though we walked blindly and headlong with the mass of humanity toward eternal destruction, reviling and scorning God along the way, God plucked us out and spared our souls. As an act of sheer generosity and predetermined kindness, God saved us. We didn't earn anything. He chose to create us. He chose to place His grace on us. He chose to make us children. Thank You, Lord!

Second, Paul says that we are *holy*. The idea should blow our minds. How on earth can God use the word *holy* to define us? It proves the depth of God's grace in Christ and how it changes us. All of our sin has been put on Christ and washed away by His blood.

All His righteousness has been put on us. Now the Father declares us righteous. We have been made clean and set apart for His glorious and eternal purposes. We have been filled with His *Holy* Spirit. He makes us holy. The Father sees us joined to Jesus Christ, filled with His Spirit, set apart for His use, and says, "Holy!"

Third, Paul told us that we are *beloved*. God did not redeem us in order to make us sit in the corner, away from Him, facing the wall of heaven. Unlike David, who brought Absalom home but refused to show his face (see 2 Sam. 14:21–24), God brings us home, sets us before Him, and without delay heaps a waterfall of affection and delight on our souls. He loves us, joyfully and passionately. He always will. We are "chosen of God, holy and beloved."

What also stands out from the passage above is the impact that these realities should have on our hearts before God and others. Since we have been "chosen of God, holy and beloved," Paul said, "put on a heart of compassion, kindness, humility, gentleness and patience." Paul seemed to assume that whenever we grasp the compassion of God toward us in Jesus Christ, we will automatically put on compassion for others. When we comprehend the kindness of our Lord toward us, then kindness toward others becomes more instinctive and unavoidable. Once we behold and marvel at the humility of our Lord Jesus, we cannot actually resist becoming more humble toward others (see Phil. 2:3–8).

God deals with us gently, so we can deal with others gently. Jesus Christ shows continual patience toward us, at great cost to Himself, so we can bear patiently with others at great cost to ourselves. The more we grasp God's forgiveness of us, the more motivated we become to forgive others out of reverence and gratitude for Christ.

We cannot begin the journey by aspiring to be more compassionate. We must begin by beholding the compassion of our Savior and by crying out for His Spirit to make us more like Him. We cannot begin the day by striving to be more humble. We must start with being overwhelmed and stirred by the humility of our risen Lord and then genuinely crying out for the Spirit to help us follow in His footsteps. We cannot grow in love for others by personal grit and effort, but instead by being filled with the Spirit of God (see Gal. 5:22–23).

We Mature Together and Face Sin Together by His Grace

In Colossians 3:14–16, Paul keeps unpacking the implications of being recipients of the grace of God through Jesus Christ.

> Beyond all these things put on love, which is the perfect bond of unity. Let the peace of Christ rule in your hearts, to which indeed you were called in one body; and be thankful. Let the word of Christ richly dwell within you, with all wisdom teaching and admonishing one another with psalms and hymns and spiritual songs, singing with thankfulness in your hearts to God.

Embracing grace does not mean we ignore transgression and wrong-doing in our marriages. On the contrary, grace provides us a means to deal with it head-on. After really soaking in the implications of being "chosen of God, holy and beloved," after "putting on love" and "letting the peace of Christ rule in our hearts," after "being thankful" for all that God has done, after "letting the word of Christ dwell richly within our souls," we are now better equipped to address any sinfulness in others, and especially the troubles we perceive in our God-given mates.

Paul provided a framework for a truly gospel-shaped intervention and intercession: "with all wisdom teaching and admonishing one another with psalms and hymns and spiritual songs, singing with thankfulness in your hearts to God."

God wants us to speak the truth in love to others. The Lord has called us to restore and reconcile sinners, but for His reasons and in His way. Without the love, peace, and Word of Christ dwelling in our hearts and ruling them, our attempts to address our spouses and their sinfulness will probably create a whole new set of troubles. We may see real problems in our mates. We may even see them accurately. We may appraise their struggles truthfully and long for them to change into something better in the eyes of God. Yet only the love of Christ keeps our own motivations in line and keeps our efforts from becoming twisted by selfish desires and vain personal interests. Only His Spirit can give us truly edifying words. Only His Spirit can give power to those words so that true restoration takes place.

Our marriages should challenge and grow us. Every day we will face and experience sin in our lives. As husbands and wives, we should be devoted to helping our spouses to face sin and change by the grace of God as they help us to face sin and change by the grace of God.

6. How have you spoken the truth in love to others? In what ways do you either run over people in criticisms and judgment or say nothing in order to avoid conflict and keep others pleased with you?

7. Identify areas in your premarriage relationship in which loving, gracious admonishment needs to happen. In what ways can you speak the truth in love more often?

The Tragedy of Covenant-Breaking Divorce

The grace of God naturally gravitates away from divorce, because grace always seeks restoration in relationships whenever the people involved are willing. Second Corinthians 5:18–19 tells us,

> Now all these things are from God, who reconciled us to Himself through Christ and gave us the ministry of reconciliation, namely, that God was in Christ reconciling the world to Himself, not counting their trespasses against them, and He has committed to us the word of reconciliation.

Christian marriage should be distinguished from other kinds of marriage not by the absence of sin but by the presence of redeeming and reconciling grace.

Living under law in marriage makes us naturally gravitate toward divorce. After all, we are sinners and are constantly breaking the law of God in our hearts and relationships. The law provides no ability or power for true repentance, forgiveness, and reconciliation. The basis for love, peace, and unity in marriage is not the law but the grace of God in Jesus Christ. Without grace, there cannot be the genuine, daily renewal of marriage. Our mates are regularly transgressing the law and thus, apart from grace, need to be judged and condemned. Divorce offers a decisive way to deliver judgment and condemnation.

Let me give a caveat or two. Unrepentant adultery is an attack on the marriage covenant so severe that divorce may not necessarily be an act of wrongful condemnation but instead an expression of love for Christ and of longing for His glory. This could be one reason Jesus offered the statement in Matthew 19:9, "And I say to you, whoever divorces his wife, *except for immorality*, and marries another woman commits adultery." His words suggest that whenever a husband or wife engages in adultery, and especially unrepentant adultery, the offended spouse can be granted freedom to seek divorce. Divorce remains tragic, but not sinful in this case for the offended spouse.

There are other situations in which divorce is not wrong for an offended spouse. If an unbelieving spouse "leaves" or divorces a believing spouse, then the believing spouse "is not under bondage in such cases" (1 Cor. 7:15). When divorce happens under these conditions, the abandoned spouse is free from the obligations of marriage and, perhaps, will be free to remarry in the future.

In cases of domestic violence, after a violent spouse has refused the attempts of legal authorities and the body of Christ to help him or her, and proves unwilling to repent and change, a church may, through the course of church discipline (see Matt. 18:15–20), cast the abuser from the Christian community and grant the offended spouse freedom to divorce. Some churches believe that Jesus' words in Matthew 18 apply to the spouse and family of the offending man or woman as well as to the rest of the church.

In each of these cases, true repentance of the offending spouse, true healing of the offended spouse, and reconciliation would be the best end. The power of God and the beauty of His grace are clearly and wonderfully seen when marriages are restored and made whole after adultery, abandonment, or abuse. Such restoration is not possible, however, when the offending person continues to walk in unrepentant pride and refuses to acknowledge his or her offense before God and the body of Christ.

Why Does God Hate Divorce?

> But not one has done so who has a remnant of the Spirit. And what did that one do while he was seeking a godly offspring? Take heed then to your spirit, and let no one deal treacherously against the wife of your youth. "For I hate divorce," says the LORD, the God of Israel, "and him who covers his garment with wrong," says the LORD of hosts. "So take heed to your spirit, that you do not deal treacherously." (Mal. 2:15–16)

In God's words through Malachi, divorce is portrayed as an act of violence against one's lifelong companion by covenant. The act involves terrible, invisible bloodshed. It covers our garments with "wrong," or violence. Since God joins together a husband and wife, then only God knows how to take them apart. When people take them apart, it gets bloody.

There are several other reasons that Malachi gives for staying faithful to the covenant of marriage. First, God is faithful to His covenant promises, and His Spirit compels faithfulness in His covenant people. People who are filled with the Spirit and led by the Spirit do not abandon their wives or husbands. Forsaking a marriage covenant requires a man or woman to reject the leading, convicting influences of the Holy Spirit. By the same token, keeping the covenant promises of marriage displays submission to the Spirit of God. Such submission wisely honors Him.

Second, the foundation for raising godly children is a godly marriage. During the time of Malachi, the men of Israel were putting away their wives for younger, foreign women. So the children of the covenant people were being reared in a strange mixture of true and false religion. This hypocrisy made it impossible to genuinely train sons and daughters in the delights of godliness and obedience to God's Word. Divorce and remarriage can fracture families and pour a host of confusing and idolatrous messages onto the next generation.

Divorce should always grieve us. It grieves God. The main reason that divorce should grieve us is this: divorce corrupts, despises, and casts aside the beauty of the union of Christ and the church. It tarnishes the expression of God's redeeming love that is meant to be visible in marriage. Divorce crushes the spirits of offended spouses, children, extended families, and church communities.

However, we can still do a great deal of damage to the glory of Christ in our marriages and can crush the spirits of spouses and children without ever getting a divorce. Marital violence, for example, provides an equally awful depiction of Jesus Christ. It can be equally crushing to people involved. Divorce is not the only evil associated with specific human marriages. It just happens to be a decisive and final one.

Are You Free to Marry?

Before you began the marriage preparation process, you should have established whether or not you and your fiancé are free to marry each other. The question should have been asked, "According to God and His Word, are you free to marry?" If neither of you has ever been divorced, then the question may not have come up. If one or both of you have been divorced, then the pastor who plans to officiate your wedding or the leaders who have been guiding you toward marriage probably asked you this question weeks ago. I hope this is the case.

If this issue somehow fell through the cracks, then you need to ask yourselves a few hard questions now. I cannot answer these questions for you or spend adequate time examining all that Scripture has to say about divorce and remarriage. I simply encourage you to make it a point of discussion. The discussion will give you and those who are guiding you an opportunity to make sure that the Lord truly ordains and honors your marriage union.

8. Have you or your fiancé been divorced in the past? If so, please briefly explain the circumstances.

9. According to God's Word, are you and your fiancé free to marry each other? If you or your fiancé have been divorced, then please read the following passages in order to help you answer this question: Genesis 2:23–24; Matthew 19:1–10; Mark 10:1–12; 1 Corinthians 7:10–16.

10. If your previous spouse sinfully divorced you, to what degree does resentment, anger, and guilt linger from your previous marriage and divorce?

Taking the Point to Heart

There are a number of covenants presented in the Scripture involving God and humanity. Marriage is one of them. The covenant of marriage involves an agreement between a man and a woman to remain faithful to each other, by the grace of God, as husband and wife during their earthly lives (see Mark 10:9). It provides a beautiful, visible picture of the glorious, invisible covenant between Christ and His bride, the church. We should take the covenant very seriously—just as God does.

What we cannot try to do, however, is to keep the covenant of marriage through our self-righteous works. We are sinners. Our best efforts to keep the law cannot redeem and transform us. The law can highlight the truth of our sinfulness, but it cannot save and sanctify us. The righteous commandments of Scripture cannot perfect us, nor can they perfect our spouses. The law leads us to Jesus Christ, and the law is satisfied and fulfilled in Jesus Christ—then it fades into the background so that Jesus Christ can have center stage.

We are saved and sanctified by His grace alone. Our marriages are forged, nurtured, and grown by grace alone.

Law suffocates. Grace breathes life. Law produces despair and death. Grace produces hope and life.

Some of this may not make sense right now. God willing, you will have many years to soak it all in. Please remember: sweetness and delight will never come to our marriages by the absence of sinfulness, but only by the presence of redeeming and reconciling grace.

6

Becoming a Husband

Husbands, love your wives, just as Christ also loved
the church and gave Himself up for her. (Eph. 5:25)

If you are a man entering into marriage, then you are about to become a
husband. It is a wonderful and serious privilege. God will be with you,
and you will need Him.

As you become a husband, *you are not to decide what this role should*
entail. God has already assigned it. Though we are free to choose or not
choose marriage, we are not free to choose our most basic roles and
responsibilities in marriage. God has already established these. While
many of the details and expressions of duties could change from man
to man, the basic responsibilities of a husband, from God's point of
view, apply to every man in every marriage. So if you are becoming a
husband, then you need to understand what God asks and requires of
you. We will all answer to Him and receive our rewards from Him in
the end.

When talking about marriage, and especially Christian marriage,
we can jump too quickly into discussions about the roles of husbands
and wives without a proper understanding of the reasons for these
roles. The previous chapters were meant to lay a foundation of the reasons for marriage. One reason stands above them all: the display and
enjoyment of the glory of God, and especially the glory of Christ and
the church. Marriage is a unique and beautiful stage for the glory of
God's redeeming grace.

The roles of marriage help to express *the reason* for marriage. God did not assign these roles in a vacuum, or simply to make marriage work better for people, or simply to make everyone get along in their marriages. He is not chiefly concerned with keeping everybody fulfilled, or keeping societal harmony, or avoiding divorce, or cutting down on fights in the kitchen. Once more, those would be *man-centered* reasons, not *God-centered* reasons. He is concerned about those things, but neither firstly nor centrally. After all, when we come to behold, praise, and delight in the glory of Christ in marriage and the beauties of His grace in our eternal marriage to Him, everything else that matters will follow. We will fight less often in our kitchens and everywhere else.

Whose Power and Ability?

As we begin our discussion about the roles and responsibilities of husbands and wives in marriage, we need to lay a little groundwork from the Scripture. The groundwork will be intended for one purpose: to let His Word highlight our desperate need for the grace of God in our ministry as husbands and wives. When reading the instructions that Scripture gives to husbands and wives, we can easily assume that they can be achieved through our ability apart from God's transformative grace. They cannot be! From the moment the human race was plunged into sinful rebellion until now, honoring these beautiful roles has been outside our reach. We need supernatural help.

Let me try to develop this idea from Ephesians 5:18–21. These four verses immediately precede Paul's classic address to husbands and wives in the body of Christ.

> And do not get drunk with wine, for that is dissipation, but *be filled with the Spirit*, speaking to one another in psalms and hymns and spiritual songs, singing and making melody with your heart to the Lord; always giving thanks for all things in the name of our Lord Jesus Christ to God, even the Father; and be subject to one another in the fear of Christ. (Eph. 5:18–21)

These are vitally important verses for us as we approach Scripture's specific exhortations to husbands and wives. They provide the fuel to power everything that Scripture asks us to be and do in marriage. After telling us not to be drunk with wine, Paul offers a serious imperative: "But be filled with the Spirit." This is the essential verb to follow in the whole text. Everything else depends on *it* happening.

So what does it mean to be filled with the Holy Spirit? Being filled with the Holy Spirit means

- being new creations in Christ and, thus, Spirit-filled (see Eph. 1:13–14; 5:18).
- trusting Him and honoring Him from our hearts according to His Word (see 1:17–19).
- remaining strengthened by His power in our daily submission to Him (see 1:18–19).
- not being ruled by worldly desires (see 5:18) or being controlled by sin and worldliness.
- being ruled by Christ and His Word.
- living by absolute faith in Jesus Christ as Savior and Lord with the power that His indwelling Spirit supplies.

Ephesians 5:19–21 names four wonderful outcomes of being filled with the Holy Spirit. In a manner of speaking, these are relational fruits of the Spirit.

1. Speaking to one another in psalms and hymns and spiritual songs.
2. Singing and making melody with your heart to the Lord.
3. Always giving thanks for all things in the name of our Lord Jesus Christ to God.
4. Be subject to one another in the fear of Christ.

If we are filled with the Spirit (and walking in the Spirit), then we will speak to one another with loving, kind, and compassionate words. We will worship Jesus Christ together from our hearts. Our interactions with others will build up the body of Christ, not tear it down. We will constantly give thanks to God in light of all that He has given us in Jesus Christ. Even when life hurts, we will praise Him and encourage others to see Him and enjoy Him. Then we will voluntarily submit ourselves to whatever authority God has assigned to us out of reverence for Christ. When we trust Christ and follow Him with the strength that the Spirit provides, all these qualities grow and flourish in us over time.

Without being new creations in Christ and walking in His Spirit, we will not (and cannot) abide with one another in this loving and beautiful manner. Whatever speech we express will spring from self-centeredness and bring forth sorrow. We may use proper theological words and speak Christian ideas, but building up others will not be our goal. Any singing that we project will be not from our hearts to the Lord but from our religious habits or something worse. Our thanksgivings will be short-lived and empty. Any obedience that we offer to God in public will be for outward show. Our hearts will be grumbling and complaining on the inside.

If we do not abide in the Spirit of Christ, we cannot honor and please God. If we abide in the Spirit of Christ, then we cannot avoid honoring and pleasing God, because His Spirit will bear fruit in our lives. Jesus promised, "I am the vine, you are the branches; he who abides in Me and I in him, he bears much fruit, for apart from Me you can do nothing" (John 15:5).

The picture of Christ and the church is too marvelous—and the glory of God in marriage too spectacular—for us to seize marriage by our own strength and endure it by our personal grit. Constant divine enablement will be required.

The questions and sections that follow are for husbands-to-be, so you ladies can feel free to skip forward to the next section.

1. In what ways do you walk in the Spirit? In what ways do you walk in the flesh?

2. In your coming marriage, are you likely to rely on Christ and His Spirit for strength, or on your own strength and abilities? Please explain.

3. Please describe your prayer life. Has it been thriving, struggling, inconsistent, desperate, heartfelt, empty, sweet, or painful? Anything else?

Husbands with Their Wives

There is no shortage of biblical truth, wisdom, and images for earthly husbands to behold and embrace as they seek to live honorably with their wives. God referred to His covenant relationship with Israel as a marriage, in which God identified Himself as the husband figure and Israel as the bride figure. Isaiah 54:5 is one example: "For your husband is your Maker, whose name is the LORD of hosts; and your Redeemer is the Holy One of Israel, who is called the God of all the earth." If we need direction as husbands, then we must study the faithful and gracious ways of God with His bride.

The story of Hosea and his wife Gomer offers a beautiful image of redeeming love in marriage and a living, vivid picture of God's covenantal love for His people.

The story begins with God commanding Hosea to "go, take to yourself a wife of harlotry and have children of harlotry; for the land commits flagrant harlotry, forsaking the LORD" (Hos. 1:2). Hosea married Gomer, and she was an unfaithful wife. She even had at least one child by another man. God called Hosea to restore her over and over: "Then the LORD said to me, 'Go again, love a woman who is loved by her husband, yet an adulteress, even as the LORD loves the sons of Israel, though they turn to other gods and love raisin cakes'" (3:1).

Hosea and Gomer did not have a bad marriage from God's frame of reference, because they served His eternal purposes with splendid and timeless precision. Their marriage was full of pain and heartache, but it was also full of grace, beauty, and divine wonder. Their marriage provided exactly what God intended it to provide: a visible, tangible display of His nature and character, and especially the nature of His grace.

If you are going to be a husband, then you are about to accept an assignment of serious and eternal weight. You are about to assume the Christ-reflecting figure in your marriage. You are about to represent Him in your home and display something about Him to the world through your relationship to your bride.

Paul pointed to this beautiful and significant responsibility in his letter to the Ephesians.

Husbands, love your wives, just as Christ also loved the church and gave Himself up for her, so that He might sanctify her, having cleansed her by the washing of water with the word, that He might present to Himself the church in all her glory, having no spot or wrinkle or any such thing; but that she would be holy and blameless. So husbands ought also to love their own wives as their own bodies. He who loves his own wife loves himself; for no one ever hated his own flesh, but nourishes and cherishes it, just as Christ also does the church, because we are members of His body. For this reason a man shall leave his father and mother and shall be joined to his wife, and the two shall become one flesh. This mystery is great; but I am speaking with reference to Christ and the church. Nevertheless, each individual among you also is to love his own wife even as himself, and the wife must see to it that she respects her husband. (Eph. 5:25–33)

A consistent word that Paul used to define the role of a husband in relation to his wife is *love* (from *agape*). This meaning of love defines or captures the way of Christ with His bride. Human marriage exists in order to help us reflect and enjoy the union of Christ and His bride. A husband's love for his wife means *joyful self-sacrifice, empowered by the Holy Spirit, that has as its aim the eternal good of his bride for the glory of his God.*

Paul conveyed this meaning in verses 25–33. We will unpack this definition using the comparisons and pictures that he offers in the text.

Just as Christ Also Loved the Church

The life, death, and resurrection of Jesus Christ offer a clear, timeless example of the love that a husband is called to display toward his wife. The giving of Himself defined Jesus' love for His bride. Jesus "gave Himself up for" the church. No one forced Him to become a human bondslave and die as a criminal in order to ransom His bride from slavery. He offered Himself willingly. John 10:11 records Jesus' words: "I am the good shepherd; the good shepherd lays down His life for the sheep."

It should help us all to remember that Jesus gave Himself gladly in marriage. It was not a begrudging service. He gave Himself gladly, because He delighted in the glory of His Father and in the redemption of His bride. Hebrews 12:2 says that Jesus "for the joy set before Him endured the cross, despising the shame, and has sat down at the right hand of the throne of God."

A husband is called to give up himself for his bride the way Jesus did for His bride. Such sacrifice is hard, but it is also good. It takes many years to learn this kind of love, and it is very worthwhile. A husband will often be tempted (and will often fall) to bitterness and resentment toward his wife, because the very nature of his calling is joyful self-sacrifice, and the sinful flesh hates nothing more than joyful self-sacrifice.

Paul built on the idea further in his letter to the Colossians: "Husbands, love your wives and *do not be embittered against them*" (Col. 3:19). A husband's disposition toward his wife should be cheerful, patient, and grace-filled, not begrudging, impatient, and law-filled.

Love delights in giving and serving, and it refuses to resent the costs of its own existence (see 1 Cor. 13:4; 1 Peter 4:8).

The aim of Christ's joyful self-sacrifice is the eternal good of His bride. His love is benevolent in nature, not self-seeking or for its own sake. He gave himself up "so that He might sanctify her . . . that He might present to Himself the church in all her glory" (Eph. 5:26–27). Jesus sanctifies and will glorify His bride. His self-sacrifice leads her in a good direction. It does not move in circles. His Word blesses His bride. It helps to deal with sin and shame in her life. His love reconciles her to the Father and helps her to grow.

So when a husband is called to love his wife as Christ loved the church, he is called to joyfully sacrifice himself for the eternal welfare of his bride. This sacrifice is an attempt to lead his bride toward the Father for her good and the Father's glory. This service leads him to pray for sanctification and growth in his bride. A husband who loves his bride this way seeks to help her glorify and enjoy her eternal husband, Jesus Christ.

A husband who is learning to love his wife just as Christ also loved the church is also learning to speak the truth in love to his wife. He learns to pay careful attention to her words and to receive her thoughts with thanksgiving. He strives to be tender and compassionate. He learns to pray with his wife and for his wife. He reads the Scripture with her and listens to her views about the Word of God. He longs to give himself sexually and exercises patience when she declines to give her body in return. He prays to serve his bride without expecting service in return. He initiates conversation. He confesses sin genuinely. He forgives her and refuses to hold grudges.

A husband who is learning to love his wife just as Christ also loved the church is also learning to confront his wife's sinfulness in a gracious way. He is learning *not to avoid* painful interactions or to pretend things are okay in marriage when they are not. If his wife thinks they need help in their marriage, he humbles himself and seeks the aid of wise friends or pastors. He leads his marriage toward Christ and the body of Christ. He leads it into regular worship and service in the church. He is learning to lead it in wise and generous use of money. He works hard at his job without living for his career. He works faithfully at his job, whether it pays well or not, simply because he loves God and his wife. He is learning not to lord authority over his wife but to serve and encourage her in Christ.

There will be many hours when your wife does not cooperate with your efforts to lead her toward Christ. Her sin will bring grief and pain, just as your sin brings grief and pain to your divine Husband, and just as your sin will bring grief and pain to your wife. At these moments, love becomes more important than ever before. At the moments when love is most difficult, it is most needed—and therefore the Spirit is most needed.

God has *not* chosen to make you a husband so that you get the respect, honor, and approval from your wife that you think you deserve. He is not providing you a wife so that she can satisfy all your sexual passions.

We must remember the greater picture: you are "chosen of God, holy and beloved" (Col. 3:12). You have been forgiven of all your sins. Christ has absorbed the wrath of God in your place. God has granted you both a new heart and everlasting life with Him. He has filled you with

His Spirit. The Lord is your Shepherd. He is your Refuge and Deliverer. What more, fundamentally and ultimately, do you really need?

Respect, honor, and approval are all nice things, but they are not essential to your life. They will be deadly to your soul when they are exalted too highly. They will wage war on your marriage. Like all created things, they will consume you if you make them the target of your affections. So if you are entering into marriage to try to get something from your wife that you think you cannot survive without, then get ready for tremendous disappointment and frustration. Marriage does not exist to be a delivery vehicle for your appetites. If selfish desires are ruling your heart, then marriage will eat you alive, and you will never really understand why.

God has chosen to make you a husband, first and foremost, so that you can display His glory and enjoy Him forever. Marriage exists, first and foremost, in order to help you and everyone else to behold and proclaim the mystery of Christ and the church. Marriage will even sanctify you and conform you to the image of Jesus Christ, over time and when you are humble. The blessings of marriage become true blessings when they are received as gifts from Christ, and they are intended to be enjoyed in the love of Christ and others.

4. List expressions of love that you can give your future wife.

5. What things are you excited for your wife to give you in marriage? How can you enjoy these things without expecting or demanding them?

As His Own Body

The glory of Christ and the church provides something exultant and resplendent for us to pray for and seek after in our marriages.

In addition to this picture of Christ and the church, Paul gives a second, related image of how husbands are to love their wives in Ephesians 5:28. It appears more basic and earthy. Husbands are called to love their wives "as their own bodies." A husband is to show the regard and respect for his wife that he pays to his own body. After all, when we are hungry, we feed our bodies. When thirsty, we provide drink to our bodies. When endangered, we guard our bodies. When exhausted, we rest our bodies.

A husband is to love his wife by serving, helping, encouraging, providing for, and guarding her the way that he would his own body. "For no one ever hated his own flesh, but nourishes and cherishes it" (Eph. 5:29). No man in his right mind has ever treated his body with cruelty and disdain. Demons may provoke a man to harm his own body (see Mark 5:1–5), and men may even harm their bodies in order to manipulate their gods (see 1 Kings 18:28–29) or to deal with emotional pain, but these are acts of self-love and blind confusion. Basic reason and sensibility compel human beings to handle their bodies with care and concern.

The words *nourish* and *cherish* grasp what Paul meant when he said that a husband is to love his wife even as his own body. A husband should provide for his wife carefully and value her highly, "just as Christ also does the church" (Eph. 5:29). When a husband nourishes and cherishes his bride, he carefully provides for her what is necessary for her eternal good and highly prizes her as a gift from God. He sees her as God's precious daughter, thus better reflecting the manner of Jesus with His bride. Once again, a husband joyfully sacrifices certain things in order to serve the good of his wife, as he would his very own body. He listens to his wife as he does his own body. He pays attention and thinks ahead in order to care for her, just as he would his own body.

There may be hours or days when nourishing and cherishing your wife becomes quite difficult and painful. There may be times when your love for your wife compels you to gently reprove and guide her as you would your own body. Sometimes your body wants foolish things— even sinful things. Sometimes your wife will want foolish things—even sinful things. Sometimes your body would like to get drunk with wine or indulge sinful passions, but you are enabled by the Spirit to walk in love and obedience. In a similar way, you may be called to lovingly admonish, exhort, and teach your wife in response to her sinful passions and desires. Christ also loves the church in this way.

With Understanding and Showing Honor

> You husbands in the same way, live with your wives in an understanding way, as with someone weaker, since she is a woman; and show her honor as a fellow heir of the grace of life, so that your prayers will not be hindered. (1 Peter 3:7)

In the verse above, Peter instructed husbands to live in a certain manner with their wives "as with someone weaker, since she is a woman." What on earth does he mean? What does he mean that a wife is "someone weaker, since she is a woman"?

Let me give four possible ways to understand these words so that we can better grasp Peter's counsel to husbands.

First, as we will see in a few moments, wives are commanded by God to submit themselves to their own husbands "as to the Lord" (Eph. 5:22). Such submission places a wife in a very *vulnerable* position. This is one way to look at the statement "someone weaker." God has commanded wives to assume a "weaker" position—a more vulnerable position. She is at the mercy of God and, on another level, at the mercy of her husband. A husband should take this very seriously.

From this point of view, "Live with your wives in an understanding way" means "Appreciate the difficult and perhaps scary position that wives assume in order to follow their human husbands." A husband must realize how hard it is to live in submission to a man in order for him to pray for understanding and empathy toward his wife.

Second, in another manner, a wife is created and enabled by God to be a suitable helper for her husband (see Gen. 2:20–24). She is, by nature, *different* from her husband. This is one way to look at the phrase "since she is a woman." She is not a man. A wife will probably think, feel, and respond to daily situations and to life as a whole in a way that is special and unique in comparison to her husband. Her way may be distinct from her husband's because she has been called by God to fulfill a role that is distinct from her husband's. Such distinction is good. Such differences can be extremely helpful in marriage, especially when those differences are treated with humility and grace.

From this point of view, "Live with your wives in an understanding way" means "Appreciate her specialness and differentness." Be patient with her concerns and objections and ideas, even though they seem peculiar to you, because she is a woman and is meant to bring something unique to the table. A husband and a wife are not meant to be the same but to complement each other for the glory of Christ and His kingdom. No husband and wife are perfect, but by God's sovereign design they can be a perfect fit for each other.

Another, third way to view Peter's words has to do with *physical delicacy.* Since God made women, as a whole, physically "weaker" and smaller than men, a husband should be careful in how he physically conducts himself with his wife. "Since she is woman," Peter says, be gentle and tender with her, "as with someone weaker." In other words, don't intimidate her with your size and strength, but protect her. Don't force your way because you are bigger and stronger, but handle her with gentleness.

Of course, there are ways that wives can be physically stronger than their husbands. If the day comes when you watch your wife give birth to a child, you will see what I mean. Certain physical tasks God has enabled women, but not men, to handle. What I believe Peter could be focusing on, however, is the reality that husbands are more physically powerful than their wives. They should use their size and strength to serve and guard their wives, not to threaten and control them.

A fourth way to see these words would be this: a wife could be, as a whole, more *susceptible* to deceit and error than her husband. This sense of meaning would be supported by Paul's words to Timothy:

> But I do not allow a woman to teach or exercise authority over a man, but to remain quiet. For it was Adam who was first created, and then Eve. And it was not Adam who was deceived, but the woman being deceived, fell into transgression. (1 Tim. 2:12–14)

One reason that Paul instructed men to lead and women to follow in churches is that women, in keeping with the pattern that Eve instituted, could be more susceptible to spiritual deceit and error.

Of course, we all know that men can also fall to deceit and error, and specific husbands can be far more prone to deceit and error than their specific wives, but we are speaking generally about men and women, just as Paul was speaking generally. Paul, and perhaps Peter, were speaking of a pattern of weakness that began in the garden of Eden and continues today.

If we believe that this is what Peter was getting after in his words "someone weaker, since she is a woman," then we should believe he is drawing attention to a wife's susceptibility to being led astray by various lusts, fears, and emotional winds of the world, and is saying that a husband needs to live with her struggle in an understanding way. (There are plenty of struggles that men bring to marriage, but we will get to these later in the book.)

There may be times when a wife believes things that do not make sense to her husband, or accuses her husband wrongly, or gets upset about something said in church and would rather not go back, or over-reacts to a difficult discussion. There may be moments when her moods are unpredictable or out of proportion. Peter tells every husband to live with his own wife in an understanding way, to be sympathetic and patient, to listen and encourage. Every husband should remember: she is a woman, not a man, and her unique strengths and weaknesses are valuable parts of the marriage gift.

For these reasons, there are two particular attitudes that every husband must be encouraged to adopt if he is going to love his wife in a way that honors the Lord. First, Peter tells husbands to "live with your wives in an understanding way." In other words, listen to, appreciate, and value your wife. She will not always make sense to you, so pray and learn to live with her in an understanding way, just as Jesus lives with you in an understanding way.

The second disposition that Peter tells husbands to adopt with their wives is this: "Show her honor as a fellow heir of the grace of life, so that your prayers will not be hindered." Although a wife is given a distinct role in marriage, she is not given a lesser role—or any lesser value, or any lower-class status. She is a "fellow heir." She is a daughter of the King just as you are a son of the King. She has been redeemed by grace just as you have been redeemed by grace. Galatians 3:28 emphasizes that "there is neither Jew nor Greek, there is neither slave nor free man, there is neither male nor female; for you are all one in Christ Jesus."

Just in case any husband might be tempted to view and treat his wife as less important than himself, Peter commanded husbands to "show her honor." God takes this so seriously that He will refuse the prayers of any man who deals dishonorably with his wife. What a terrifying and humbling reality! In a way, God is telling husbands this: "If you will not show your wife honor, then neither will I show you honor. If you will not live with her in an understanding way, then neither will I live with you in an understanding way. If you will not hear her petitions, then neither will I hear your petitions. I will receive you in the same way that you receive my daughter."

These words from Peter remind me of Malachi 2. God spoke through Malachi to help the husbands of Israel understand why He was not hearing their tearful prayers. The prophet said,

> This is another thing you do: you cover the altar of the LORD with tears, with weeping and with groaning, because He no longer regards the offering or accepts it with favor from your hand. Yet you say, "For what reason?" Because the LORD has been a witness between you and the wife of your youth, against whom you have dealt treacherously, though she is your companion and your wife by covenant. (vv. 13–14)

The God of Israel was refusing the offerings and prayers from men in Israel because those men were dealing treacherously with their wives (divorcing them in order to marry foreign women, for example). These men were expecting God to hear their petitions and bless their work. They were expecting God to honor their prayers even though they had dishonored their wives of covenant. God saw into their homes. He saw into their hearts. He responded to their prayers accordingly. God is no less holy or serious or attentive to our marriages today.

Indeed, let us all remember, as husbands, to "show her honor as a fellow heir of the grace of life, so that your prayers will not be hindered." God loves us, but He also loves our wives. God loves us, and He will discipline us and chasten us until the very end. Let us praise Him for His persistent love.

6. As a man, do you have a track record of respecting and valuing women as a whole? How do you treat your mother? Your sisters?

7. Share about a few men who were key examples for you growing up—for better or for worse. How did they treat the women in their lives? What did you see in them and learn from them?

8. How has God prepared you for the lifelong journey of learning to love your wife just as Christ also loved the church? What do you expect this journey to look like for you?

A Brief Note on Leaving Your Parents

For this reason a man shall leave his father and mother and be joined to his wife, and the two shall become one flesh. . . . So they are no longer two, but one flesh. What therefore God has joined together, let no man separate. (Matt. 19:5–6)

No man can love his wife freely and in a Christ-exalting way while remaining wrongly attached to his parents. God knows this. He designed it this way. Immediately after recording the creation of marriage in Genesis 2, God inspired Moses to insert the directive "A man shall leave his father and his mother, and be joined to his wife" (Gen. 2:24). Jesus quoted from this passage before adding, "What therefore God has joined together, let no man separate" (Matt. 19:6).

Biblical marriage requires men to grow up. A husband is asked by God to love his wife just as Christ also loved the church: by giving himself up, by speaking the truth in love, by leading humbly, by charting a course for his home that serves the eternal good of his wife and the glory of his God. In order for a man to accomplish this, Christ, not his parents, must be his Head. The Spirit, not the ambitions and entanglements of his parents, must fill his heart. He must be learning to depend on God, not his parents, for provision and protection.

What it means for a man to honor his father and mother changes over time. It modifies from dependency on his parents in numerous areas of life into a call to provide and care for the physical needs of his parents once they are *unable* to care for their own physical needs. Biological children are supposed to care for their aging parents when their aging parents have legitimate physical needs. First Timothy 5:4 clearly directs us, "But if any widow has children or grandchildren, they must first learn to practice piety in regard to their own family and to make some return to their parents; for this is acceptable in the sight of God." A husband and his wife may even live with his parents or have his parents live in his home, but not under the authority of his parents. He must be learning to love, lead, and care for his wife as the Lord has designed.

The instruction for a son to honor his father and mother also changes from a call to obey and follow his parents into a call to show them respect and gratitude but not obedience. A son may seek wisdom from his father or mother, but he is never again to place himself beneath their direction and control. He may continue to receive biblical counsel and encouragement from his parents, but only as he would from brothers or sisters in Christ.

Each man will have to pray and seek God regarding how these truths apply to his own heart and life. Some men have parents who love Jesus, hold marriage in high regard, and refuse to threaten the marriages of their children in any form. Other men have parents who couldn't care less about Christ and His glory and have little regard for the covenant of marriage. They have no qualms about intruding into, disrupting, and breeding conflict in the marriages of their children. Disobedient parents can reduce your marriage vineyard to ash if you let them loose inside the fences.

You may have parents who really think that they honor your marriage, but in reality they cross the fence lines of your marriage far more often than they realize. They may try to respect the integrity of your marriage, but then cannot help themselves from giving direction and exerting their influence. Often they will not even notice. Perhaps your parents will share opinions very freely and thus will offer regular advice about how you should spend money, decorate your house, raise your children, cook food, clean the kitchen, and otherwise live as a married couple. Perhaps they will expect you to come over for Sunday lunch every weekend for the next fifteen years. Maybe they expect a daily phone call or updates on the events of your life and home. You and your fiancé will know, better than anyone else, what to anticipate from the parents in your lives.

Please don't wait for the battle to come to you. Initiate prayer, thoughtfulness, and conversation about what will need to change in your relationship with your father and mother during the days ahead. It may be helpful to find out from them what they are expecting from you after your wedding day. No matter what, you will need to take the words of Christ very seriously: "What therefore God has joined together, let no man separate" (Matt. 19:6). You must consider deeply what it means to leave your father and mother, become one with your wife, and love her with the love of Christ.

9. Share some obstacles you foresee in your own heart and life to leaving your parents in order to become one flesh with your wife.

10. Share some ways that your parents may, consciously or not, create problems and difficulties in your marriage.

11. How do you intend to face these challenges with your wife?

Taking the Point to Heart

What a privilege husbands have been given in marriage—to reflect Christ by their joyful, benevolent self-sacrifice for the eternal good of their brides and the glory of their God! Marriage exists, foremost, to help tell the story of Christ and His church. A multitude of delights come alongside, but they are not the ultimate reasons for marriage. Sex, companionship, and procreation are all wonderful gifts of marriage, but they are not the main point. It will be important for you as a husband to remember these things. Jesus is enough for you. You are "chosen of God, holy and beloved" (Col. 3:12). The more you believe this, the better equipped you will be to truly love your wife. You are less likely to use your wife and more likely to serve your wife.

Here is another vital point: You cannot fulfill your calling as a husband in your own strength. The road is too long and the task too difficult. Dependence on the Spirit will be essential. Only by His grace will you glorify and enjoy your God in marriage and love your wife just as Christ also loved the church.

7

Becoming a Wife

But as the church is subject to Christ, so also the wives
ought to be to their husbands in everything. (Eph. 5:24)

If you are a woman entering into marriage, then you are about to become a wife. It is a wonderful and serious privilege. God will be with you, and you will need Him.

As you become a wife, *you are not to decide what this role should entail. God has already assigned it.* Though we are free to choose or not choose marriage, we are not free to choose our most basic roles and responsibilities in marriage. God has already established these. While many of the details and expressions of duties could change from woman to woman, the basic responsibilities of a wife, from God's point of view, apply to every woman in every marriage. So if you are becoming a wife, then you need to understand what God asks and requires of you. Every wife will answer to Him and receive her reward from Him in the end.

The previous chapter began our discussion of roles in marriage. The roles of husbands and wives in marriage are simply expressions of the primary reason for marriage: to provide a temporal, visible, and living picture of the eternal, invisible, and living reality of Christ and His church. Husbands are called to be a reflection of Christ in their marriages. They are called to love their own wives the way that Christ also loves the church. We looked at this charge in the previous chapter. Wives are called to be a reflection of the church in their marriages—to display the affections, attitudes, and activities that the church should have toward Jesus Christ. A wife displays this through her attitude and conduct toward her own husband.

Once Again, Whose Power and Ability?

Before we jumped into the proper attitudes and actions of husbands toward their own wives in chapter 6, we identified *the only means* by which husbands and wives can truly fulfill their God-given responsibilities in marriage for the glory of Christ: through the work and enablement of the Holy Spirit. This is the same power that fills the wife.

Paul wrote these verses right before his instructions to husbands and wives in Ephesians 5.

> And do not get drunk with wine, for that is dissipation, but *be filled with the Spirit*, speaking to one another in psalms and hymns and spiritual songs, singing and making melody with your heart to the Lord; always giving thanks for all things in the name of our Lord Jesus Christ to God, even the Father; and be subject to one another in the fear of Christ. (Eph. 5:18–21)

The power for obeying the Word of God comes from God. Namely, it comes by the Holy Spirit living and working inside our hearts. Gracious speech, genuine corporate worship, gratitude in our relationships, and cheerful submission to our authorities flow from our souls when they have been redeemed and filled by Christ. There is no other way to produce the kind of fruit that the Lord seeks. His power must abide in us, and we must abide in Him. Jesus made certain His disciples heard this loud and clear: "I am the vine, you are the branches; he who abides in Me and I in him, he bears much fruit, for apart from Me you can do nothing" (John 15:5).

Not from ourselves, but from Him, comes our ability to accomplish His will and pleasure in our lives and marriages. Even our desire to please Him comes from Him. God redeems and works in us. We follow and obey Him. We accomplish this through the strength He supplies. Philippians 2:12–13 says,

So then, my beloved, just as you have always obeyed, not as in my presence only, but now much more in my absence, work out your salvation with fear and trembling; for it is God who is at work in you, both to will and to work for His good pleasure.

The beautiful instructions that wives are given in marriage and the wonderful challenges that wives are asked to face in marriage are utterly impossible for wives to tackle by themselves. God designed it this way. Wives were never meant to run the course alone or in their own strength. Complete dependence on the Spirit of God is the only way to obey the Lord with a joyful disposition. It is the only way to be a wife for His glory.

Wives with Their Husbands

Wives, *be subject* to your own husbands, as to the Lord. For the husband is the head of the wife, as Christ also is the head of the church, He Himself being the Savior of the body. But as the church is subject to Christ, so also the wives ought to be to their husbands in everything. (Eph. 5:22–24)

After saying to every member of the church in Ephesians 5:21, "And be subject to one another in the fear of Christ," Paul then says, "Wives, be subject to your own husbands, as to the Lord" (v. 22). The position of a wife in relation to her husband has been defined in Paul's words by the phrase "be subject . . . as to the Lord." Paul repeats the idea in Colossians 3:18, and Peter expands on it in 1 Peter 3:1–6. A great deal can be said about the attitudes and actions of a wife toward her husband, beyond the instruction to "be subject," but we will begin here because the Scripture puts so much weight on this particular attitude and activity.

Everyone in the household of God is called to be in subjection to someone. The place of submission is not unique to wives. Husbands are called to be subject to Christ, their Head (see 1 Cor. 11:3). Children are called to obey their parents "in the Lord, for this is right" (Eph. 6:1). Younger men are called to be subject to their elders in the church (see 1 Peter 5:5). Slaves are called to be obedient to their masters "as to Christ" (Eph. 6:5). And a wife is called to be subject to her husband "as to the Lord."

This instruction may not be popular in some families and cultures, but it continues to play a crucial role in God's design for relationships. Words like *obedience, submission, subjection,* and *headship* rub against the sinful flesh like nails against a chalkboard, but these words come from the Lord and remain vital to the health and God-glorifying purposes of relationships in the body of Christ.

A wife's being subject to her husband is a *joyful honoring of her husband's will and position, empowered by the Holy Spirit, that has as its aim the eternal fruitfulness of her husband for the glory of her God.* She wants to help show the world what the relationship between Christ and His church is really like. It means that *she longs to help her husband make much of Christ,* not much of herself. She prays for her marriage to honor Christ and His kingdom, not her own.

It means that her deep appreciation for Christ and His sacrificial love for her soul overflows into her attitude and activities toward the man who most visibly represents Jesus Christ in her life. Even when her husband acts selfishly, the Christian wife wants to do her part to portray the wondrous, invisible reality of the church in relation to Christ. It means that she wants to see and enact a little bit of heaven on earth.

On Earth as It Is in Heaven

Headship and submission begin not on earth, but in heaven. They begin not with humanity, but with God. First Corinthians 11:3 says, "But I want you to understand that Christ is the head of every man, and the man is the head of a woman, and God is the head of Christ."

Though all three persons of God are fully God, equally divine, and equally worthy of eternal worship, there is a dynamic of leadership and obedience between them. God is the head of Christ. The rest of Scripture reveals how the Father, Son, and Holy Spirit relate uniquely to one another (see Luke 22:42; John 5:30; 8:28–29, 42; 1 Peter 2:21–25). They love one another and assume distinctive roles in the work of salvation. The Son joyfully submits to the Father and the Father joyfully loves the Son, just as the church submits to Christ and Christ loves the church.

This is really important for us to realize and embrace. The reality of one person being the head of another person originates in the Godhead. The reality of one person being submitted to another person also originates in the Godhead. This way of relating did not begin on earth between men and women. It started as something beautiful in the very nature of God. We as humans have given submission and lordship ugly meanings. They did not originate that way.

Christ submits to the Father. His submission produced our salvation. He longs to glorify and honor the Father. First Corinthians 15:28 explains that "when all things are subjected to Him, then the Son Himself also will be subjected to the One who subjected all things to Him, so that God may be all in all." The Spirit also submits to the Father. He submits to the Father by bringing glory to the Son so that the Son may bring glory to the Father. Jesus made this clear when He spoke of the Spirit's coming:

> But when He, the Spirit of truth, comes, He will guide you into all the truth; for He will not speak on His own initiative, but whatever He hears, He will speak; and He will disclose to you what is to come. He will glorify Me, for He will take of Mine and will disclose it to you. (John 16:13–14)

Husbands are therefore called to be subject to Jesus Christ, their Head and Savior. In marriage, this subjection to Christ can be expressed through a husband's *joyful self-sacrifice, empowered by the Holy Spirit, that has as its aim the eternal good of his bride for the glory of his God.* The Spirit of God fills husbands and enables them to joyfully submit themselves to Jesus Christ and to follow Him daily. The very call of the Christian life is a call to surrender self, take up the cross, and follow Him. Jesus said this plainly in Luke 9:23–24:

> And He was saying to them all, "If anyone wishes to come after Me, he must deny himself, and take up his cross daily and follow Me. For

whoever wishes to save his life will lose it, but whoever loses his life for My sake, he is the one who will save it."

Wives, therefore, are called to be subject to their own earthly husbands out of reverence for Christ, in keeping with the pattern of authority that exists in God. The pattern begins in heaven, not on earth. Married women who are redeemed by the grace of God have been filled and enabled by the Spirit of God to visibly enact on earth what already exists in heaven.

The questions for this chapter are for women only. So men, please feel free to read this chapter without answering the questions.

1. If you were painfully honest, would you say that your goal for marriage is to help your husband make much of Christ, or for him to make much of you? What evidence do you see in either direction?

2. What is the earthly view of submission in your culture?

3. In what way do you see marriage as a means for you to love and submit to your husband for the glory of Christ and His kingdom?

As to the Lord

Wives, be subject to your own husbands, as to the Lord. For the husband is the head of the wife, as Christ also is the head of the church, He Himself being the Savior of the body. But as the church is subject to Christ, so also the wives ought to be to their husbands in everything. (Eph. 5:22–24)

The beautiful and ultimate reason for the instruction "Wives, be subject to your own husbands, as to the Lord" is built into the passage itself: "For the husband is the head of the wife, as Christ also is the head of the church." Wives are called and enabled to respect and honor their husbands as they would respect and honor Christ *because* marriage is a visible picture of the invisible relationship between Christ and the church.

Whenever a wife finds herself fighting to maintain a joyful posture of submission to her husband, God gives her this image to behold and remember: Christ and His church. Believing wives have been asked to submit to their husbands not as the husband deserves but as Christ deserves. The Father asks His daughters to honor their earthly husbands not according to the behavior and spiritual maturity of those earthly husbands but according to the behavior and glory of their heavenly husband. Jesus always deserves our full and happy obedience. A wife's heart attitude toward her husband *always* reflects her heart attitude toward Jesus Christ. The manner of a wife with her earthly husband *always* expresses her manner with her heavenly Husband. The former gives visibility to the latter.

You may be marrying a man who will make this attitude of heart and way of life a little easier. You may be marrying a man who, whether you realize it or not, will make this quite difficult. Either way, the aim of your attitude and actions toward your husband should be to help him live for the glory of God. They do not have as their aim your personal comfort and desires on earth. They do not have as their aim the satisfaction of your husband's selfish appetites and glory. They do not seek to conform your husband to your ideas of what he ought to be, even if your ideas for him are biblically upright. You are not your husband's head—Christ is!

A wife who is learning to be subject to her husband "as to the Lord" is learning to speak to her husband in kind and respectful ways. She seeks to fulfill his desires for their household without begrudging them or resenting what they cost. She is learning to give herself more freely in sexual union. She appreciates the opportunity to serve him. She is praying to be "a suitable helper" (see Gen. 2:18), in every sense of the phrase.

The wife who is learning to honor her husband "as to the Lord" longs to speak the truth in love to her husband. She refuses to nag and criticize him. She shares concerns with her husband but tries not to demand or threaten. When he sins against her, she gently confronts him for his own good and the pleasure of Christ. If he responds in pride and rejects all her petitions, then she carefully, courageously, and prayerfully seeks help from a trusted friend or from others in the body of Christ.

She prays for reconciliation with her husband, not retribution. When she is afraid, she prays and runs to God for strength, faith, and wisdom. When life seems to be crumbling, she runs to Christ first, then to her husband. She trusts the Holy Spirit with the sanctification of her husband.

The wife who loves her husband does not expect him to provide her sense of value and purpose in life. She looks to God to be her God and Savior. She believes herself to be "chosen of God, holy and beloved" (Col. 3:12), and longs to walk securely in the promises of God. She is learning to repent often and to seek God's forgiveness. She even repents before her earthly husband and seeks his forgiveness.

If she understands and walks in the Scripture with more maturity than her husband, then she also walks humbly before God and refuses to view her husband in a condescending way. She wants to help her husband love God according to God's sense of time and perspective.

Increasingly she views her place in marriage as a privilege and gift from God, not as a chore and certainly not as a punishment. She is learning to keep her home well—to be faithful in every duty that the Lord assigns. A wife who loves her husband is learning to view her every attitude, thought, and action toward her husband as an expression of her love for Jesus Christ.

4. What kinds of attitudes about marriage, men, and a wife's relationship to her husband have been modeled, taught, and expressed to you over the course of your life?

5. What obstacles do you foresee to honoring, respecting, and submitting to your husband just as the church submits to Christ?
How do you plan to face these obstacles?

In Everything

In light of everything we have said so far, it may be worth clarifying
the limits of a wife's submission to her husband—especially since Paul
seems to remove all limits to this submission in Ephesians 5:24: "So
also the wives ought to be to their husbands in everything." In everything! What does that mean?

The first half of this verse provides an extremely important context
for us to understand what Paul means by "everything" here. He calls
our attention to the relationship between Christ and His church: "But
as the church is subject to Christ, so also the wives ought to be to their
husbands in everything." Christ never asks the church to think, feel,
or do anything sinful. He never has and He never will. This may not
always be the case between a fallen husband and his wife.

On occasion, a husband may ask his wife to think, feel, or act sinfully toward her God or toward others. In these moments, a wife should
feel free to respectfully and sincerely decline his request. If ever a wife's
submission to Christ and her submission to her husband conflict, she

should obey Christ. She should express this carefully and respectfully, but also without shame. Such devotion to Christ expresses love for her husband, though he may not know it at the time.

Let me offer a few examples. A wife should not agree to watch pornography with her husband. A wife should not agree to sign a fraudulent tax return so that the family can pay less money to the government. A wife should not agree to lie to leaders in the church about her husband's violence or infidelity so that he retains his reputation and position as a Bible study teacher. A wife should not agree to keep his abuse of their children a secret, or to help him steal something, or to otherwise participate in immoral or illegal activities that bring dishonor to Jesus Christ. A wife should not go and buy beer for her husband because he is too drunk to go out and buy it himself. I think these kinds of situations are rare, but they happen.

Submission to Christ overrules submission to a husband. The two are meant to operate in unison, but sometimes they don't.

What I am not saying is that a wife is free from her call to honor and submit to her husband whenever he is acting like a sinner. After all, we are all sinners! What I am saying is that a wife is free from her call to submit to her husband in those moments when *he asks her* to think, feel, or live sinfully. Although he is redeemed by the grace of God, he will be a sinner until the day of his death. God knows that the Scripture directs you to respect and submit to a sinner. Some days will be harder than others. The Word of God is not invalidated in your life when your husband's attitude is lousy. It may be far more difficult to honor God and obey Scripture when your husband is proud and selfish, but the Holy Spirit will help. Often these are the moments when the gospel takes deeper root and shines more brightly in your life than ever before.

Fitting in the Lord

In Colossians 3:18, Paul includes an interesting phrase in His instruction to wives: "Wives, be subject to your husbands, as is fitting in the Lord." The phrase "fitting in the Lord" deserves some of our time and energy to digest.

There are two particular questions I would like us to consider. First, what does Paul mean? Second, why is this important for wives today?

In the words "fitting in the Lord," I believe Paul invited wives to see how voluntary and joyful submission to their own husbands becomes and beautifies women of faith. It *fits* a Christian wife. For a woman "chosen of God, holy and beloved," (Col. 3:12), the apparel of happy obedience in her marriage makes an appropriate covering. A wife who is redeemed by the blood of Christ and is looking forward to an eternity in her Lord's presence sees her relationship to her husband as a wonderful opportunity to express her gratitude and love toward God.

Just as immodest dress or coarse language does not suit a woman of faith, so an attitude of irreverence and bitterness toward her husband does not suit a woman of faith. Love, joy, and peace belong to those who are beloved of Christ. God celebrates and delights in His daughters who honor and respect their husbands with the strength He supplies. Such clothing *befits* His children.

So why is this exhortation important for wives today? The exhortation remains important because it runs quite contrary to the prevailing winds of our day. We live in an age when the prevailing messages and ideas of culture run violently against the notion that a wife's submission to her husband is a glorious and wonderful thing. If you become a wife who follows the Word of God in your marriage, then you will probably be seen by the world as weak or foolish. You may be treated by the world as strange and absurdly behind the times. Let me encourage you not to doubt, but to persevere! As we are about to see, "A gentle and quiet spirit . . . is precious in the sight of God" (1 Peter 3:4).

Precious in the Sight of God

In the same way, you wives, be submissive to your own husbands so that even if any of them are disobedient to the word, they may be won without a word by the behavior of their wives, as they observe your chaste and respectful behavior. Your adornment must not be merely external—braiding the hair, and wearing gold jewelry, or putting on dresses; but let it be the hidden person of the heart, with the imperishable quality of a gentle and quiet spirit, which is precious in the sight of God. For in this way in former times the holy women also, who hoped in God, used to adorn themselves, being submissive to their own husbands; just as Sarah obeyed Abraham, calling him lord, and you have become her children if you do what is right without being frightened by any fear. (1 Peter 3:1–6)

The world at large refuses to offer good, godly examples of how a wife should relate to her husband. Rarely (or perhaps never) will we hear the popular voices of our day proclaiming the beauty and importance of a wife honoring her husband with perseverance and joy. If you really want encouragement down this road of faith as a wife, then you will have to look to God, His Word, and the "holy women" of past ages. I pray that the Lord has supplied your church community with godly women to whom you may look as examples as well.

Even if this is not the case, the Lord gives an abundance of encouragement in His Word and power in His Spirit in order to help you assume the role of a believing wife in peace and gratitude.

No woman should be ashamed of the Word of God or of the glorious role that God assigns to her in relation to her husband and home. It is a privilege and a gift.

Peter begins chapter 3 by connecting his statement to wives with statements he has made in the previous chapter. "In the same way" that Christian citizens submit themselves to their governments (see 1 Peter 2:13–17), and Christian servants submit themselves to their masters (see vv. 18–20), and the Lord Jesus Christ submitted himself to the Father (see vv. 21–25), so a Christian wife has been called to submit herself to her husband.

Even if a woman comes to faith in Jesus Christ and is married to an unbeliever, Peter says that this wife is to give her husband honor and respect in hopeful prayer that Christ would use her loving, reverent attitude and actions to bring him to salvation. This can be painful, but it is also glorious. Jesus Christ was willing to joyfully submit Himself beneath the Father's will all the way through torture and death in order to purchase your salvation. God asks a Christian wife who is married to an unbelieving husband to be willing to do something similar. He asks her to joyfully submit herself to the Father's will in marriage to an unbelieving man in hope for his salvation.

If you are a Christ-believing woman who is preparing to marry, then you should not be marrying an unbelieving man. You should be marrying a Christ-loving man. I am assuming that this is the case for you. Since you are marrying a believing man, you have been given the same charge as a wife who is married to an unbelieving man: "Be submissive to your own husband." It may look a little different, because you are not trying to "win" your husband "without a word." You are trying to paint the grand portrait of Christ and His church.

Peter uses a number of beautiful words to define how faithful women can satisfy and enjoy this charge: *chaste*, *respectful*, *gentle*, and *quiet*. These words express the inward adornment that God seeks from His daughters. These words also fly in the face of almost every culture of women in the history of the world. They are the very opposite of fleshly instinct and desire. They will not come easily to you.

Chaste means "pure or uncorrupted by the sinful passions of the world." It means that you are not ruled by sensual desires. It means that you are learning to humbly combat sensual desires for the attention of men, or for material possessions, or for social glory. Even though the world beckons you to manipulate and control your husband in order to get what you want, chastity compels you to respect him instead. It means that you refuse to use your beauty to bring glory and attention to yourself, but that you pray to be able to use your life and body for giving honor to your husband instead.

Respectful means "reverent." It means that you hold your husband in high regard, even when your girlfriends mock and run down their husbands. Whether away from his face or to his face, behaving respectfully means that you treat him just as you would treat Christ. Again, this can be very difficult. There will be many days when your husband speaks, feels, and acts in an irreverent manner. Seeing and treating him respectfully will require God's supernatural help.

Gentle means "tender and mild." It means that you refuse to escalate into rage and apply emotional force in order to get your husband moving in a certain direction. It means that you handle his sinfulness the way that God has handled your sinfulness: with the utmost care and grace.

The phrase *quiet spirit* conveys a similar idea. Having a quiet spirit implies that you live with your husband in *a restful and peaceful way*, ruled not by fears and frustrations but by the Spirit of Christ. These qualities are neither common nor weak but are rare and courageous. They are "precious in the sight of God."

In fact, only women who are filled with the Spirit of Christ, resting in the unwavering love of God for them and committed to the further-ance of the gospel in their homes, will be able to honor God's purpose for them in marriage. Husbands are too sinful, selfish, and frustrating for their wives to love and honor in their own strength. In fact, any sensible woman who is married for long could hear these words from Peter and seriously question her ability to love her husband. What if he is rude or unkind? What if he stops following God and starts following his flesh? What if he "falls in love" with another woman and leaves me? Who will take care of me if he doesn't take care of me?

These are good questions. They arise from common fears and worries that wives can face every day in their marriages. By submitting to a husband, a woman runs the risk of being mistreated, neglected, and misunderstood. This can arouse a host of questions. Peter offered wives the only real comfort and energy that can help them maintain an inward beauty and peacefulness with their own husbands: a persevering "hope in God" (see 1 Peter 3:5).

The women of faith from ages past adorned themselves with chaste, respectful, gentle, and quiet spirits *because* they hoped in God and not in their husbands. They sought their peace from God, not from marriage. Their daily fears were battled back by *trusting in the Lord* for their ultimate protection and provision. A Christ-fearing husband is a gift from God. Being married to a patient and kind man could make marriage a little easier. But marriage to such a man is not promised by God, nor is such a man even necessary for you to enjoy your marriage. God intends to be the absolute hope, comfort, and joy of His daughters in their temporal marriages to their earthly husbands.

6. Think of a recent time when someone wronged you. Did you cover the transgression or speak the truth in love and seek reconciliation through the gospel? Or did you avoid, criticize, become bitter, or push the offenders away?

7. Reflect on the words *chaste, respectful, gentle,* and *quiet in spirit.* To what degree do these words describe your way with others? How do you see the Lord cultivating these qualities in your heart today?

8. When you dreamed of marriage, how did you imagine your husband would interact with you? Respond to you? What do you think is more realistic?

A Brief Note on Leaving Your Parents

Joyfully honoring your husband's will and position for the sake of his spiritual fruitfulness and God's glory assumes that you leave the authority, oversight, and other entanglements of your parents or caregivers. A wife cannot sincerely and fully serve Jesus Christ through the honor she gives to her husband while also following the leadership of her parents—not for long, at least.

At some point in the days that follow your wedding, the interests of your husband and the interests of your parents will collide. Parents must be respectfully and tenderly ushered to the outskirts of your marriage vineyard. What it means to honor your father and mother always changes over time, but at no time does it change more drastically than your wedding day.

There is a common question both men and women ask regarding the instruction that men are given to leave their parents. Here is the question: why are men given the commandment, but not women? Genesis 2:24 says this: "For this reason a man shall leave his father and his mother, and be joined to his wife; and they shall become one flesh." Why is the man instructed to leave, but not the woman?

Let me offer one broad explanation. A wife who joins to her husband *assumes* that she leaves the leadership of her parents, because, by definition, her husband becomes her head and leader from God's point of view. The nature of biblical marriage assumes that a woman will leave home in order to place herself under her husband's care and devote herself to his leading. Since a wife comes under the protection, provision, and direction of her husband, she no longer comes under the protection, provision, and direction of her parents. Most wedding ceremonies make this shift quite visible and clear. At some point early in the ceremony, the father of the bride *gives her* to the bridegroom.

The same may not be safely assumed for a man. A husband must be commanded to leave his father and mother in order to be joined to his wife, because he can still function as a husband, theoretically at least, while practically living under the authority and leadership of his parents. Bridegrooms are not usually given away during the wedding service. They "leave." Becoming married does not naturally assume that a man leaves the protection, provision, and direction of his parents. God must remind him to leave. Since remaining under the protection, provision, and direction of his parents is devastating to a man's marriage, God instructs him to leave.

Sometimes this leaving is easy for a wife, or seems so, but sometimes it can be quite difficult. You may have trusted your family for a long time—but what about this new man? Capture those foxes that may sneak in here! It may be tempting, when disagreements arise, to go to one who "knows you better" or "has lived longer," like your daddy. But now it's time for you and your husband to pray, talk, stand, and work together. By all means, love your parents. Seek their wisdom together. But, when it comes to decision-making time, God would have you cleave to your husband instead of to your father and mother.

9. Share some obstacles that you foresee in your own heart and life to leaving your parents in order to become one flesh with your husband.

10. Share some ways that your parents may, consciously or not, create problems and difficulties in your marriage.

11. How do you intend to face these challenges with your husband?

Taking the Point to Heart

What a gift wives have been given in marriage—to express their devotion to Jesus Christ through their attitude and manner toward their respective husbands! The heart of a wife toward her husband is always an expression of her heart toward Jesus Christ. Marriage provides a stage on which God tells the awesome story of Christ and the church. And wives are called to assume the church-reflecting role in this story. The affections, thoughts, and actions of a wife toward her husband tells the world, "This is the proper manner of the church toward her eternal Husband."

The glorious role of a wife is so serious and substantial that no woman can possibly achieve it apart from the grace of God. Her role requires the *joyful honoring of her husband's will and position, empowered by the Holy Spirit, that has as its aim the eternal fruitfulness of her husband for the glory of her God.* It is an impossible task. Only by walking in the Holy Spirit can any wife respect and honor her husband *as to the Lord.* She must learn to hope in God, not herself. She must learn to hope in God, not her husband. She must learn to continually entrust herself to her eternal Father in her daily battle with pride, fear, and frustration. Praise God for His promised and certain help!

8

Understanding
Marriage Conflict

What is the source of quarrels and conflicts among you?
Is not the source your pleasures that wage war in your members?
(James 4:1)

When Mike and Tanya first walked into my counseling study more than fifteen years ago, they were *wearing* conflict and contention. Their faces were sour, their were bodies tense, and their jaws were set. As soon as they settled into their seats, their arms were crossed. They refused to look at each other. Each gave "their side" of the story. Mike shared a long list of offenses and shortcomings that he saw clearly in his wife. Tanya shared an equally long list of wrongdoings and problems that she clearly saw in her husband. Both offered a list of justifications for why they thought, felt, and acted the way they did toward their mate. Their view of their own offenses and wrongdoings, ironically, was not so clear. If their spouse would just improve, each believed, then their marriage had a chance. It would be so much easier! More enjoyable!

Sometime during our meeting I asked the question, "Why do you believe there is tension and fighting in your marriage?" Both Mike and Tanya had answers. The person sitting next to them was the main problem. The families they grew up in and the experiences they endured before marriage were, from their perspective, also reasons for their struggle. The stresses of children, financial debt, and extended family members were other "causes." If these areas could be changed for the better, they believed, then their marriage would be changed for the better. If the circumstances around them improved, then marriage could finally improve. They had explanations for their conflict. Their explanations just happened to be wrong.

Why does fighting happen in marriage? It seems to be an important question. It is a question that most people ask, in some form, from time to time. Everyone seems to have an answer, whether it is spoken or not. Personality differences, failure to meet needs, and poor communication are often blamed for our marriage battles. Sometimes we identify family upbringing or physical makeup as the basic reasons for marital miseries.

But what does the Bible say about relational wars? How does God explain our marital conflicts?

The Heart of Marriage Conflict

One of the great biblical texts for understanding and resolving relational conflict of any kind, including marital conflict, may be found in James 4. In my early meetings with Mike and Tanya, we spent a lot of time in the first ten verses of this chapter.

> What is the source of quarrels and conflicts among you? Is not the source your pleasures that wage war in your members? You lust and do not have; so you commit murder. You are envious and cannot obtain; so you fight and quarrel. You do not have because you do not ask. You ask and do not receive, because you ask with wrong motives, so that you may spend it on your pleasures. You adulteresses, do you not know that friendship with the world is hostility toward God? Therefore whoever wishes to be a friend of the world makes himself an enemy of God. Or do you think that the Scripture speaks to no purpose: "He jealously desires the Spirit which He has made to dwell in us"? But He gives a greater grace. Therefore it says, "God is opposed to the proud, but gives grace to the humble." Submit therefore to God. Resist the devil and he will flee from you. Draw

near to God and He will draw near to you. Cleanse your hands, you sinners; and purify your hearts, you double-minded. Be miserable and mourn and weep; let your laughter be turned into mourning and your joy to gloom. Humble yourselves in the presence of the Lord, and He will exalt you. (James 4:1–10)

The text begins with a very basic and significant question: "What causes fights and quarrels among you?" What is the source, the root, or the real core of dispute among you, Christ's people? James gives the answer: selfish desires. The selfish passions, longings, and fears of our souls drive our wars with one another.

In order to understand why they were fighting in marriage, Mike and Tanya needed to begin where the Scripture begins. We have to begin there too.

Selfish Desires

Selfish desires in our hearts can fix themselves to any created thing in the world. They show what we crave or lust for as well as what we are afraid of losing or fearful of facing. We can lust for approval, respect, money, or sexual pleasure. We can fear failure, pain, or disapproval. *Selfish desires are those desires that are so strong and self-interested that we are willing to sin in order to achieve or preserve them, or to sin in attitude or action when our efforts to achieve or preserve them fail.*

Mike expressed his desire for a wife who was respectful and patient. He wanted her to "make his life easier, not harder." Tanya desired a husband who "parented God's way" and "considered her feelings." She wanted him to do things the right way. They had desires for good things. They just didn't realize how those good desires far outweighed their desire for God's glory and eternal purposes. Their personal desires had consumed their hearts. Their good desires had turned into evil desires.

What causes fights? God's Word gives the answer: it is your desires that battle within you. James offered an extremely simple yet profound truth. When we want something badly enough, most of us are willing to sin in order to achieve or preserve it, or to sin when we don't achieve or preserve it. Mike and Tanya were angry. The bitterness and resentment that they carried toward each other was obvious. On occasion, Tanya had prayed for Mike's death. In moments of rage, Mike had seriously considered abandoning Tanya altogether. These are examples of the coveting and killing that James referred to in the verses above.

No matter what object we seek—whether approval, money, power, position, sexual pleasure, children, a certain kind of spouse, or any other idol—the elevated desires of our hearts will send us to war for that idol. The spiritual and relational costs of this don't usually hold us back. Even our prayers can become contaminated by these lusts and longings. God gets reduced in our hearts and minds to some kind of personal butler or private waiter. Under the guise of spiritual devotion, we beg and plead with Christ to serve our selfish appetites.

Over the years, Mike had been praying for a better Tanya. She had been praying for Mike to grow up and love her the way he was supposed to. They wanted God to intervene in their marriage on a practical, tangible level. They sought His help in keeping their unwanted in-laws at bay. They asked for better sex. They asked God to help their mate become more patient, humble, and willing to change. They pleaded with God to improve the climate of their home. It had never dawned on Mike or Tanya that their motivations for these prayers were actually proud and selfish.

James can help us to see this danger. He exposes the underlying motive for our misguided prayers in verse 3: "that you may spend what you get on your pleasures" (NIV). What a troubling idea! We can pray to God for bad things. Even worse, we can pray to God for good things but with evil motives in our hearts. We can cry out to Him in desperate-sounding prayers, all the while being ruled by selfish desires (see Num. 11:4–6).

When James refers to "your pleasures" in verse 3, he does not refer exclusively to explicit sins like sexual immorality, drunkenness, and gluttony. He refers to the wrongful elevation of any desire for any created thing. The elevation itself, according to James, is idolatry. It is the worship of something or someone other than God. In verse 4, James calls this "adulterous" (NIV).

James goes on to explain his thinking: "Friendship with the world is hatred toward God" (see v. 4). The kind of desiring that would provoke quarreling and fighting among the people of God is a kind of desiring that involves a deep love for the world and its things. It is, therefore, spiritual adultery. Being bitter and angry when our personal goals are thwarted is "hatred toward God." It is *choosing* friendship with the world. It is *choosing* to be an enemy of God. We are choosing to love something more deeply and passionately than our Lord Jesus Christ. Our anger, irritation, hostility, and fighting provide the necessary evidence.

Although the quarrels and disputes are being played out between humans, James points to the more critical war being waged in our hearts with God. Namely, our proud self-interest is colliding with the will of God. James draws from Psalm 138:6 and Proverbs 3:34 when he says, "God opposes the proud" (v. 6 NIV). We fight in marriage because of our pride. We quarrel and bicker because we love ourselves more than Jesus Christ. Our marriages fail to work and function well because God refuses to make them work and function well when our hearts are proud and self-serving.

The Grace of God Is Our Only Hope

A wonderful and refreshing contrast is given in James 4:6: "But he gives us more grace" (NIV). Here we find a breath of fresh air and hope for the warring person. The problem is pride, the solution is humility, and God gives grace. While God works against the proud, He gives unmerited favor, wisdom, and help to the humble. Quarreling people are free to relax and be humble, because God will preserve, help, sanctify, and lift us when we lower ourselves, give up our selfish desires, and consider God's pleasure in whatever conflict we face.

Even more, we have been justified in Jesus Christ and declared righteous before God as the result of Christ's death and resurrection. We are forgiven. We are new creations. We are now adopted children of God and recipients of grace upon grace. What more do we really need?

God has given us Himself. Is He enough? He has shown us incredible compassion. Will we show compassion to one another? He has been forbearing and forgiving toward us. Will we be forbearing and forgiving toward one another?

If we are sinners saved by grace alone and clothed in the righteousness of Christ, then why on earth are we so eager to defend ourselves when criticized, to justify ourselves when our wrongs are pointed out, and to condemn others who fail to meet our standards? If we really believe the gospel, then why are we fighting?

For this reason, James counsels us, "Submit yourselves, then, to God. Resist the devil, and he will flee from you" (v. 7 NIV). In every marriage dispute, James is calling us to identify that which we cherish more than Christ, in order to repent, receive His grace, and yield ourselves to His will and plan for the moment. This may include losing the immediate relational battle or giving up whatever treasures we have come to desire so strongly. Attitudes and actions of this kind signify submission to God and resistance to the devil.

I will never forget a scene from my home several months ago. Two of my sons were fighting over a toy. What struck me when I entered the room was this: they were standing in the middle of the room, surrounded by dozens and dozens of beautiful toys, while quarreling over a single army figure no bigger than my thumb. It was an amazing and ridiculous scene—a scene we each help to enact whenever we fight and quarrel in our marriages. We stand in the middle of the riches and blessings that God has given, fighting over some created thing—a thing no more eternal than a blade of grass.

If we really believe the gospel—that we have been reconciled to God through His Son and that *in Him* we are forgiven and are co-heirs in all the benefits of God's family—then we really do have enough. He has given us the universe in Christ. We don't need to fight over a grain of sand, do we? We must remember who we are *in Him*. We are sons and daughters of God, redeemed by His grace. We don't have to cling to or fight for the things of this world anymore.

1. What do you tend to get angry about? How have you handled being hurt, disappointed, and angry in your relationships?

2. Share ways that you try to punish, manipulate, or otherwise train people to handle you the way you want to be handled and to give you what you want.

3. In what ways do you love the world more than God? What are some idols that you worship in your heart?

The Expression of Conflict in Marriage

Relational conflict can express itself in a great many forms. The particular things we can say and do in marriage that create and sustain conflict are too many to number, yet within these many forms and expressions there are certain threads or qualities that remain somewhat consistent. These qualities receive consistent attention in Scripture—that is, there are particular relational battles that are commonly addressed in the Word of God. Learning to notice, grieve, and repent from these qualities of your interactions will equip you to face conflict and suffering in your marriage with a humble and gospel-centered heart.

Expression 1: Corrupt Words

Perhaps the most common expression of conflict in marriage is verbal fighting. More likely than not, this form of conflict will need to be dealt with in your marriage on a regular basis. In order to deal with your speech biblically, you must develop a true understanding of where it comes from and how it can be redeemed.

Our words come from our hearts. Jesus said this very plainly in Luke 6:45: "The good man out of the good treasure of his heart brings forth what is good; and the evil man out of the evil treasure brings forth what is evil; for his mouth speaks from that which fills his heart." Proud words express a proud heart. Humble words express a humble heart. Selfish speech expresses selfish desires in our hearts. Cheerful words display a cheerful heart. Words do not primarily express our culture or family upbringing or biochemistry—they primarily express our souls. When our words are unkind and ungrateful, no one else is to blame. Such words come from inside us.

Other people may provide the context through which our hearts show themselves, but they do not determine what comes out of our hearts. Our spouses may act selfishly, or sin against us, or otherwise cause us pain, but they are not the reason for what we say and how we say it. They are not the reason for our cold silence or hot anger. What rules our hearts rules our lives. If sin rules our hearts, then sin will rule our mouths. When the Spirit of God rules our souls, then good and fruitful words will pour out (see Gal. 5:16–24).

After all, whether we realize or not, we are all masters at passing responsibility for our thoughts and words onto other people. We are skilled at justifying ourselves and making excuses.

So be ready for this in your marriage. You will be tempted to think and speak all kinds of corrupt words toward your mate. And there will be no time when you are more prone to justifying corrupt words than after your mate commits some kind of perceived evil against you.

Returning evil for evil tends to be the main reason our verbal arguments escalate. Like a tennis opponent, you will quickly volley all kinds of proud speech against your mate once he or she serves up proud speech of his or her own. Our spouses say something unkind to us, so we return the favor, blaming them for the whole thing. Returning evil for evil will probably represent one of the most common reasons for verbal conflict in your marriage.

Another reason we go to verbal war in our marriages comes from our thirst for victory and spoils. We like to win. We hate to lose. Our desires, we believe, are the right desires. We think our desires should prevail. Pride, by nature, is competitive.[1] We love to prove ourselves right. We hate to be proven wrong. So we argue and contend.

One of the most natural lusts of the human heart is the lust for victory over others, especially in areas that are dear to us. Where to spend money, how to handle the children, how often to have sex, and how to spend leisure time can provide the topics of conflict, but getting our way is the real energy behind the battle. Words can be made into our tools of battle. Articulate speech can make an effective weapon of war.

Go into any courtroom in the world and watch two highly skilled, well-trained lawyers contend with one another. You will probably find that both lawyers listen very carefully. They hear everything that their opponent speaks. They may even take notes. Whenever they speak, I promise you, they will calculate everything. They will measure their

---

1. C.S. Lewis addresses this relationship quite clearly in *Mere Christianity* (1952; repr., New York: HarperCollins, 2001) 121–23.

ideas carefully and try to deliver their words with precision. All great lawyers are masterful communicators. They are not at war because they are lousy at communication. They are at war because their clients' desires are opposed. Lawyers are paid to go to war for those desires. This means that they both want to win. This means that their primary relational goal is not love but victory. Bringing edification to people and relationships is not the traditional objective of courtroom litigation.

Sometimes a living room or kitchen can look like a courtroom where a husband and wife litigate the desires of their hearts. They may listen very carefully. The may speak with precision and clarity. Their mode of reasoning and style of speaking may be brilliant. But all of this will simply bring more anguish and destruction. Communication is not the problem. Better communication is not the solution. Hearts that are fixed on their personal desires is the problem. Transformed hearts that are fixed on Jesus Christ, as we will see shortly, is the solution.

Expression 2: Rejection of Correction

Another common expression of conflict in marriage is hard-hearted responses to feedback from spouses. One or both spouses refuse to receive correction, feedback, rebuke, or counsel without becoming proud and defensive. One spouse may offer correction or concerns to the other, but the recipient consistently rejects the counsel. The rejection could take many forms, from changing the subject to making excuses to self-justifying to shifting blame to simply staring back in silence. Either way, humility and repentance are cast aside and the proud defense of self becomes more important.

All of us, by sinful nature, have an aversion to correction. Our flesh hates being shown its errors. It longs to look good and to "save face." We would rather the sins of others be brought to light, not our own. When we hurt others or fail in some way, we run for the shadows, create diversions, and cover up. Much of the conflict we will ever face in our marriages arises from our proud, hard-hearted refusal to genuinely hear the concerns of others—especially the concerns of our spouses.

The Bible tells us this is an extremely foolish way to live. Proverbs

12:1 says, "Whoever loves discipline loves knowledge, but he who hates reproof is stupid."

We all need admonishment, since we are, by human nature, sinful, flawed, and prone to error. We depend on regular correction and instruction from people around us in order to repent and grow. This is especially true in marriage, because marriage exposes our sin more consistently and clearly than almost any other relationship we will ever know. God uses this for our good!

4. How do you receive correction from others—whether from parents, friends, or anyone else?

5. Do you value the feedback of the man or woman you are preparing to marry? Are you grateful when he or she shares concerns? If so, how have you expressed such gratitude?

6. Once you are married, in what ways can you cultivate an atmosphere in which your mate feels comfortable speaking the truth in love to you?

Expression 3: The One Acting as Two

God intends all of us to understand the concept of *union*. The idea is apparent in the phrase "they shall become one flesh" (Gen. 2:24). The act of sexual union between a husband and wife expresses and celebrates that God has joined them together for earthly life in a holy covenant. Jesus Christ highlighted this in His teaching: "So they are no longer two, but one flesh. What therefore God has joined together, let no man separate" (Matt. 19:6).

The ultimate reason that God designed marriage to be a one-flesh union is to display the one-spirit union that exists between Christ and His church (see 1 Cor. 6:16–17). The temporal union points to a grander, more eternal union. A husband and wife are to function interdependently, just as Christ and the church function in union with each other.

While we all exist as individual beings, we also exist in relationship to other beings. Even though a husband and wife exist as separate souls, they also exist in this life joined to each other as individual parts of a single unit.

So when a man and a woman marry each other, their lives are to change in relation to everything else. The way that we steward our God-furnished bodies, time, energy, money, words, friendships, possessions, and everything else should now have our God-given mates in consideration. We are not to live *for* each other but to live *beside* each other *for* the Lord. Our lives are not meant to *revolve* around each other, but they are meant to *revolve together* around Jesus Christ. Like partners training for a marathon and encouraging each other toward a shared goal, so a husband and wife can encourage each other by serving Christ and His kingdom together, praying with each other, admonishing each other, and helping each other along the way.

Along with corrupt words and rejection of correction, a third expression of conflict in marriage arises from our resistance to the reality of marital union. It happens when one or both spouses think, feel, and act without regard for the welfare or edification of the other, as if God had not really joined them together. It means that we spend our time, energy, money, and emotions without concern for the good of our mates and the glory of Christ in marriage. It means that we live divided under the same roof. The division can take a thousand forms, but in every form we are choosing to regard lightly the instruction of Jesus Christ, "What therefore God has joined together, let no man separate" (Matt. 19:6).

Expression 4: Trusting Our Own Eyes

Each of us walks through life with some sense of what is right and good, which is not necessarily a bad thing. The critical question is, on whom and on what do we base our sense of right and good? Who guides us? Whose words do we depend on? The wise person understands his or her proneness to folly. The fool doesn't. Proverbs 28:26 teaches us, "He who trusts in his own heart is a fool, but he who walks wisely will be delivered." The wise person accepts the truth about human nature: "The heart is more deceitful than all else and is desperately sick; who can understand it?" (Jer. 17:9). The fool refuses to accept this truth.

So the fool trusts his own view of God and the world. The fool believes what he wants to believe and sees, perhaps unawares, what he wants to see. The wise person depends on the Word and Spirit of God to illumine his or her vision. The righteous person tries to see the world by faith through the lens of Scripture. "Behold, as for the proud one, his soul is not right within him; but the righteous will live by his faith" (Hab. 2:4).

Whether you see and hear by faith according to the Word of God or by your own wisdom will impact your marriage deeply. There will often be days when nothing makes sense in your home and when everything seems to be going wrong. There will be days when you don't know what to do. You will feel upside down and inside out.

What do you plan to do? Will you trust the Lord and cling to His Word through the power of His Spirit, or will you trust your own vision and perceptions?

I remember taking a white-water rafting trip many years ago. While we were putting on our life vests and preparing to cast out downriver, the guide shared an interesting piece of advice. "If ever you are thrown into the rapids," he said, "and find yourself underwater or caught in a current, don't panic! Don't try to swim and thrash around, even if you think you know which way is up. Trust me: you will not know which way is up . . . but your life vest will. Relax and let the vest ride the current and bring you to the surface."

Sometimes marriage can be like a trip down the rapids. Sometimes you will get thrown over the side. When our personal, human perceptions (rather than the Spirit and Word of God) govern our judgments and our path, all of life becomes folly and conflict. We only add sorrow to sorrow when we panic and navigate the water according to our personal instincts, intuitions, and feelings rather than *submitting to* the Spirit and Word of God. We are too easily deceived to be able to live in such a way without inflicting pain and creating chaos.

7. How do you depend on the Lord, hour by hour and day by day, for truth and understanding? How does His Word shape your view of human life—not in theory, but in practice?

8. In what ways do you lean on your own understanding? In what ways do you judge yourself and others by your own wisdom?

Expression 5: Following Our Own Counsel

Trusting our own understanding is the first step down a path of life that is wrought with folly and destruction. Proverbs 14:12 says, "There is a way which seems right to a man, but its end is the way of death." We each have a sense of what is right and good, and we tend to live accordingly. We like to follow our own counsel. This approach to life presents another cause and expression of conflict in marriage—on in which one or both spouses think, feel, and act according to whatever seems right in their own eyes.

The people of Israel during the days of Judges were defined by this philosophy. "In those days there was no king in Israel; every man did what was right in his own eyes" (Judg. 17:6; see also 21:25). The nation was in chaos, and the people plunged into waves of war and divine judgment.

Even earlier in human history, this heart sickness prevailed. Though God warned Cain about sin "crouching at the door" (Gen. 4:7), Cain thought he knew better. His hostility toward God and jealousy toward his brother distorted his view of the world and compelled him to reject the counsel of God. He had plans of his own: "Cain rose up against Abel his brother and killed him" (v. 8).

Later in the Bible story, when God forgave the Ninevites after the preaching of Jonah, the prophet became extremely angry. He felt so justified in his attitude that he argued with God. He felt so strongly about how God should run the universe that he fumed in anger and despaired even to death whenever God acted against his wishes. He felt justified in disobeying God's instructions. He felt justified in raging about God's grace. He felt no qualms about pouting in isolation, praying for death, and clinging to his anger until the end (see Jonah 4:1–4, 9).

Be ready for this in your life and marriage. Be ready for those moments when you justify everything that you do and stand convinced that your way is right. Be ready for the conflict that will follow. Your spouse will probably stand equally convinced of his or her own counsel. Are you willing to be challenged and changed? Are you praying for humility of heart and a softening of all your opinions? Can you be receptive to the Word of God and the views of your mate in order to follow God's counsel rather than your own?

9. In what ways do you tend to lean on your own wisdom and understanding in life?

10. When you set your heart on a certain object or course in life, how do you handle being confronted with opposing views? Are you too easily persuaded? Are you unwilling to be persuaded? Please share examples.

Taking the Point to Heart

There will be conflict in your marriage. Of this you can be certain. You are a sinner. You are marrying a sinner. Your marriage will exist in a sinful, fallen world.

The main reason for your fighting will be the selfish desires of your heart. Often these desires will be good desires that are sinfully exalted. Your flesh will constantly labor for its own pleasure and security. Your flesh will strive to view and use God and others as vehicles to serve your personal passions and concerns. These battles will begin in your private interactions with God. Whatever rules your heart will also rule your life.

Now, your weapons of warfare can take many forms. More often than not, you will use corrupt words. When you want something bad enough, you will probably say almost anything in order to get it or almost anything when you don't. When you become fearful and worried, you may justify your words as a means of self-defense and survival. Again, these struggles are not communication struggles. They are heart struggles. They are expressions of a heart that is living for its own kingdom and glory. Only Jesus Christ can redeem your words, because only Jesus Christ can redeem your heart.

Sometimes your proud heart will reject correction and stand defensively against your mate. When admonished, you may get angry and accusatory. When your spouse points out your sins or failures, you will make excuses and create diversions.

Perhaps you will neglect the reality of marital union and live your life without regard for the eternal welfare of your mate, as if you were not joined to your mate in Christ.

At times you will trust your own eyes, and at other times you will follow your own counsel rather than the Lord's.

Ask the Lord to grant you wisdom and insight into the way that you fight and quarrel.

All the expressions of conflict that we have covered begin with the condition of your heart before Jesus Christ. They are first about you and God, not you and your spouse. Praise God that He has given us a way out! God is redeeming us and redeeming the way that we deal with troubles in our marriages.

9

Resolving Marriage Conflict Biblically

Humble yourselves in the presence of the Lord,
and He will exalt you. (James 4:10)

How do we resolve conflict in marriage? We wish there were an easy answer. Fighting happens in human relationships. We know this. So what are we to think, feel, and do about it?

In the previous chapter, we learned about the source of conflict in marriage. We garnered from James 4 that fighting and wars in our relationships happen because of selfish desires ruling our hearts. When the functional mission of our lives becomes "My kingdom come, my will be done," then our lives will overflow with conflict. Our kingdoms will clash with everyone else's kingdoms. Most significantly, our kingdoms will clash with God's kingdom.

Here is how James put it: "You ask and do not receive, because you ask with wrong motives, so that you may spend it on your pleasures. You adulteresses, do you not know that friendship with the world is hostility toward God?" (James 4:3–4). A husband's war with his wife actually arises from his war with God. The war may not be visible, but it is real and the effects are real. A wife's war with her husband actually arises from her battle with God. Again, this battle may not be out in the open, but it always takes a tangible toll. The ultimate *problem* begins in the relationship between each spouse and his or her Lord.

The *solution*, James goes on to tell us, begins in the same place (see James 4:7–10).

This chapter will not tell you everything you need to know about resolving marriage conflict. It will, by the grace of God, begin you down a road of learning to address conflict in your marriage while keeping Jesus Christ and the gospel at the center of the discussion. It will impart to you a few essential truths for navigating the unavoidable realities of being a sinner who is married to a sinner while living in a broken world.

The Resolution of Conflict in Marriage

When we as redeemed people fight with one another, we are displaying just how poorly we understand the gospel. All of us can safely admit that we regularly fail to grasp the full meaning of our salvation. Our bitterness, coldness, and disputes with those around us provide all the evidence we really need. Quarreling in our marriages means we have forgotten our salvation. We do not suffer first from poor communication skills, but from a poor or selective memory.

The apostle Peter tried to help us see this and deal honestly with the evidence.

> Now for this very reason also, applying all diligence, in your faith supply moral excellence, and in your moral excellence, knowledge, and in your knowledge, self-control, and in your self-control, perseverance, and in your perseverance, godliness, and in your godliness, brotherly kindness, and in your brotherly kindness, love. (2 Peter 1:5–7)

We should probably ask, why should we be progressing along the list that Peter provided? The answer may be found in the preceding verse: "He has granted to us His precious and magnificent promises, so that by them you may become partakers of the divine nature, having escaped the corruption that is in the world by lust" (v. 4). We should grow in moral excellence, knowledge, self-control, perseverance, godliness, brotherly kindness, and love because we have been saved by the grace of God. We have been given a host of promises that lead to eternal life. We have been filled with the Holy Spirit. We have been reconciled to the Father and now partake of His nature every day.

The promises of the gospel compel us to become more like the Father.

The message of our salvation stirs our affections for God and others. The gospel reminds us that we have escaped the corruption that comes through worldliness, and it keeps us from that corruption. We grow into the image of Jesus Christ by regularly receiving His grace and believing His promises.

The list Peter offered in verses 5–7 simply catalogues and charts the growth that happens when we deeply trust the Lord and His promises.

The idea shows up again in verse 9: "For he who lacks these qualities is blind or short-sighted, having forgotten his purification from his former sins." So then, experiencing horizontal peace with others comes from understanding the vertical peace with the Father that we have been given through Jesus Christ. We learn to minister grace horizontally when we comprehend the grace that has been given to us vertically.

Consider an illustration. If our earthly father has given us $50 billion as an undeserved gift, then we should be far less likely to dispute with our neighbor over his $5 debt. If our earthly parents lavish on us grand banquets of food at every meal, then we should never be heard raging about an apple that someone stole from our table or bemoaning the quality of our vegetables. We are recipients of grace upon grace. We have been given eternal life, even though we deserved wrath instead.

In Matthew 18, Jesus tells a parable about a slave who owed his master a great sum of money. Evil use of his master's property had finally caught up to him. Now it was time to settle the account. He couldn't. The slave, his wife, and his children were to be sold for repayment. Although the slave could never come close to repaying the debt, he proudly and desperately asked for more time. No time remained.

It is amazing to see how the master responded: "The lord of that slave felt compassion and released him and forgave him the debt" (Matt. 18:27). The master gave more than patience; he gave forgiveness. At great cost to himself, the master absorbed the debt and released the slave. What an incredible gesture of mercy! We can only imagine how wonderful the slave felt leaving his master's presence that day. What freedom! Even his family was spared. All his debts had been canceled.

Sadly, the meaning and significance of the gesture did not really soak into his soul. The events that follow in the story make this clear. "But that slave went out and found one of his fellow slaves who owed him a hundred denarii; and he seized him and began to choke him" (v. 28). We should be stunned by how quickly and aggressively the pardoned slave fell, without mercy, on another debtor. The second slave asked for patience, but the first slave refused. Then he threw the indebted slave into prison until payment could be made.

The onlookers were shocked. Fellow slaves quickly reported the whole event to their master.

When the master called the first slave back, here is what he said: "You wicked slave, I forgave you all that debt because you pleaded with me. Should you not also have had mercy on your fellow slave, in the same way that I had mercy on you?" (vv. 32–33). The master was angry because his grace had not stirred and compelled his slave to show grace. The master wanted the mercy he had placed on his servant to shape the way that the servant approached other debtors. Grace received, he believed, should produce an eagerness to give grace to others.

This should certainly be true for each of us. Think about the worst things you have ever done. Think about the most evil thoughts you have ever conceived. Think about all the good you have failed to feel and do. The Father has forgiven it all in Jesus Christ. Your account has been settled by His blood. You are free. When your heart is moved by this grace in Jesus Christ, you should be moved to respond to other sinners in a similar way. A proper understanding of the gospel in your heart moves you to forgive and reconcile in your relationships.

This is the basis for resolving conflict in our marriages. Our hearts must be in tune with the love we have been shown in order to love God and others in return. Resolving conflict is not firstly about articulate speech. Clever conflict-resolution strategies are not the key. Hearts that love God and others, because they are so deeply moved by God's love for them, is the key.

Hearts That Love God

We love, because He first loved us. If someone says, "I love God," and hates his brother, he is a liar; for the one who does not love his brother whom he has seen, cannot love God whom he has not seen. And this commandment we have from Him, that the one who loves God should love his brother also. (1 John 4:19–21)

Good communication skills and clever strategies for romance could be helpful, but these devices are never enough in the end. Really, they are nowhere near enough and can actually be deadly. When skillful communication and clever romance grow and thrive under the sway of sinful desires and personal power, they will become manipulative and sinister.

Give a scalpel to a selfish, angry man with no medical training, then ask him to do surgery on someone he despises, and he will be far more likely to bring injury than healing. He is far more likely to bring death than life. Give smooth words and skills at romance to proud, self-serving souls and you will get the same thing: injury and death. We need radical heart change first, and then skills. We need love for God and people, then strategies.

When our hearts love God, we will love other people, and this should include our mates. The apostle John helps us to see the connection: We will love *because* God has first loved us. And the love with which we love our mate will be God's love because His love will flow from His Spirit living in our hearts (see 1 John 4:11–13, 19).

The essence of conflict resolution in marriage is abiding in Christ and yielding to His Spirit's power in our hearts. When we abide in Him, by definition, we will be learning to love the way that He loves. And we love the way that He loves *because* He first loved us.

When are hearts are growing in love for God, we will be learning to *repent, forgive others,* and *trust the Lord* with our lives. These are three vital ingredients of conflict resolution. They invite the grace of God into our relationships. They break down enmity. They are expressions of how the gospel is moving and controlling our hearts.

Humble Repentance

Shortly after the wedding ceremony finishes, you should begin to realize how hard it is to love your spouse the way that Christ loves you. Someday soon, you will probably sense cold words, quickness to anger, and overall selfishness bubbling in your heart.

You will lust for other people—whether sexually, emotionally, or financially. When you spouse sins or makes mistakes, you may become judgmental, critical, and bitter. You will want what you want the way you want it whenever you want it, and you will resent your spouse for wanting it a different way. There may be times when you are deceptive, manipulative, or otherwise dishonest in the way that you handle time, money, thoughts, and your body. You will be selfish. You will be proud.

Conflict will happen as a result. God will allow it. He will call you to repentance. God will call you to confess your sinfulness to Him and then confess it to your spouse. This represents a critical first step in resolving the troubles of marriage.

Next time you dispute with another person, ask yourself these questions: What does my heart love so strongly that I am willing to fight for it? Is it Jesus or some worldly treasure? What good desires have become so sinfully exalted in my heart that I am willing to war for their acquisition or protection? What good gifts of God have I fashioned into demands and cravings in my soul? In answering these questions honestly and repenting honestly, as shown in God's Word and among God's people, you will be well down the road of reconciliation with God and others.

Eager Forgiveness

> Be kind to one another, tender-hearted, forgiving each other, just as God in Christ also has forgiven you. (Eph. 4:32)

Forgiving your spouse will sometimes mean *covering* offenses. It will mean absorbing a debt that your spouse accrued and not asking him or her to pay it back, then striking it from the balance sheet as if it never happened. There will be evils and wrongs your spouse commits that love covers over—just as Christ has covered your sins, even sins you were never aware of.

There will be times when your mate is irritable and says rude things. There will be times when he or she forgets responsibilities or neglects little acts of service. There may be times when your spouse embarrasses you in front of others or makes decisions without considering your interests. At times, your mate may spend more money than you agreed on or may fail to listen to your voice over the sound of the television. These could all be opportunities for you to *cover* transgression.

Sometimes, on the other hand, there are sins your spouse commits that should not and cannot be covered, because of the actual or potential harm that they bring to the name of Christ, your spouse, or you. To cover the transgression of your mate under these circumstances would be an expression not of love for Christ and others, but of apathy, avoidance, and love for self. If we see a valued friend playing near a pit of vipers, then love intervenes. Love does not say, "I don't want him to be offended and angry at me for ruining his fun." Nor does it say, "Oh well; I guess he will have to learn the hard way." It may eventually say this, but only after serious and gracious steps have been taken to call him away from peril.

Sometimes your spouse will speak rudely. Perhaps your spouse will neglect the Word of God and prayer. There may be times when your spouse drinks to excess, tells crass jokes, or looks at pornography. Perhaps your spouse will blow up in anger whenever he drives across town. Maybe she will go on spending or eating binges when she is stressed. He may be prone to gossip, or she may be extremely selfish with her time and energy. These could be moments when the Spirit calls on you to admonish and confront your spouse with humble and wise words from Scripture (see Col. 3:12–16). We all need help dealing with sin. Your spouse will need help dealing with sin.

"Winning" our brother or sister back to Christ and Christian fellowship is the heartfelt desire of such a conversation. Matthew 18:15 says, "If he listens to you, you have won your brother." This should always be our goal when we bring sin to light in our marriages: being used by God to bring a beloved and wandering sheep back to the fold, for God's pleasure. Our chief motivation should never be the alleviation of personal irritations. It should not be to conform our spouse to our version of a good spouse. It should be to help him or her to love and enjoy God more deeply.

Once repentance comes, by the grace of God, we are called by God to forgive, "just as God in Christ also has forgiven you" (Eph. 4:32; see also Col. 3:13). Rather than *covering* the transgression, at this point we are *cancelling* the transgression. We are declaring that the sins of our mate have been acknowledged by him or her and have been washed away by the blood of Christ. We are restoring fellowship with our spouse as the Lord continually restores us to Himself. "If we confess our sins, He is faithful and righteous to forgive us our sins and to cleanse us from all unrighteousness" (1 John 1:9).

If repentance does not come, then we must prayerfully and humbly decide whether to absorb the offense and wait in the hope that God will soften our spouse over time (see Prov. 10:12), or whether to bring one or two people with us to confront our spouse in love once more (see Matt. 18:16). There are times when we tenderly confront struggles or troubles with our mate but then leave them at our mate's doorstep if he or she is unable or unwilling to see. At other times, for one reason or another, we bring another saint along and try again. The wisdom of the Spirit, the Word of God, and godly saints will help you to discern a loving course of action.

1. As you consider your life to this point, do you confess sin openly to God and to others? What are ways that you hide, cover up, and seek to preserve a righteous external image?

2. In what ways are you a forgiving person? How do you hold grudges and crave personal justice? Why do you forgive others? Why do you refuse to forgive others?

3. How do you wisely discern between times to cover sin and times to confront sin? Which do you tend to do more often?

Trusting the Lord

Trust is essential in marriage—but not the kind of trust you are probably thinking about. You may be thinking that a thriving trust in each other will be critical to the health of your marriage, but this is not the case. The kind of trust that is critical to the health of your marriage is *trust in Christ.*

Trust in your spouse could certainly be helpful, but it is not required. Trust between you and your spouse is good. It could make marriage a little easier to endure, but trust in humans has never been the sort of trust that makes marriage glorifying to God and reflective of Christ and the church.

Consider this question: where is trusting your spouse commanded in the Bible? God never asks us to trust other people. He calls us to love them, not to trust them. He calls us to submit to our human authorities but not to put our hope in them. Jeremiah 17:5 tells us, "Cursed is the man who trusts in mankind and makes flesh his strength, and whose heart turns away from the Lord."

Trust in your spouse is not simply futile; it could also be sinful. To look to our mates as the source of our hope, deliverance, and strength is to turn our hearts *away from the Lord*. So whatever trust we place in our human spouses needs to be a humble, small, and honest trust that recognizes that we are married to sinners. While they may be filled with the Spirit of God, they are not God. To place *trust* in our spouses equals false worship and idolatry.

We are called to cheerfully love our spouses. We are commanded to joyfully serve our spouses. And we love and serve our spouses not because we trust them to take care of us but because we trust God to take care of us.

When God commanded Hosea to "take to yourself a wife of harlotry" (Hos. 1:2), He was calling Hosea to trust and follow Him, not to trust his wife. His love for Gomer was rooted not in her trustworthiness but in God's trustworthiness. The "holy women in former times" were submissive to their husbands because those women "hoped in God," not in their husbands (see 1 Peter 3:5–6). Since their trust and hope was in their God, not their mates, they were free to love, honor, and serve their mates just as God desired.

I am not saying that trust between a husband and wife doesn't matter or can't be a good thing. Being a trustworthy spouse is very important to the health of your marriage, and being married to a trustworthy spouse is a wonderful thing. Gaining trust over the years and decades of marriage can be a delightful gift from God. It can make marriage so much easier and sweeter. Yet human trust is not the root or source or cause of our love for one another in marriage. Faith and hope in God is!

Feet That Walk by His Spirit

Marriages in which husband and wife obey the Word of God will, by definition, grow in godliness and delight. Much can be said for plain and simple obedience that flows from simple devotion to the Lord. It is the inevitable reflex of the one who loves and trusts God. Christ made this clear in John 14:21: "He who has My commandments and keeps them is the one who loves Me."

Healthy conflict resolution in our marriages requires that we learn to walk in the Spirit of God under every circumstance while in a world full of temptation. Walking in His Spirit means learning not to love the world or be intoxicated by the things of the world (see Eph. 5:18; 1 John 2:15–16). Relational conflict feeds on worldly desires.

Fighting and warring erupt when our hearts are intoxicated by the world and consumed with satisfying our personal passions (see James 4:1–5). It stands to reason, then, that living peacefully with others requires us to put to death all our idolatrous loves for the world. Only Jesus can bring this about in us.

No marriage ever suffered from a lack of television, a lack of pornography, or a lack of expensive cars. No family in the history of the world ever crumbled due to poor technology, the absence of choice meats on the dinner table, the absence of exciting vacations, or low social status. No redeemed child in his or her right mind ever grows up and resents his or her parents because those parents weren't able to provide private schooling, expensive clothes, and fame. Walking humbly with God and rejoicing in His provision never destroyed anyone's soul.

Marriages crumble because the men and women inside them refuse to deal humbly and repentantly with their fleshly cravings and passions. Families get broken apart because the people inside them live their lives according to fleshly longings. Lose the war for our hearts, and we will lose everything else as well (see Luke 9:23–24).

When we believe fully that "the LORD is my shepherd, I shall not want" (Ps. 23:1), we are far less vulnerable to the temptations of the world. No person is better equipped to resist temptation than the totally-satisfied-in-Jesus person. When our souls are consumed in Him, we will find ourselves far less easily offended by others. We will find far less need to defend our reputation, be first in line, be esteemed by the world, or live without pain. What need do we have for riches, sensual pleasures, the praise of mankind, or emotional ease in life when our hearts feed constantly on Jesus Christ and drink deeply of His Spirit?

When we walk in the Spirit, we learn to enjoy and express the fruits of the Spirit (see Gal. 5:22–23; Eph. 5:18–21). If our mates are troubled and worried, we will learn to listen with love, joy, and peace. When someone cuts in front of us at the grocery store, we will express patience and kindness. When our children nag and defy us, self-control and gentleness will come from our hearts—not because of our ability to produce them, but because of God's Spirit controlling our souls.

Hands That Serve Cheerfully

> Calling them to Himself, Jesus said to them, "You know that those who are recognized as rulers of the Gentiles lord it over them; and their great men exercise authority over them. But it is not this way among you, but whoever wishes to become great among you shall be your servant; and whoever wishes to be first among you shall be slave of all. For even the Son of Man did not come to be served, but to serve, and to give His life a ransom for many." (Mark 10:42–45)

The words that Jesus spoke above were set in the context of a dispute among the disciples. Their dispute was over who was the greatest—a question expressing the very nature of human pride.

Jesus swiftly identifies this competitive spirit as the mark of pagan leaders and, therefore, as unbecoming to leaders of His church and members of His household. Rather, *humble service* is to define those who claim fellowship with Him, and humble service is quite reasonable for a redeemed saint since God the Son, taking on human flesh, came to serve rather than to be served.

Remember how Jesus served His disciples on the eve of His betrayal and death?

> Jesus, knowing that the Father had given all things into His hands, and that He had come forth from God and was going back to God, got up from supper, and laid aside His garments; and taking a towel, He girded Himself. Then He poured water into the basin, and began to wash the disciples' feet and to wipe them with the towel with which He was girded. (John 13:3–5)

What an image! Though He deserved service and honor, He gave service and honor.

This is the example that Jesus has left us to follow:

> For I gave you an example that you also should do as I did to you. Truly, truly, I say to you, a slave is not greater than his master, nor is one who is sent greater than the one who sent him. If you know these things, you are blessed if you do them. (John 13:15–17)

The pattern of humble service that Jesus offered to His followers is the same pattern we are given for relating to each other in marriage. Humble service defuses conflict, and it leaves no room for fighting. It's hard to argue when you are washing someone's feet. Bond servants don't fight for their personal rights and interests. They lay them down. They obey the desires of those they serve. They sacrifice their cravings for higher purposes.

I have come to believe that our attitude and manner in serving determines the amount of joy, peace, and unity we experience in our relationships with others. When we delight in helping others and do not require anything in return, every moment of life becomes another opportunity for happiness. When we genuinely value giving over receiving and serving over being served, it becomes almost impossible for others to agitate and irritate our souls or to move us to despair.

Adopting the attitude of Jesus in your home will dissolve most disputes before they truly begin. If conflict does begin, then serving your mate with joy and eagerness will, by the grace of God, bring hostilities swiftly to a close. Fights tend to linger because our pride lingers. Disputes will grow hotter and deeper because our affection for service grows colder and shallower. We must pray every day for the grace to sacrifice joyfully in marriage. We are not greater than our Master, and He took the form of a bondslave. Winning and being right just don't matter nearly as much as serving and sacrificing for His name's sake.

4. Evaluate your attitude about service, especially when no one notices or cares. To what degree are you selfless, joyful, and thankful in your service to Christ and others?

5. What interferes with your cheerful service to others? What attitudes, activities, and desires of your heart get in the way? How might you combat these problems through the Word of God?

Lips That Edify

"There is one who speaks rashly like the thrusts of a sword, but the tongue of the wise brings healing" (Prov. 12:18). The tongue can be an implement of surgery or of warfare. Like a scalpel in the hand of a surgeon, the tongue can produce words that heal and build up. Or, like a sword in the hand of an assassin, the tongue can cut people to pieces. In one moment we speak to heal, and in the next moment we speak to injure. Observing this common reality, the apostle James was confounded that "from the same mouth come both blessing and cursing. My brethren, these things ought not to be this way" (James 3:10).

Certainly in marriage, "these things ought not to be this way." A husband who loves God will love his wife (no matter how she treats him), and his love will be evident by the manner in which he speaks to her and of her, because "his mouth speaks from that which fills his heart" (Luke 6:45). A wife who loves God will love her husband (no matter how he treats her), and her love will be evident by the manner in which she speaks to him and of him.

The truth must still be spoken in marriage, but spoken in love (see Eph. 4:15). Problems should be addressed, but with loving speech. Wrongs should be confronted, but with loving speech, because loving speech is an expression of an infinite, loving God abiding in the heart of the speaker.

6. When life gets a little difficult, what kind of speech flows from your heart? Do you talk more or less? Do you speak the truth in love, speak the truth in anger, or withdraw in cold silence? Please explain and give an example.

7. In what way are you an ambassador for Christ—someone whose words speak for Him and about Him in this world? Over the course of your life, how have your words represented Him in your relationships?

8. In what ways might you be tempted to speak unkindly about your mate? Do you tend to run to other people to gripe and complain when your fiancé offends you? What might help you take a more loving approach?

Taking the Point to Heart

Fighting in marriage happens when proud hearts clash. Our hearts become proud when Christ does not rule them and when His kingdom is in a subordinate place to our kingdoms. Our clashing proud hearts can display themselves through corrupt speech, unwillingness to receive feedback, disunity, reliance on our own wisdom, and following our own counsel rather than God's. While our hearts are the problem, the expressions of this problem take many forms.

The real and difficult task of resolving our marital disputes biblically involves seeing through the many topics of dispute in order to deal with the issues of our hearts beneath. Anything can be the topic— but how we talk, listen, unify, pray, and serve around that topic is the true display of our hearts and, thus, should be the focus of our words. Learning to remain undistracted by the many opinions or ideas that are available, in order to focus on heart attitudes and love for each other amidst disagreement, presents the greatest obstacle.

Rarely will we agree on all the topics of marriage. Rarely will we agree on the exact proper use of money, the exact proper amount of sexual intimacy, or the exact proper way to handle the children. God did not design everyone to agree exactly on all these matters. Rather, God redeems and enables husbands and wives to reflect Christ and the church amid their disagreements and to grow in love for each other under every circumstance. This love tends to be expressed through gracious speech, humble listening, eagerness to serve, and longing for Christ to be magnified in our marriages.

10

The Glory of Christ
in Sexual Union

For He says, "The two shall become one flesh." But the one who joins himself to the Lord is one spirit with Him. (1 Cor. 6:16–17)

These inspired words of Scripture contain one of the most radical, life-changing, and exultant truths about sexual union we can ever embrace: "'The two shall become one flesh.' But the one who joins himself to the Lord is one spirit with Him."

These words can forever reshape our view of sexual immorality by granting us a vision for our bodies and sexual union so Christ-centered, lovely, and worshipful that we resist every form of perversion out of humble and holy fear—troubled lest we do anything to forfeit or taint the glory that God has revealed in the gift of sexual union.

The Place of Sexual Union in Marriage

A marriage covenant between a husband and wife is consummated, or completed, by sexual union. We are not fully married until we have become "one flesh" (Gen. 2:24). God-honoring sexual union happens between one man and one woman, within the marriage covenant, as an expression of faith and worship toward God. It offers an intimate expression and enjoyment of the marriage covenant. It symbolizes a man's departure from his family of origin in order to be joined to his wife (see, again, Gen. 2:24).

Sexual union during the years of marriage does not make the marriage. It does, however, express the marriage. It encourages the marriage. It offers a unique form of physical pleasure in marriage. It is an expression of love and service in marriage. Above all else, sexual union provides a wonderfully visible, temporal, one-flesh picture of the invisible, eternal, one-spirit reality of Christ and His church. It is an extremely important aspect of marriage.

Now, there may be cases in which sexual union between a husband and wife is not possible. Perhaps there are physical or medical reasons that prevent a husband and wife from joining to each other. There could be special circumstances in which special considerations have to be made. These are rare, but they happen. In the cases I have seen of married couples who have never been able to complete sexual intercourse, God has been gracious. Their marriages have been blessed. The husbands and wives love each other, enjoy each other, and see God glorifying Himself through their marriages in unique ways.

In this chapter, we will look at several biblical truths pertaining to sexual union in marriage that apply to most marriage situations. Some of these truths will be quite general and broadly applied. You will be asked to apply the Scripture with sensitivity and wisdom in your own preparation for marriage.

The Two Shall Become One Flesh

For He says, "The two shall become one flesh." But the one who joins himself to the Lord is one spirit with Him. (1 Cor. 6:16–17)

It is worth stating the truth again that sexual union in marriage provides a beautiful, visible picture of the invisible union between Christ and the church. Essentially, sexual union in marriage is worship. It provides an opportunity to celebrate our union with the Lord by serving and enjoying union with our spouse. Through sexual union, the oneness of our physical bodies parallels our oneness of spirit with the Lord.

Every form of sexual perversion (through which God's pattern for sex is rejected and replaced with a defiant pattern) is false worship.

Self-serving masturbation is false worship. It displays my deep concern for myself above the dignity and welfare of my spouse. It says to the universe, "Jesus is self-serving and chiefly concerned with gratifying himself!" Pornography expresses idolatry of the highest kind. It says, "Jesus uses other people to pleasure Himself without having to love or sacrifice." It lowers God and exalts the creation. Adultery, by definition, displays something about Christ and the church that is irreverent and phony. It says, "This is how Jesus is with His bride, and this is how His bride is to be with Him—unfaithful and deceitful." Fornication is qualitatively the same as going into the temple of a false god in some foreign country and bowing low before its altar. It elevates the gift of God—namely, sex—above the Giver by using the gift in a form that God forbids.

Yet there is more! If we have been saved in Jesus Christ, then we are now members of His body. First Corinthians 6:15 asks, "Do you not know that your bodies are members of Christ?" So when we enter into sexual union with our God-given mate as fellow members of Christ, we are joining our mate to the Lord and our mate is joining us to the Lord. It provides one of the most sacred and unique pictures of Christian fellowship we could ever imagine. We are helping each other to enjoy our union with Christ by offering ourselves in union to each other.

On these grounds, Paul questioned all forms of fornication and adultery: "Shall I then take away the members of Christ and make them members of a prostitute? May it never be!" (1 Cor. 6:15). By joining our blood-bought, Spirit-filled bodies to another person in sexual immorality, we are actually joining Christ to that other person in immorality, since we are members of His body. We are using a part of His body in false worship—to fulfill our sinful cravings. Whether we realize it or not, we are implicating Him in the event. After all, it is His body we are offering on that bed-shaped altar.

So then, sexual union between a husband and wife is an expression of worship. It celebrates our spiritual union with Christ. In addition, sexual union in marriage expresses love for our mate. It offers service to our mate. Sex is designed to be enjoyable, pleasurable, and fun. What a wonderful gift!

Render the Affection Due

> The husband must fulfill his duty to his wife, and likewise also the wife to her husband. The wife does not have authority over her own body, but the husband does; and likewise also the husband does not have authority over his own body, but the wife does. Stop depriving one another, except by agreement for a time, so that you may devote yourselves to prayer, and come together again so that Satan will not tempt you because of your lack of self-control. (1 Cor. 7:3–5)

Sexual union is an act of love, service, and ministry to our respective mates. It expresses our belief that our bodies are not our own but belong first to Christ (see 1 Cor. 6:19–20). After this, our bodies belong to our respective mates (see 1 Cor. 7:4). Sexual serving is meant to be a joyful and selfless act. Abstaining from sexual union in marriage, therefore, requires mutual consent. And a good reason to abstain, according to Paul, is to engage in undistracted devotion to God through fasting and prayer for a time.

Aside from this reason, God gives us the call and privilege of the ministry of sexual service to our mates. Faithfulness in this area of ministry even strengthens our marriages against the temptations of Satan. When we withhold ourselves from our spouses, we are opening a door for Satan to bring increased temptation into our lives and the lives of our mates. We should take this seriously. God takes it seriously.

Now, this does not mean that adultery is unavoidable or excusable in cases when one spouse withholds his or her body from the other. No human being needs sex so deeply that sin becomes necessary. It is a gift from God, not a need. Our seeking out and indulging in sexual immorality (whether through lust, masturbation, pornography, adultery, or anything else) arises from our proud and sinful flesh. It is never anyone else's fault. Other people, including our spouses, can make this easier or harder, but the Scripture puts all the weight of responsibility for our own lives onto our own hearts. In verse 5 above, Paul points us in this direction when he gives the ultimate reason for falling to sexual temptation: "your lack of self-control."

1. Do you think it will be easy or difficult to give your body freely to your spouse? If your spouse desires more sexual union than you do, how do you plan to handle it?

2. Do you think it will be easy or difficult to restrain your sexual desires out of love for Christ and your mate? If your spouse desires less sexual union than you do, how do you plan to handle it?

Potential Obstacles to Sexual Union in the Early Days of Marriage

The sections below highlight a few common and possible obstacles to the sanctity of the marriage bed in the early days of your marriage. There are plenty of other obstacles throughout marriage that can take their toll in this area, such as adultery, but we will not have time to address those here. I have chosen to focus on premarital sexual immorality, pornography, past sexual abuse, and significant problems in other areas of marriage, because you may have to face these concerns right away. If you have experienced any of these firsthand, then you will want to prepare for their potential effects on your marriage.

Premarital Sexual Immorality

> I adjure you, O daughters of Jerusalem, by the gazelles or by the hinds of the field, that you do not arouse or awaken my love until she pleases. (Song 2:7)

Premarital sexual sin awakens pleasures and indulges privileges that are reserved for the sanctity and security of the marriage union. By premarital sexual sin, I mean sexually immoral acts that happen outside of and prior to the marriage covenant—whether this involves going as far as fornication (sexual intercourse while both parties are unmarried), or oral sex, or any number of other activities. (We will talk about pornography in the next section.)

Solomon entreated his bride, along with all of us, to save the privileges of sexual union for the marriage bed. "I adjure you . . . do not arouse or awaken my love until she pleases."

The first reason to save these privileges for marriage is this: God commands it. And He commands it, first of all, to guard and promote His own glory. He commands it in order to guard the precious image of Christ and the church in marriage. Even for an unmarried person, sexual perversion is an attack on the majesty of Christ and the church.

Yet God has also commanded sexual purity in order to guard something else. Sexual purity guards our bodies and souls from destruction. Reserving sexual pleasure for marriage promotes our eternal good. Sex has been given by God in order to be enjoyed. And it can be truly enjoyed only when received in the form in which God gave it. To take it any other way brings spiritual destruction—as all sin does. Think about the extremely sobering words Solomon used to describe a man walking into sexual immorality:

> Suddenly he follows her
> As an ox goes to the slaughter,
> Or as one in fetters to the discipline of a fool,
> Until an arrow pierces through his liver;

As a bird hastens to the snare,
So he does not know that it will cost him his life. (Prov. 7:22–23)

Paul put it this way: "Flee immorality. Every other sin that a man commits is outside the body, but the immoral man sins against his own body" (1 Cor. 6:18). These are strong words meant to shake us up. Immorality does something to us that many other sins don't.

In one sense, Paul meant that sexual immorality *harms the physical body*. Sexual immorality can take a heavy toll on the body itself, whether through sexually transmitted diseases or through general decay due to the judgment of God (see Gal. 6:7–8). It is a sin against the body that takes a severe, though sometimes hidden, toll on the body. Many of us have experienced this pain.

Paul could also mean that sexual sin that is committed in the body *sticks on the body* like no other sin. It lingers with us long after the sin has been indulged. The body keeps craving and desiring more. It leads our bodies down a road from which only Christ can save us (see Prov. 7:27).

Sexual sin distorts the true joy, purity, and purpose of sexual union and pleasure for the body. It usually attaches guilt or shame to behavior that God has given us to enjoy freely in marriage. There can be a great many natural consequences to premarital sexual sin. Some of these can be felt in marriage long after the sin has occurred.

Another layer to Paul's meaning here is that the physical body of a redeemed person has been "bought with a price" (1 Cor. 6:20) and now belongs to God. Our bodies are temples of the Holy Spirit. To commit sexual immorality in the body is to sin against the new and eternal purposes of the body. Sexual immorality takes what belongs to God for His glory in order to use it for self-worship and self-glory. It abuses and misuses the body. It employs the body as the instrument of sin. This could also be what Paul meant by "the immoral man sins against his own body."

All sins that are committed, whether past or present, can be forgiven in Christ. God promises to forgive the sins of His children (see 1 John 1:9). No matter how ugly, frequent, or flippant they are, all our sins have been nailed to Jesus Christ on the cross, washed away by His blood, and put away from us as far as the east is from the west (see Ps. 103:12). Romans 8:1–2 declares,

> Therefore there is now no condemnation for those who are in Christ Jesus. For the law of the Spirit of life in Christ Jesus has set you free from the law of sin and of death.

What this means is that you can be honest with God and the man or woman you are marrying about the sexual sins you have committed in the past. You can confess the sins of your past, be forgiven, and be healed by the grace of God (see James 5:16; 1 John 1:9). You can ask God to help you to walk with Him in purity. As a couple, if you have walked in sexual sin with each other in the past, then Christ has freed you to be honest and to walk in the light. You can repent, be forgiven, and be healed by the grace of God. Deal honestly with sexual sin in your past in order to repent, be cleansed, and be transformed for the future.

Keeping past or present sexual sin concealed will only create bigger problems down the line. David made this clear:

> When I kept silent about my sin, my body wasted away
> Through my groaning all day long.
> For day and night Your hand was heavy upon me;
> My vitality was drained away as with the fever heat of summer. (Ps.
>   32:3–4)

Then he offered a sweet and simple solution:

> I acknowledged my sin to You,
> And my iniquity I did not hide;
> I said, "I will confess my transgressions to the LORD";
> And You forgave the guilt of my sin. (v. 5)

So, if need be, please face your sin now through the gospel of Jesus Christ. Don't avoid it. If what we have said here applies to you, bring hidden sins to the open and ask God to wash you anew. Then you can sing with David,

> How blessed is he whose transgression is forgiven,
> Whose sin is covered!
> How blessed is the man to whom the LORD does not impute iniquity,
> And in whose spirit there is no deceit! (vv. 1–2)

3. If need be, share the sexual sins you have committed in the past that you believe are important to share. If you bear any guilt or shame, take a moment and talk to God. Repent and leave them at the cross. Celebrate how God has forgiven these sins in Jesus Christ.

4. If need be, bring to light any sexual sins you are walking in right now. Share how you intend to bring these to the Lord in humble repentance.

5. In what ways might the sexual sins from your past impact your marriage in the future? How do you intend to face these effects?

Pornography

By *pornography*, I am referring to sexually illicit material, either written, auditory, or visual, which includes the categories of photographic, cinematic, virtual, or real. Pornography aims to make show and sport of the human body and human sexuality. It aims to gratify the partaker by creating and enacting illicit scenes and ideas.

Technology has made pornography available all over the world. The use of pornography has reached epidemic levels. So the likelihood of you or your fiancé (or both) having a level of contact with pornography in your past is quite high. The likelihood of you facing the temptations of pornography in your present or future is equally high. I encourage you to be alert and to talk about this danger to your marital life. This little fox can wreak havoc in your marriage vineyard.

Physical sex usually pleases the body. Images and thoughts of sex can please the body, too. Arousing another person sexually can be intoxicating because it feeds our pride and glory. Enticing another person to give him or herself to us in physical ways feeds our pride. It should not surprise us, then, that pornography can be so attractive and enticing to our flesh. It takes a good gift of God—one that is meant for true worship (sex in marriage to the glory of God)—and fashions it into an idol for false worship. It grabs a beautiful sculpture of Christ and the church that is designed to give glory to God and reshapes it in order to give humanity all the glory. It takes a wonderful possession of God that is intended to give humanity pure delight and makes it a possession of man to be used as he pleases.

Pornography corrupts the relationship between a person and his or her Creator. Like all sin, it offends God and sours our fellowship with Him. Job understood this:

> I have made a covenant with my eyes;
> How then could I gaze at a virgin?
> And what is the portion of God from above
> Or the heritage of the Almighty from on high?
> . . . .
> Does He not see my ways
> And number all my steps?" (Job 31:1–2, 4)

Job valued his covenant relationship with God, so he made a covenant with his eyes. He realized that lusting after the bodies of other people would bring enmity into his relationship with his God and Savior.

Indulgence in pornography equals adultery of the heart. Jesus put it this way:

> You have heard that it was said, "You shall not commit adultery"; but I say to you that everyone who looks at a woman with lust for her has already committed adultery with her in his heart. (Matt. 5:27–28).

God is not interested merely in pure bodies, but also in pure hearts. He wants our hearts. He has redeemed our hearts. And when the Lord rules our hearts, He will rule our bodies as well.

Pornography fastens on our hearts and lives when we indulge it. It claws at us. It cries out for more. It refuses to simply slide off our souls and fade into oblivion.

David understood this. He wrote, "I will set no worthless thing before my eyes; I hate the work of those who fall away; it shall not fasten its grip on me" (Ps. 101:3).

Contrary to what many people believe, viewing pornography is never contained in a room or locked away inside a computer. Once we feed on it, we carry it. It fastens to us—perhaps in ways that we fail to see. We bring it to bed. The sensual images and ideas can change the way that we view God, our spouses, the sexual union, and other people.

Then it takes us somewhere. Pornography *deceives* and *leads* our hearts further astray (see Prov. 7:22–23). Giving into sexual cravings will cost the fool his life—because, without the supernatural grace of God, he will keep going back. It will consume him. It will lead him to destruction.

The flesh has no power to refuse itself. God must intervene. True repentance comes through the Holy Spirit working in our hearts. We cannot conceive it ourselves. This presents a real danger when we play with pornography and assume that we will get out eventually. We are presuming that God will intervene. We are presuming that He will come to get us. We are presuming that God will not let our sin have its way in us.

6. Share your past contact with pornography and how you believe that it impacts you today.

7. What wise safeguards can you and your fiancé place around your marriage when it comes to pornography?

Past Sexual Abuse

Many people have been hurt by past sexual abuse—sexual violations that were committed against them during their childhood, adolescent, or previous adult years. This may have been a single event at a single moment in time or a number of events covering a great length of time. It may have been at the hands of strangers or perhaps at the hands of an immediate family member. You may have learned to speak about these experiences with ease and comfort, or you may have kept them hidden in your heart. You may have enjoyed years of healing from the pain, or the memories may continue to stir agony and discomfort in your soul.

The effects of sexual abuse on a person can be diverse and painful. The effects on a marriage can be equally diverse and painful. If you or your fiancé have experienced sexual abuse in the past, it will be important for you talk and pray through these experiences using a suitable level of disclosure. I don't think you need to use great detail, but tell your story so that your fiancé knows how to pray for you and support you. You don't want to wait until the later years of marriage to open up and face this together.

The goal in this brief section is not for you to resolve every hurt you have suffered or come to complete healing from abuse before your wedding day. The goal is to help you continue the journey to put relevant events on the table before your fiancé so that you can both be aware of your experiences, pray over them, and gather a sense of how they could impact your married life. Hopefully you have already begun sharing with your fiancé any sexual abuse that you endured in your past. If not, then now is a good time to carefully begin that process. You cannot cover everything here, but you can at least engage in gracious conversation and humble prayer concerning possible pains and fears you may have regarding marriage, sex, and intimacy.

8. If you have endured sexual abuse in your past, please share the parts of your story that you are comfortable sharing.

9. Have you received counseling to help you address sexual abuse from your past? If so, please share the nature and outcome of the counseling. What conclusions or resolutions did it bring to your heart?

10. In what way(s) do you believe your experience of abuse impacts you today?

The grace of God in Jesus Christ cleanses us from the defiling effects of sin. First Corinthians 6:11 says, "You were washed, but you were sanctified, but you were justified in the name of the Lord Jesus Christ and in the Spirit of our God."

The grace of God in Jesus Christ frees us from the defiling effects of other people's sins against us. However dirty and ashamed we may feel as the recipients of sexual sin, we are cleansed in Jesus Christ. This is important. Even though we are not guilty for sins that are perpetrated on us, we may *feel* guilty. All sense of dignity can be lost in the wake of abuse. We can feel less than human. David expressed this very sentiment: "But I am a worm and not a man, a reproach of men and despised by the people" (Ps. 22:6).

While we do not need forgiveness for sins committed against us, we may feel cheapened or lessened in the eyes of God because of the nature of sexual abuse. The gospel comforts us in such affliction. It reminds us that we are "chosen of God, holy and beloved" (Col. 3:12). It tells us that we have been washed by His grace and made whiter than snow (see Ps. 51:7). No kind or degree of others' sin against us can ever change this. Nothing "will be able to separate us from the love of God, which is in Christ Jesus our Lord" (Rom. 8:39).

You may recall the story of the Good Samaritan in Luke 10. Jesus uses the story to illustrate what it means to love our neighbor. The story also illustrates how Jesus loves us. Remember how the Samaritan cared for the abused traveler? "When he saw him, he felt compassion, and came to him and bandaged up his wounds, pouring oil and wine on them; and he put him on his own beast, and brought him to an inn and took care of him" (Luke 10:33–34). This is how Jesus cares for our hearts and lives when we are crushed beneath the atrocities of others. He sees us, feels compassion for us, and cleanses our wounds. Then He bandages us and carries us to a place of rest.

If you have experienced sexual abuse in your past, then sexual union in marriage may bring particular struggles for you. It may not. No matter what, though, I pray that the grace of God in Jesus Christ and His love will be sufficient for you.

If your spouse has experienced sexual abuse in his or her past, then sexual union in marriage may bring another set of struggles for you. It may not. Either way, God's grace will still be sufficient. And His love is deep, strong, and unending.

Talk. Pray. Trust God. Be patient. Learn to love the way Jesus loves. Let your marriage tell whatever story God may be seeking to tell through it. Let it be a testimony of His grace and power in the midst of whatever obstacles and sorrows may be present.

Significant Problems in Other Areas of Life

Another threat you will face to the glory of Christ and to marital joy in sexual union is *significant problems outside the bedroom*. If you walk in selfish pride, then you can expect difficulty in your marriage bed. If there is ever aggression or violence in your home, then your sexual intimacy will be threatened. If there is bitterness or resentment in your hearts toward each other, then sexual intimacy, more often than not, will be shallow, frustrating, or nonexistent. If you are disconnected spiritually and emotionally, then making love to your spouse may seem like making love to a stranger (which will probably bother at least one of you). God has designed sexual union to work in concert with the rest of your marriage. When most of your marriage is in trouble, then sexual union with your spouse will probably be in trouble as well.

If your heart and marriage are in trouble but your sexual union thrives, then something far more dreadful and frightening is happening. If this occurs, then you should tremble, not rejoice. It means that you and your spouse enjoy sex as mere entertainment rather than as an expression of godly love and true worship. It means that you and your spouse could have sex with almost anyone and not really care. It means that you could have great fun in bed with a complete stranger, provided that he or she is skilled in sexual technique. If your life and marriage are suffering as a whole, then you want your sexual union to suffer too. This is healthier than the alternative.

The condition of your heart before God will, by His design, impact your sexual relationship with your mate. If you are ruled by fears and worries, then sexual intimacy could be threatening to you. If you are preoccupied with your image, prone to performance anxiety, or insecure about your body, then sex could be intimidating for you. It will take humble prayer, a deepening trust in the Lord, and faithful service to your mate over time to grow in comfort and joy in sex.

If you are selfish and impatient, or even proud and demanding in getting your way, then sex in your marriage will probably expose these qualities in your soul. Your frustration with your spouse when he or she declines your sexual invitations will be evidence enough.

Or you might become irritated when sex is challenging. Your spouse may not "perform" up to your standards. You may not "perform" up to your standards either. What are you going to do? Who will you run to? How will you and your spouse address the normal obstacles to sexual intimacy? God provides sexual union as a gift to your marriage, but He will also use it as a means to expose and sanctify your hearts.

Selfless lovers make the sweetest lovers. They glorify Christ and experience all the blessings that God intends them to enjoy over the life of their marriage. Gracious words, cheerful service, and good conversation carry over into the marriage bed. So if you desire a growing and thriving sexual union with your mate, you will need to begin in your heart with God. The next major section builds on this idea.

The Nature of Human Life

Joyful, consistent, and satisfying sex in marriage can be easily and often interrupted by the basic realities of human life. Sickness, exhaustion, and other daily burdens make sexual intimacy between a husband and wife more challenging. Start adding children to the mix and you might find personal time and energy far more difficult to come by.

Sometimes these daily burdens cannot be avoided. Sometimes they result from our self-imposed way of life, which is far too busy and distracted by the world. Sometimes the Lord brings us into circumstances that make sexual union impossible for periods of time. It can be frustrating. It can be confusing. Either way, you will need to learn as a couple how to best navigate the particular landscape of marriage you have been given.

A Process of Sanctification and Learning

Sex with your mate may be uninhibited and pleasurable on your wedding night and in the days to follow. Or it may take time to get there. It will probably be a mix of both. You can enjoy wonderful sex in marriage and yet still have a lot to learn. This is important for you to realize. You may have sexual intercourse on your wedding night, or it may take you several days. There is plenty of time. Treat sexual union seriously. Make it a priority—just don't make it *the* priority. Approach it with humility and patience.

The joys and pleasures of sexual union in marriage develop over time. Like a good wine, it usually gets even better with age. Young people aren't necessarily having the best sex. Spiritually immature people certainly aren't having the best sex. Unmarried people don't have a chance. They are not even capable of sex in its purest and most glorious forms (see Prov. 9:16–18). The whole point of it is lost on them (see 1 Cor. 6:12–20). They think they are savoring vintage wines given to them by master winemakers. In reality, they are gulping down cheap and soured dregs that were recently scooped from the bottom of someone else's barrel. The initial taste seems sweet and fun, but the aftereffects are sour and shameful.

Godly, humble, and Spirit-filled people who are married to each other are having the best sex. You won't see any research or movies portraying that notion. The world's view of sexual fulfillment and delight is based mostly on lies. Its view promises unending sexual pleasures to proud, vain, and unmarried people without cost. God has promised quite a different result:

> For this is the will of God, your sanctification; that is, that you abstain from sexual immorality; that each of you know how to possess his own vessel in sanctification and honor, not in lustful passion, like the Gentiles who do not know God; and that no man transgress and defraud his brother in the matter because the Lord is the avenger in all these things, just as we also told you before and solemnly warned you. (1 Thess. 4:3–6)

As with all other gifts from God, you must be redeemed in order to fully enjoy sex. Couples who are being sanctified together and learning to love the way that God loves are, by definition, being taken by God to new heights of sexual satisfaction and delight. How can I say this? Because people who really grasp the beauty and wonder of Christ and the church, who really grasp the sweetness of their salvation, will really grasp the beauty, wonder, and sweetness of sexual union in marriage (see Song 2:1–6; 4:10–12; 1 Cor. 6:17–20). The more fully like God you become, the more fully you will enjoy His gifts.

Of course, there are exceptions. There will be men and women who grow in Christ, grow in love for their spouses, and yet lose their ability to have sex in certain ways. The effects of chemotherapy, for example, or damage to genitalia from an accident can reduce a married couple's sexual capacities. What I would argue, however, is that those very couples can be every bit as satisfied and delighted in their sexual relationship as ever before, simply because the grace of God prevails on their souls and blesses whatever forms of sexual celebration they continue.

Most people who marry will not have to face these kinds of unique circumstances. More likely than not, you and your spouse will enter into your wedding night planning to consummate your union as God designed from the beginning (see Gen. 2:24–25). It is meant to be a loving and joyful experience. And it is also meant to be a selfless and joyful process.

A Few Thoughts to Consider

- Your first hours and days in bed together could be a little clumsy, especially if you have no experience. If the bride is a virgin, then sexual intercourse could be quite painful in the early going. Be prepared for this. Be prepared to cry and pray together if your first night or two hurt a bit. It will be totally worthwhile. So trust God through it. Enjoy His gift!
- One of you may be quite experienced at sex while the other is not. If you are a virgin and your spouse is not, please be gracious. Remember that all sins are paid for in Christ. If your spouse has

confessed his or her sexual sins of the past, then please forgive him or her and celebrate the redemption you have been given in Christ. The sacrifice of Jesus on the cross was enough to satisfy the Father. It should be enough to satisfy you.

- If your spouse is a virgin and you are not, then please be gracious. I cannot say this enough. Pray that you never compare him or her to anyone else! Don't be disappointed because your spouse isn't a skillful lover in the early days! His or her lack of skill comes from a lack of experience—and the lack of experience comes from sexual purity, innocence, and saving his or her body for you.

- If you both bring past experiences to the bedroom, then certain aspects of sexual union may be easy while other aspects could prove more difficult. You may know what to do and how to do it. Intercourse may happen without pain. These parts could be easier. Missing out on the excitement of "the first time" happening on your wedding night may be difficult. Facing the twinges of regret and shame concerning your sexual past could sour the moment. God knows what you will face on that night and in the days to follow. Talk to Him and trust Him! Talk to each other and be kind!

- In the hours between the wedding ceremony and the marriage bed, try to relax. Enjoy all that God has done. Take in the scenery. Try to enjoy a meal and leisure time together. Talk and pray together. Maybe read a little Scripture. Assume a pace toward sexual union that seems comfortable for both of you.

- In the space below, please share any other tips and ideas that come to your mind for the wedding night and the days to follow.

11

The Glory of Christ in Financial Stewardship

For where your treasure is, there your
heart will be also. (Matt. 6:21)

A steward is someone who manages and cares for the property of another person. Stewards do not own this property, but they maintain and cultivate it. They oversee the households and riches of their masters. Good stewards are usually free to enjoy the property of their masters in one form or another. They are positioned, trained, and instructed to manage the property of their masters in whatever form seems best. It is a serious and privileged position.

The life of Joseph provides a beautiful picture of faithful stewardship. After his brothers sold him into slavery, Joseph was taken to Egypt and placed into service inside the household of Potiphar. The Lord was with Joseph, and Joseph was faithful. Genesis 39:3–4 tells us,

> Now his master saw that the LORD was with him and how the LORD caused all that he did to prosper in his hand. So Joseph found favor in his sight and became his personal servant; and he made him overseer over his house, and all that he owned he put in his charge.

Although Joseph had no long-term financial stake in Potiphar's estate, he still managed the estate with diligence and integrity.

God calls us to handle everything He has given us in this life with the same attitude and effort. God refers to His redeemed people, and especially to leaders in His household, as stewards. Titus 1:7 says, "For the overseer must be above reproach *as God's steward*, not self-willed, not quick-tempered, not addicted to wine, not pugnacious, not fond of sordid gain."

Jesus used a parable of stewardship to encourage faithfulness in all His followers:

> And the Lord said, "Who then is the faithful and sensible steward, whom his master will put in charge of his servants, to give them their rations at the proper time? Blessed is that slave whom his master finds so doing when he comes. Truly I say to you that he will put him in charge of all his possessions." (Luke 12:42–44)

Paul saw himself and his fellow apostles as stewards of God's grace and glory. In 1 Corinthians 4:1–2, he said,

> Let a man regard us in this manner, as servants of Christ and stewards of the mysteries of God. In this case, moreover, it is required of stewards that one be found trustworthy.

The salvation we have been granted and spiritual gifts we have been given are to be handled in a manner that builds and strengthens God's household. First Peter 4:10 says, "As each one has received a special gift, employ it in serving one another as good stewards of the manifold grace of God."

While being a steward of God's manifold grace involves faithfulness to the ministry of the gospel, it also involves faithfulness to the management of earthly wealth. Eternal life and earthly wealth are both gifts from God. They are both means to enjoy God. He gives treasures in heaven and treasures on earth. He owns all of it. He entrusts them to us. The temporal gifts are to be enjoyed. They are also to be invested for eternal gains.

In the years of marriage ahead, you and your spouse will likely be entrusted with property and possessions. And God has called and enabled you to steward them well. He wants you to enjoy them. He also wants you to invest them for the sake of His name. His does not want them to be sources of contention and strife, but raw material that you use to express your love for Him and for others.

The Heart of Wise Stewardship in Marriage

Whatever rules our hearts will rule our lives. If the Spirit of Christ rules our hearts, then He will also rule our bank accounts. He will control our attitudes about earthly resources, and every created thing in our possession, because He will first control our hearts. As we begin to think about financial stewardship in marriage, we must remember what is truly important. Money and possessions actually exist to serve the glory of our God and His kingdom.

Dealing faithfully with the resources God has assigned to us in marriage begins when we embrace a shared mission in life. Philippians 2:2 says, "Make my joy complete by being of the same mind, maintaining the same love, united in spirit, intent on one purpose." God wants husbands, wives, and all His people to agree on the critical matters of life: the glory of God, the spread of the gospel, the salvation of souls, the edification of His church, the authority of Scripture, love for one another, and other critical matters from His Word. He wants our hearts to be firmly committed to these things. When this happens, all the little details and differences among people fall into their proper place; we learn to work them out; we learn to bear patiently with one another.

The Heart of Foolish Stewardship in Marriage

Disputes and divisions about money and possessions in our marriages arise when we lose sight of Jesus Christ and His eternal purposes for our lives.

The problem isn't primarily about money and budgeting. Money and budgets are simply the *topics* of dispute. The foxes to be wary of don't take form as purses or wallets or credit cards. The foxes that would wreak havoc in the vineyard of your marriage come in the form of pride, selfishness, fear, control, and a host of other heart conditions.

Fighting over money does not arise, first, from poor techniques with money or better ideas for using money. It arises from hearts that use money based on sinful cravings and fears. Finding better techniques for managing wealth will not remedy this problem. Only Jesus Christ can remedy this problem. In fact, techniques for managing wealth can just as easily be used as a means to satisfy our cravings and fears. Good techniques may help us to save a lot of money and manage to stay out of debt, but they will not make us love God and people through our use of money.

So, by all means, use wise strategies for stewarding the resources that God has entrusted to your care. Develop a budget. Get financial guidance. Just remember that these are simply aids to good stewardship. They are not the key. The Spirit of Christ ruling your souls will be the key.

After all, you and your spouse will probably disagree about many aspects of earning, saving, and managing money. You will probably have different strategies for budgeting. Marriage leaves room for these kinds of differences. In Christ, you can handle this—you can even enjoy and celebrate the differences. If Christ rules your hearts, then you will work it out.

1. Do you live as though everything in your possession belongs to God and is intended for His glory? In what ways do you act as a steward of God's resources? It what ways do you mistakenly act as the owner?

2. What are the essential things in life? Which ones do you and your fiancé agree on? About which ones might you disagree?

3. What do you wish to accomplish with your mate in this life?

The Example of the Philippian Church

There is no grander mission to share in life than living for the glory of Christ and His kingdom. This will not tell you exactly where every penny ought to be spent, exactly which couch to buy, or exactly where to live and what to eat, but it will orient your hearts toward God in your approach to life and will join you together in such a way that conversations about stewardship become a joy rather than a source of strife.

The church at Philippi had been joined together in such a way.

Nevertheless, you have done well to share with me in my affliction. You yourselves also know, Philippians, that at the first preaching of the gospel, after I left Macedonia, no church shared with me in the matter of giving and receiving but you alone; for even in Thessalonica you sent a gift more than once for my needs. Not that I seek the gift itself, but I seek for the profit which increases to your account.

But I have received everything in full and have an abundance;
I am amply supplied, having received from Epaphroditus what you
have sent, a fragrant aroma, an acceptable sacrifice, well-pleasing to
God. And my God will supply all your needs according to His riches
in glory in Christ Jesus. Now to our God and Father be the glory
forever and ever. Amen. (Phil. 4:14–20)

The planting of the Philippian church is recorded in Acts 16. Paul
and Silas were beaten and thrown into prison shortly after its con-
ception. After departing the city, Paul and his team "traveled through
Amphipolis and Apollonia" (Acts 17:1) before coming to Thessalonica.
They reasoned in the synagogue for three Sabbaths before jealous men
incited a mob and "set the city in an uproar" (Acts 17:5). Paul and Silas
were then sent by night to Berea. They were in Thessalonica for less
than a month.

It is astounding to consider, then, that during Paul's brief stay
in Thessalonica, the Philippian church "sent a gift more than once."
Within weeks of coming to Christ, the church at Philippi was giving
money to support gospel ministry in the surrounding cities. The glory
of Christ and His gospel had taken over their souls. By necessity, then,
the glory of Christ and His gospel had taken over their finances.

Giving to gospel ministry from what God had already given the
Philippians was not, from Paul's perspective, a burdensome chore. It
was a privilege. It was a sweet opportunity. They "shared with him" in
the work. In fact, their generosity in earthly things translated to their
"profit" in eternal things. Their sacrifice was "well-pleasing to God."
They could be assured that God would supply all their needs "according to His riches in glory in Christ Jesus." They were helping to further the gospel and, therefore, storing up for themselves "treasures in
heaven, where neither moth nor rust destroys, and where thieves do
not break in or steal" (Matt. 6:20).

Adopting a Christ-focused, kingdom-expanding mission will be an
important step as you begin to talk about financial stewardship in marriage. With this mind-set, your conversations about money will be less
likely to devolve into debates about material possessions, retirement,

and wealth management. Your conversation is more likely to focus on using and enjoying all that God provides in a manner that honors Him.

Enjoying God and His Provision

For everything created by God is good, and nothing is to be rejected if it is received with gratitude; for it is sanctified by means of the word of God and prayer. (1 Tim. 4:4–5)

When a father and mother give gifts to their children, they want their children to enjoy them with gratitude. They will feel no joy or honor if their children hang their heads in guilt and shame before throwing the gifts into the trash because they feel unworthy of them.

Gifts are undeserved. We are not supposed to *feel worthy of them.* Gifts are not earned. No one pays for a gift; you just receive and enjoy it. God intends for us to enjoy the created things He provides. We are not meant to be ashamed of material comforts. Everything that God created is good. Everything that God created shows His goodness. All that God has given to mankind is to be used and enjoyed wisely.

So then, every created thing that God has given for our possession has been given for the sake of His glory and kingdom. They have also been given for our good and enjoyment. God wants us to enjoy the gifts He has given and to use those gifts to honor His name and love people. We are to enjoy and employ His gifts with thankful and cheerful hearts.

4. Identify possible ways that you might feel guilty and ashamed of having money or possessions. In what ways do you fail to enjoy God's gifts because of a guilty conscience?

5. Do you give to your church? To the poor? If not, then please share why not. If you do, then please share what compels you to give.

The Practices of a Faithful Steward

Hopefully we have come to realize that every created thing in our possession, including our lives, has been given to us as a gift from God and is meant to be faithfully used for His glory. This means that we use created stuff as an instrument for loving Him and loving others. This means that we use created stuff as an instrument for enjoying God and enjoying others.

There are hundreds of tools and systems for helping people to manage money and material possessions. These can be very helpful. It will be up to you to decide what tools and systems are most helpful for your household. This premarital training will not try to address these tools and systems. In this section, we will simply try to highlight a few important principles that will help you to steward material possessions in a wise and biblical manner, knowing that there will be a thousand nuances and details that every couple will encounter and have to address on their own.

Diligent Work

For you yourselves know how you ought to follow our example, because we did not act in an undisciplined manner among you, nor did we eat anyone's bread without paying for it, but with labor and hardship we kept working night and day so that we would not be a burden to any of you; not because we do not have the right to this, but in order to offer ourselves as a model for you, so that you would follow our example. For even when we were with you, we used to give you this order: if anyone is not willing to work, then he is not to eat, either. (2 Thess. 3:7–10)

One way that we honor Christ as stewards of His creation is through diligent and honest work. Paul tried to be a model to the Thessalonians in how he worked each day and provided for his own physical needs. He refused to exercise his right as an apostle to ask for financial support, in order to set an example.

Some of the able-bodied men, probably believing that Jesus would return any moment, had ceased from working. So they had no money to care for the physical needs of their households. They were eating the bread of other people's labors (see 2 Thess. 3:11).

These men were setting aside one of their God-given roles: to provide for the physical needs of their households, which is both a privilege and a serious responsibility.

Paul even said, in 1 Timothy 5:8, "But if anyone does not provide for his own, and especially for those of his household, he has denied the faith and is worse than an unbeliever." From God's point of view, laziness and refusal to work hard are not merely rejections of godliness, but even rejections of humanity (see Prov. 18:9).

Of course, seasons of unemployment or physical injury may create complications. There may be periods of time when a wife, an extended family, the government, or a church is asked to provide financially for a household. Certainly there are exceptions, but these are rare. Men are called and enabled to work diligently and provide for their homes.

Now, these exhortations from Scripture do not provide justification for a man to work an insane number of hours each week for the sake of achieving a high standard of living for his family (see Prov. 23:4). Providing for the physical needs of his home, while essential, is not the most essential provision that a husband and father is to make. Husbands and fathers, first and foremost, are appointed to be spiritual leaders and shepherds in their homes. As we talked about in previous chapters, God has already assigned this role.

Providing material things for his home is an important task for every husband and father, but providing spiritual things is an even greater one. In fact, assuming this role of the spiritual shepherd in their respective homes happens to be a necessary qualification for leaders in the church (see 1 Tim. 3:4).

A wife and mother's primary responsibility, according to Scripture, may be found inside the home. Titus 2:3–5 says,

> Older women likewise are to be reverent in their behavior, not malicious gossips nor enslaved to much wine, teaching what is good, so that they may encourage the young women to love their husbands, to love their children, to be sensible, pure, workers at home, kind, being subject to their own husbands, so that the word of God will not be dishonored.

Now, this does not mean that a wife is not allowed to work outside the home or earn money at all. The excellent wife of Proverbs 31 conducted business outside the home (see v. 16), yet her primary role was to her husband and children.

Some women feel free and able to labor outside the home while fulfilling all God has called them to fulfill inside the home—with the consent of their husbands as well. This is probably a rare and special calling. Most families cannot live with both father and mother working full-time outside the home without compromising the Word of God or falling prey to the trappings and distractions of the world. Some women feel called to school their children at home and to manage their homes in such a way that requires their full-time attention and effort. Every couple must prayerfully consider the glory of God and His will for their marriage and home.

6. In what way do you show a track record of diligent work? Or of laziness? Whether inside or outside your home, are you learning to be a hard and cheerful worker? Briefly explain your answer.

7. In what ways are you tempted to overwork? In what ways is God teaching you to rest when it is time to rest?

Faithful Giving

> Now this I say, he who sows sparingly will also reap sparingly, and he who sows bountifully will also reap bountifully. Each one must do just as he has purposed in his heart, not grudgingly or under compulsion, for God loves a cheerful giver. (2 Cor. 9:6–7)

Generous and faithful giving is another way through which we honor Christ as stewards of His creation. God is generous. He wants His children to be generous. God is more devoted to His name and eternal mission than to accumulating material stuff. He wants our hearts to be oriented the same way. God loves people more than things. He wants us to love people more than things.

Faithful giving in our lives begins when we *purpose in our hearts to give* and then follow through with whatever our hearts have purposed to give. This may be a set amount every week, or it may be a percentage of your income every month, or it may be whatever the Lord burdens you to give. It does not have to be the same percentage or amount as everyone else. It should be sacrificial. It should be cheerful. If we are unable to give anything cheerfully, then we need to repent and ask for the Lord's help with becoming a joyful giver.

Loving God and pleasing Him should control our giving. His pleasure is our chief reason for sharing His resources wisely.

8. When you consider the life you have lived so far, have you been generous in your giving?

9. Do you believe it is better to give than to receive? Share ways that this belief been expressed in your life.

A Sensible Lifestyle

Assuming a sensible standard of living represents another way that we steward God's creation well. Being wise with money and material things is, I believe, not very complicated. It is hard, but not complicated. It requires commitment to one very simple guideline: *wisely spend less money than you possess*. Every human being on earth is accountable to this principle. We invite serious financial trouble once we start spending money that we don't actually have in our possession.

Of course, there are areas of life and seasons of life in which bank loans and lines of credit could be wise and helpful. These areas and seasons are rare. Buying a house using a bank loan could be a good decision, provided that your down payment and ability to pay the note are substantial enough. Using a line of credit to expand a business can be a wise investment, provided that the landscape of the marketplace supports such a decision. Life-and-death medical treatments could require money that we don't possess at the moment. We must consider these case-by-case.

Again, these are situations that most people don't face every day. Talk to the Lord about these special circumstances when they arise. Talk together as a couple. Seek the wisdom of older men and women who have struggled well.

The real wisdom of being a good steward involves how we approach material things day to day and hour to hour. The financial mistakes that we make usually happen one little step at a time: the kind and amount of clothing we purchase; the kind and amount of restaurant eating we do; the types of cars we drive; the monthly cost of the homes we purchase; the sports our children play; the cost of our vacations, entertainment, electronics, and other gadgets; and other items we consume such as sodas, alcohol, coffee, and cigarettes. These are, if you will, areas of stewardship in which we make decisions every day. They can add up quickly. They represent the areas in which living sensibly under the control of the Holy Spirit proves vital.

> But we urge you, brethren, to excel still more, and to make it your ambition to lead a quiet life and attend to your own business and

work with your hands, just as we commanded you, so that you will behave properly toward outsiders and not be in any need. (1 Thess. 4:10–12)

In the passage above, Paul encourages us to lead simple, sensible lives. He tells us not to aim for an extravagant lifestyle, but for something basic and reasonable. He wants us *to lead a quiet life*. He means for us to be levelheaded in the way we work and play. Mind your daily business, plod along in your duties, and pay your bills. This, he argued, offers an example of godly wisdom to the world.

Living this way also validates the truthfulness of the gospel. The gospel declares that we are saved through Jesus Christ and are being conformed to the image of God. Since God works with integrity and upholds His promises, His followers should follow in his footsteps. He fulfills His commitments. So should we. We are to work hard and provide for the basic needs of our households as an expression of obedience to the gospel. Taking on foolish loans and working ridiculously long hours so that we can live in fancy houses, drive fancy cars, and eat at fancy restaurants makes the gospel look no different than many other ideologies of the world.

Adopting a sensible lifestyle can prove difficult, because our sinful flesh prefers to feed its lusts rather than to starve them. It refuses to be content. It wants more, which means that it won't stop wanting to add material things and financial burdens to our lives. The sinful flesh covets. It craves. And it won't care about financial wisdom, budgets, and responsibility. After all, it's far easier to buy material things than it is to pay for them.

So in order to live a sensible lifestyle for the glory of Christ and His kingdom, we must learn to say no to the desires of the flesh. We must learn to drive cars, eat food, and wear clothing that fits our income. Worrying about our image and striving to impress our neighbors must be noticed, repented from, and left behind. The love of the world is the surest way to add financial complication and pressure to your life. Even more, it's a signal that the love of God is not abiding in us.

Do not love the world nor the things in the world. If anyone loves the world, the love of the Father is not in him. For all that is in the world, the lust of the flesh and the lust of the eyes and the boastful pride of life, is not from the Father, but is from the world. (1 John 2:15–16)

10. In what ways are you sensible with money? In what ways are you frivolous or extravagant?

11. What pressures do you feel to achieve or maintain a certain social status or image? Who are you trying to impress by being successful or having money?

Wise Preparation for the Future

A final way for us to honor Christ as stewards of His creation is to prepare for the future wisely. Of course, there are many other truths that we could mention, but the truths we have covered provide a substantial foundation for understanding biblical stewardship in marriage.

In offering this principle of preparing for the future wisely, I am not suggesting that you save money for the sake of your financial glory or for building lots of assets to assuage your fears about the economies of the world crumbling. These are simply other forms of covetousness under the guise of wise saving (see Luke 12:13–21). The resources that you are given in this life are intended to be used for loving God and loving others. They do not deserve our trust and hope (see Prov. 11:28). God alone deserves our trust and hope.

Rather, I am encouraging you prayerfully to understand the needs of the road ahead and to prepare to care for those needs with biblical wisdom. Saving for the birth of a child, for a vehicle, or for a down payment on a home can be proper and right. Proverbs 24:27 instructs us to "prepare your work outside and make it ready for yourself in the field; afterwards, then, build your house." We are to work diligently, live sensibly, and prepare for the future.

12. In the appendix, you will find an outline for a budget. Please take some time this week to sit down with your fiancé and fill out this budget outline.

13. Are there financial counselors who are available through your church community? If so, write down their contact information below for your future reference.

12

Getting a Grip on Your Expectations

According to my earnest expectation and hope, that I will
not be put to shame in anything, but that with all boldness,
Christ will even now, as always, be exalted in my body,
whether by life or by death. (Phil. 1:20)

Expectations impact our marriages. They shape how we approach and view marriage, as well as how we react when our married life starts unraveling before our eyes. We might expect to feel a certain way about our mate. We might expect our mate to feel a certain way about us. We could set our hopes on a specific number of children, on specific kinds of children, or on a specific kind of spouse who will parent our children in a specific manner. There could be a particular way that we think money ought to be handled and a particular way that we believe our in-laws ought to be handled. Sex should happen at least four times a week, from our point of view—or maybe less, or maybe more.

Who cooks and who cleans? What style and quality of food will we eat? How clean will the house be kept? Will we go to bed at the same time, or can we go separately? Who will do the grocery shopping? Who will do the laundry? How should I talk to you when you hurt me, or when I hurt you? How should you talk to me? What church should we attend? How involved should we be together? Are we going to pray together each night, in the morning, or not at all? These questions begin to draw out the expectations that we carry into marriage.

What Are Your Expectations?

Expectations in marriage are closely related to, and tend to arise from, our desires for marriage. When our desire for something is strong enough, and we are convinced the desire is good, we will probably expect our spouse to deliver that desire. When we desire a certain kind of marriage and believe that our desire is right, we can easily expect our spouse to make it happen. At the very least, we expect him or her to not interfere with our dream.

Our marriages run full of expectations, because our hearts come into our marriages loaded with desires. We may even generate entirely new desires and expectations for marriage once we get on the inside.

Please realize that most of these expectations are unspoken, and that you may not even realize that you have them. They usually go unnoticed for a while, just as most of our desires for marriage can go unnoticed. Often they remain unnoticed until they are threatened or violated.

You may have trouble really identifying what you expect. A few of the statements below that you are asked to respond to may make very little sense to you right now. They will make far more sense later.

Expectations for the Wedding Day

The wedding you have in mind may be a small affair. It may be something rather massive. No matter what its scale is, however, you will knowingly or unknowingly be bringing a whole list of expectations into your wedding ceremony and the hours around it.

Please estimate the strength of your expectation for each item below. Circling the number 1 means that you have little to no expectation. Circling the number 5 means that you have a very strong expectation for that event to happen.

	Strength of Expectation
	Low High
The ceremony will be smooth and wonderful	1 2 3 4 5
There will not be any serious humiliation	1 2 3 4 5
The wedding day will revolve around me	1 2 3 4 5
Our parents will behave and get along	1 2 3 4 5
I will have no doubts about getting married	1 2 3 4 5
My spouse will have no doubts about our marriage	1 2 3 4 5
Events will start on time	1 2 3 4 5
I will look and feel glorious	1 2 3 4 5
Other people will honor and respect me	1 2 3 4 5
Everything, mostly, will go according to plan	1 2 3 4 5
The wedding and reception will be a lot of fun	1 2 3 4 5
Our families will be happy for us	1 2 3 4 5
No one will do anything stupid	1 2 3 4 5
God will be with us and for us	1 2 3 4 5
The wedding will honor Jesus Christ above all things	1 2 3 4 5
The wedding will bring great glory to God	1 2 3 4 5

Please consider other expectations that you bring to the wedding day:

Expectations for the Wedding Night

The wedding night can be full of expectation: the romance of a first evening as husband and wife, the excitement of a new life, the beginning of a lifelong journey together, the anticipation of sexual pleasures, an evening away in a restful place, and much more. Most husbands and wives expect sexual intercourse to happen on the wedding night. Many expect it to be easy and pleasurable. Some couples expect intoxicating emotions, physical fireworks, and deep celebration. All these expectations could, by the grace of God, happen without a glitch. Or, by the grace of God, things could all unfold in the opposite direction. As surprising as it may sound, the wedding night can bring disappointment and heartache. It can be stressful and difficult. It can be wonderful and restful, but it can also be painful. You may not be able to control which way it goes, but you can prepare to love, serve, sacrifice, repent, and forgive no matter what the Lord brings.

	Strength of Expectation				
	Low				High
The wedding night will be romantic	1	2	3	4	5
The wedding night will be fun and relaxing	1	2	3	4	5
We will have sex	1	2	3	4	5
Sexual intercourse will be pleasurable	1	2	3	4	5
My spouse will be really thrilled to be married to me	1	2	3	4	5
I will be really thrilled to be married to my spouse	1	2	3	4	5
My spouse will feel as I do about being married	1	2	3	4	5
There will be no guilt and shame over past sins	1	2	3	4	5
No one will cry	1	2	3	4	5
We will pray together	1	2	3	4	5
My spouse will be patient with me	1	2	3	4	5
We will read and speak of Scripture together	1	2	3	4	5
We will be grateful and joyful	1	2	3	4	5
I will feel comfortable being physically naked	1	2	3	4	5
I will feel comfortable being emotionally vulnerable	1	2	3	4	5
I will be well-rested	1	2	3	4	5

Please identify other expectations you may bring to the wedding night:

1. What is a wife supposed to be like on her wedding night?

2. What is a husband supposed to be like on his wedding night?

It will be important to talk through these expectations with the man or woman you are marrying. The two of you may anticipate something very similar on the wedding night, or you may not. One of you may be charging into the evening eager and zealous to consummate your marriage sexually. One of you may be terrified or at least hesitant about sex. One of you may require very little time and non-sexual touch to get into the mood. One of you may appreciate several hours of conversation and relaxation.

Pray for God's grace. Pray to be humble and flexible. Any number of delights and difficulties could arise.

Expectations for the Honeymoon

Sometimes newlyweds are not able to go on a honeymoon right after their wedding. Special circumstances can happen. I hope this is not the case for you. I hope you are able to take a number of days after your wedding to spend in undistracted time with each other and the Lord.

In the table below, please respond to each statement with your strength of expectation for the honeymoon.

	Strength of Expectation		
	Low		High
There will not be any problems	1 2 3 4 5		
There will be no interruptions	1 2 3 4 5		
There will not be any serious marriage conflict	1 2 3 4 5		
We will be grateful and joyful	1 2 3 4 5		
There will not be any suffering	1 2 3 4 5		
I will not have to serve anyone	1 2 3 4 5		
We will pray together	1 2 3 4 5		
We will read and speak of Scripture together	1 2 3 4 5		
My spouse will be kind and considerate	1 2 3 4 5		
I will have no regrets about getting married	1 2 3 4 5		
My spouse will not regret getting married	1 2 3 4 5		

Please identify any other expectations that you believe could impact your honeymoon:

Expectations for Extended Family in the Early Months of Marriage

Eventually you will return from your honeymoon. Life will keep going. You will return to neighbors, church communities, job or school responsibilities, and so much more. More likely than not, you will return to an extended family. You will probably return to new parents and siblings (maybe even new stepchildren). This will be an adjustment.

Take a few moments to consider your expectations for your extended family before responding to the statements in the table below.

	Strength of Expectation		
	Low		High
My in-laws will accept me	1 2 3 4 5		
Our extended family will like me	1 2 3 4 5		
My parents-in-law will be happy about our marriage	1 2 3 4 5		
Everyone will get along right away	1 2 3 4 5		
My in-laws will not interfere in our marriage	1 2 3 4 5		
In conflicts with in-laws, my spouse will take my side	1 2 3 4 5		
My spouse will enjoy my parents	1 2 3 4 5		
My spouse will want to spend time with my family	1 2 3 4 5		
My parents will not interfere with our marriage	1 2 3 4 5		
My parents will accept my spouse	1 2 3 4 5		

Please identify any other expectations that you have concerning extended family:

Expectations for Home and Spiritual Life in the Early Months of Marriage

The early days and weeks of marriage will start exposing just how much you want certain things to go a certain way at a certain time in your marriage and household. The amount of time that you spend together, the order and cleanliness of your house, who takes care of various responsibilities, how to spend and save money, and a host of other details will provide both opportunities for dialogue and opportunities for frustration. You will begin to experience married life on a practical level, with all the joys and growing pains that come alongside.

From what you know about yourself and the way you like things done, what might you expect from your mate in daily life? In the chart below, please identify how strongly you expect certain things in the day-to-day operations of your household.

	Strength of Expectation		
	Low	High
Our home will be clean and tidy	1 2 3 4 5
There will be lots of people visiting	1 2 3 4 5
In household chores, we will share the load equally	1 2 3 4 5
The husband will handle the finances	1 2 3 4 5
The wife will do the dishes	1 2 3 4 5
I will be required to serve constantly and cheerfully	1 2 3 4 5
We will not be away from each other	1 2 3 4 5
We will see eye-to-eye on managing money	1 2 3 4 5
The wife will not work outside the home	1 2 3 4 5
Most nights we will go to bed at the same time	1 2 3 4 5
There will be sex at least several times a week	1 2 3 4 5
The wife will be cheerfully submissive	1 2 3 4 5
We will have quality conversation every day	1 2 3 4 5
Most days we will pray together	1 2 3 4 5
The husband will be a good spiritual leader	1 2 3 4 5
We will read and talk about Scripture together	1 2 3 4 5
There will not be much conflict	1 2 3 4 5
We will do lots of ministry together	1 2 3 4 5
We will resolve conflict quietly	1 2 3 4 5
We will resolve conflict quickly	1 2 3 4 5
We will confess sin, repent, and forgive each other	1 2 3 4 5
We will attend church every week	1 2 3 4 5
We will be very involved in biblical community	1 2 3 4 5
Relationships with our single friends will stop	1 2 3 4 5
Our circle of close friends will change	1 2 3 4 5
We will have close relationships with other couples	1 2 3 4 5

Please consider any other expectations that you have concerning your home life during the early months of marriage:

The Chief Desire

Jesus Christ helps us to see that all human desire and expectation finds its perfect meaning and shape in being submitted to a single chief desire: "Your kingdom come. Your will be done" (Matt. 6:10). He told His disciples to desire and pray for the Father's kingdom and will.

The desire for the glory of His Father controlled all Jesus' other longings. We see this most clearly when He prayed in the garden of Gethsemane on the eve of His execution: "My Father, if it is possible, let this cup pass from Me; yet not as I will, but as You will" (Matt. 26:39). So, on one level, Jesus did not want to drink the wrath of God. Yet, on another level, He wanted whatever brought glory to the Father and served the Father's eternal purpose. Jesus surrendered His little desire to His ultimate desire: "Not as I will, but as You will." The longing to love and glorify His Father ruled everything else.

Now that you have identified a number of expectations that you may be bringing into marriage, we need to spend some time examining the root of those expectations and how they can serve your marriage in the years ahead instead of destroying it.

"One thing I have asked from the LORD, that I shall seek: that I may dwell in the house of the LORD all the days of my life, to behold the beauty of the LORD and to meditate in His temple" (Ps. 27:4). To behold, worship, and enjoy the Lord should be the one ruling desire of our souls. It should consume us. All our little desires are best sub-mitted to this one big desire. The one big desire should give birth to all our little desires, which will give birth to all our little expectations for marriage.

If the chief desire of my soul is something like "my own glory and pleasure," then all my little desires will be shaped and fueled accord-ingly. I will desire respect from my wife (not for God's reasons, but for my own). I will desire a certain amount of sexual intimacy, or a certain amount of leisure time, or for things to go a certain way in my marriage that will serve my glory and pleasure.

Expectations that I place on my wife and marriage will usually fol-low suit. I will expect her to provide respect, or a certain amount of sexual intimacy, or a certain amount of leisure time, or to help things go my way in our home. If she doesn't, then I am justified in being angry, frustrated, and critical in order to help her to love me better. After all, God commands her to be my helper, right? Since God gave her to be my helper, it seems reasonable to expect my wife to serve my desires—especially my desires for good things. Under this kind of reasoning, all my little expectations will run riot in my home. All my little desires will beat my marriage to death.

If God's glory and pleasure rule my desires, then I should see every situation in my marriage as an opportunity to love and enjoy Christ through loving and enjoying my mate. I will love my wife more than I need her to respect me, validate me, or do things my way. No matter what circumstances we face, I should respond to her with just the same grace and patience that Jesus Christ grants to my soul every day. The desire for His will and glory should shape—in a good, healthy way—all my attitudes and actions toward my wife.

If we don't want our desires to govern our marriages in a sinful way, then we probably need to understand how wrongly motivated our desires can become whenever our hearts are not submitted to the Spirit of God. All our wants and expectations in marriage have to be exam-ined carefully under the lens of Scripture. They must be submitted to the Spirit of God and shaped by the Spirit of God.

The Holy Spirit feeds our desire for Christ and His glory. The Holy

Spirit concerns Himself with exalting and glorifying Jesus according to the Father's will and pleasure. Jesus made this evident to His disciples:

> But when He, the Spirit of truth, comes, He will guide you into all the truth; for He will not speak on His own initiative, but whatever He hears, He will speak; and He will disclose to you what is to come. He will glorify Me, for He will take of Mine and will disclose it to you. (John 16:13–14)

When we walk in the Spirit, we will long to see Christ magnified in our lives. We will "seek first His kingdom and His righteousness" (Matt. 6:33), trusting Him with everything else. All our little desires will be submitted to and invigorated by our delight in Him and our longing for His exaltation—and all our expectations will follow along.

The sinful flesh wants to use marriage to serve its cravings and fears. The Holy Spirit wants to use marriage to exalt Jesus Christ and bless God's people. This is the battle that Paul spoke of in Galatians 5: "For the flesh sets its desire against the Spirit, and the Spirit against the flesh; for these are in opposition to one another, so that you may not do the things that you please" (v. 17).

The specific objects of our desires are oftentimes good, but our reasons for wanting them can be evil and false. For example, I can want my wife to be loving and kind (which is a good desire) because of my selfish concern for being loved (making it a sinful desire). I can want my children to obey (a good desire), not for the glory of God but for my own convenience and ease of life (making it a sinful desire). I can desire a physically healthy and strong body (a good desire) to help me feel better about myself and look good to others (turning it into a sinful desire). I can desire prayer, Scripture memory, and holiness in my life (good desires), not because I treasure Jesus Christ, but in order to feed my personal righteousness and glory (making them evil desires).

Learning to see when a good desire becomes a sinful desire is essential to a humble, repentant life in Christ. We all need God's help in discerning the difference between *Spirit-motivated desires* and *flesh-motivated desires*. Our expectations—and our heart response when our expectations are shattered—can help us discern the difference. They can help us to see where we need God to reorient our desires to Him. They can help us to see where the Spirit has done good work in our souls and where we need Him to keep going.

The Story of Ethan

I met with Ethan for two hours in my study. He wanted to meet because "anger had finally gotten the best of him." Someone had cut him off on the highway several days beforehand, and it provoked a fiery outburst. After speeding alongside the offending vehicle, he made an obscene gesture with his hand and screamed a creative array of curses at the driver. He accelerated past the vehicle without a second thought. Looking into his rearview mirror, Ethan caught sight of his five-year-old son sitting in the back seat. Ethan had forgotten that his son was travelling with him—a son who was now peering at his father with confusion and alarm in his eyes. Following that event, Ethan realized that, just as his wife had been telling him for years, he needed to get help.

So he called me, and we sat down to talk. About an hour into our conversation, Ethan recounted the incident that I just shared. Then I asked Ethan a question: "Why did the other driver's actions bother you so much?"

Ethan was a little perplexed by the question, but he answered anyway. "Because he cut me off?"

"But why did that bother you so much?" I replied.

He thought a little longer. "Because what he did was wrong and careless and disrespectful."

All very true! We kept digging, "And why, do you believe, does someone being wrong, careless, and disrespectful toward you bother you so much?"

Ethan replied, "It just does."

Most of us stop reflecting at this point. We don't examine deeper. We know that we are offended. We know someone just did something that hurt our feelings or provoked anger in our hearts. We can usually identify exactly what the other person said or did or failed to say or do that irritated us so deeply. The way that we think about it tends to make perfect sense to us. The other person did something wrong (A), I got offended and angry (B), and then I lashed out or got cold and withdrawn (C). So A is the reason for B, and B is the reason for C, thus A is the root problem that started the whole mess. It seems reasonable.

Ethan and I decided to look a little further. In our following meetings, he and I began digging into the war that was going on in his heart before A ever happened. Even though he was a professing Christian and was deeply involved in the Scriptures, prayer, and service in the body of Christ, Ethan also craved the praise of man. He cherished the approval of others. He hated looking silly. It was critical to Ethan that other people respect, honor, and like him. It was equally critical for people not to disrespect, dishonor, or dislike him. Another driver disrespecting him on the road struck a really big nerve in his soul.

Although his spoken mission was "God's kingdom come, God's will be done," his day-to-day functional mission in life was "My kingdom come, my will be done." He was more concerned with people honoring him than with people (even himself) honoring the Lord. His name was more precious to him than the name of Jesus Christ. This really showed up when people offended him. There was a clash of kingdoms in his soul. God's kingdom and his own, practically speaking, were working in different directions.

All that it took was a complete stranger cutting in front of Ethan on the highway to expose this hidden war. The other driver was rude and insensitive. The other driver was disrespectful and careless. There is no denying these realities. Yet the other driver's sin doesn't really deserve the focus of Ethan's immediate attention. The other driver was out of line, but that wasn't the reason for Ethan's explosion. The other driver's sinfulness simply exposed Ethan's idolatrous craving for respect and good treatment from others. The painful circumstances provided the perfect environment for Ethan's heart to be flushed into the open.

If repentance was going to happen for Ethan, then it needed to go deeper than "I got mad—forgive me, God!" In the same way, change for him would need to go deeper than a trite little vow: "I will not get so angry when other people wrong me." His heart needed radical change. His outburst of rage certainly called for confession, repentance, and forgiveness in Christ, but the outburst only scratched the surface of the story. There was an idolatrous love for respect and glory churning beneath his angry reaction. Anger was a symptom. A heart that was set on his personal kingdom rather than Christ's was the source.

This is good news. It may be painful news, but it is good news. The "driving incident" provided a laboratory where God could expose Ethan's proud expectations and desires in order to highlight his need for the grace of Christ. His audible words and visible behavior in the car offered an X-ray view of the invisible sin-cancer that was eating him from the inside. God wants to deal with that invisible part, too—not just the visible behavior.

The gospel promises a supernatural transformation of the invisible part: "Though our outer man is decaying, yet our inner man is being renewed day by day" (2 Cor. 4:16).

The Holy Spirit can help Ethan to adopt a functional mission in life that matches his professed mission in life. The gospel promises forgiveness and redemption to Ethan. God offers His grace through Jesus Christ as a means to purge the pride and idolatry from Ethan's heart over time, filling it with His grace and love instead. As this begins to happen, Ethan will be free to enjoy the peace and joy of Christ, on the highway and everywhere else, no matter what all the other sinners of the world are doing.

What Does This Mean for You?

We are all just like Ethan. There is a war being waged in our hearts. Two kingdoms and wills are clashing.

Paul was aware of this war within himself: "I find then the principle that evil is present in me, the one who wants to do good" (Rom. 7:21). He alerts us to this war in Galatians 5:17: "For the flesh sets its desire against the Spirit, and the Spirit against the flesh; for these are in opposition to one another, so that you may not do the things that you please."

The battle is very real. It is costly, and it can take many forms: God's glory versus my glory, God's kingdom versus my kingdom, hope set on Him versus hope set on the world, treasure in heaven versus treasure on earth. No matter what form it takes, this war will drastically impact our desires and, therefore, our expectations for marriage.

The real test of your heart will come when you don't get what you want. It will come when your spouse offends you. It will come when your mate fails to meet your expectations. After all, marriage will disappoint you. Of this you can be certain. At some point in the days ahead, your spouse will cut you off on the marriage highway. It will probably happen on a regular basis. And at those moments, the real desire of your heart will be exposed. When your spouse dishonors you, refuses sexual intimacy, shuts you out emotionally, blows the budget, or confronts sin in *your* life, whatever rules your heart will become more evident than ever before.

Please feel free to have expectations. Just make sure they are the right ones and that they are submitted to the right Person! Expect yourself to sacrifice. Expect God to be faithful. Expect Him to ask you to forgive your mate as He has forgiven you. Expect moments of joy at the most unlikely times. Expect disappointment in marriage and God's grace to love your spouse the way that He loves you. Expect to be amazed when your mate loves you far more than you actually deserve.

Expect your sin to create a lot of trouble, and expect to repent often. Expect your enjoyment of God and of your mate to grow as you grow closer to Him. Plan on God being near to you and being for your marriage. He promises to give you His Spirit's power for the road ahead. We should expect and know that He will be faithful.

3. Why do you want to get married?

4. Whose kingdom do you want your marriage to serve? How can you tell?

5. What little desires feed your expectations going into marriage (e.g., desire for success, respect, honor, sexual pleasure, or money; desire to cure loneliness; desire to love or serve another person; desire to enjoy the gifts of God with another person)?

6. What big desire do you see yourself living for right now (the glory of Christ, your own glory, the kingdom of Christ, your own kingdom, or a mix of these)?

The Hope of Glory

According to my earnest expectation and hope, that I will not be put to shame in anything, but that with all boldness, Christ will even now, as always, be exalted in my body, whether by life or by death (Phil. 1:20)

Above all other ambitions, Paul wanted to display the magnificence of Jesus Christ. Whether he was free or imprisoned; whether he was hungry or well fed; whether in health or in sickness; whether he lived or died—these details were basically irrelevant. Paul didn't really care about them too deeply. He knew that Jesus could be exalted in his life under any circumstances. His ultimate desire was that Christ would be glorified in him. It shaped and motivated everything else in his life.

Another way to talk about expectation, according to Paul's words, is to use the word *hope*. When we set our expectation somewhere, we are setting our hope in the same place.

Earthly marriage has been a massive disappointment for many followers of Jesus Christ because they have placed their hope in it. They have worshiped the created, temporary picture rather than the Person it portrays.

We are meant to marvel at what marriage means far more than at marriage itself. Marriage means Christ and the church. It expresses the reality of Christ living in us. Marriage intends to help us set our hope on Jesus Christ—a hope that "does not disappoint, because the love of God has been poured out within our hearts through the Holy Spirit who was given to us" (Rom. 5:5).

Only God can fulfill our deepest needs and satisfy our deepest longings. Put those needs and longings onto someone else, and the burden will crush him or her, frustrate you, and destroy any good relationship that you hope to achieve.

Not only does marriage represent the union that Christ and His church enjoy now, it also points to the ultimate, completed union and fellowship of Christ and His people for eternity. We hope and wait for what He promises will come: a new heaven and earth, a holy city, God dwelling with us, and us as His forgiven and reconciled people—no more death, no more mourning, no more crying, and no more pain (see Rev. 21:1–4).

I say all this as your wedding approaches so that you will see and enjoy marriage for what God intends it to be, without fixing your hope on it. Love your God-given mate. Enjoy your God-given mate. Serve, take pleasure in, and receive blessings from your beloved spouse. Just make sure not to worship your mate, demand from your spouse what only Christ can supply, or seek marriage as an end to itself. Relish marriage as a beautiful picture. Cherish it as a glorious display. Only remember whom it displays and who makes the picture so beautiful. May the Lord make your days of marriage full and rich in Him!

Taking the Point to Heart

You are likely to bring a great many expectations into your marriage. I don't believe you can avoid it. But do you realize where your expectations come from? Do you know who gave birth to them? All your little expectations have grown from your little desires, and your little desires have their roots in your ultimate desire.

Your ultimate desire could be the glory of Christ and His kingdom, or it could be your own glory and kingdom. God wants to help you discern the difference so that your heart can become more fully His, so that your selfish desires don't burn your marriage to the ground, so that you can be free to enjoy your marriage and love your spouse the way God intends.

Our expectations lead us to where we have placed our hope. Our hope will tell us where to put our expectations. Both of these belong firmly fixed on Christ. If your expectations and hopes are set on Him, then you will probably expect to sacrifice in marriage. You will expect to lay your life down for your mate, just as Christ laid His down for you.

Are you ready for this? Will you trust God in such sacrifice?

If you are ready and willing, then marriage will prove to be far more glorious and delightful than you can ever imagine. It will prepare you for your eternal marriage to Christ far better than you could ever imagine.

A Final Note before the Wedding

Now that you are wrapping up the premarital portion of this workbook, please let me convey my thanks and congratulations to you! In recent weeks, you have covered a lot of material and, more likely than not, enjoyed some really challenging conversations. Finishing this part of the journey is a real accomplishment. I hope it has been worthwhile and convicting for your souls. I hope you have been able to identify and address real and significant "foxes" that are preying on your marriage vineyard. At the same time, I pray it has been, by the grace of God, strengthening and transformative to your hearts.

Please don't stop now. There are three chapters remaining. They are intended to help you during the weeks and months that follow your wedding ceremony. Chapter 13 fits best if you work through it two to three weeks after your wedding. Chapter 14 belongs about two months after the wedding, and chapter 15 works well at around four to five months after the wedding. The goal should be for you to at least meet with your discipling couple after you complete each of those chapters—and hopefully more!

PART 2

After the Wedding

The final three chapters of this book are for you to complete during the weeks after your wedding. Please do not neglect these chapters and meetings. They are as important to the marriage preparation process as the chapters you accomplished and the meetings you attended before the wedding. They are intended to help you celebrate all that Christ has done in your lives, look at potential troubles that are already brewing or inflamed in your marriage, and provide an open and loving means for you to face any difficulties in the days ahead.

13

In the Wake

Everyone who comes to Me and hears My words and acts on them,
I will show you whom he is like: he is like a man building a house,
who dug deep and laid a foundation on the rock; and when a flood
occurred, the torrent burst against that house and could not shake it,
because it had been well built. (Luke 6:47–48)

So . . . how did it go? A great multitude of people may have already asked you that question, and there are many different answers you may have given them.

You may have wonderful and pleasing experiences to share. The wedding ceremony, the wedding night, the honeymoon, and your interactions with people along the way may have been encouraging and joyful. Perhaps you saw the love and faithfulness of God shining on you at every step. The previous few weeks may not have been perfect, but you are deeply grateful for how smoothly you entered into marriage.

Or you may have a different kind of story to share. There may have been flashes of delight and encouragement, but also flashes of pain, frustration, and disappointment. The wedding ceremony may have been hard and difficult from your point of view. The wedding night and honeymoon may have fallen tragically short of your hopes and expectations. Family members may have been thorns in your side. Your spouse may have said or done something hurtful. You may have said or felt or done something sinful and embarrassing.

What Is Your Appraisal?

Each of the many people who were involved in your wedding ceremony and the days thereafter will have a unique perspective. To some degree this will be true for you and your spouse, too. The two of you may look back and notice the same events, and you may interpret them the same way. Or you may see very different things and draw very different conclusions from what has transpired. This is okay.

By the grace of God, you are about to spend the next several decades of your life together focusing on different events and expressing different views of the same events. You might as well start dealing with this now!

On the pages to follow, you will be asked to respond to a number of statements about your wedding day, the wedding night, and the days that followed. The particular statements were chosen not because they themselves are vital to the early days of marriage, but as a means to generate helpful conversation about your past few weeks. Please feel free to add any additional ideas, concerns, or experiences that you believe were significant.

The Wedding Day

I have seen weddings in which Jesus Christ was exalted and the body of Christ encouraged in remarkable ways. I have seen weddings in which Jesus Christ was reviled and people humiliated by the whole program. I have heard of wedding ceremonies in which particular parents of the bride or groom were so cruel and selfish that both bride and groom were left in tears by the end.

Yet here you are on the other side. It may have been the best day of your life. It may have been the worst. More likely than not, it fell somewhere in the middle. Remembering this day may be a cause for celebration. It may need to be a cause for repentance and reconciliation. You, your spouse, and the Lord will decide together how to remember and handle everything. Now is a good time to begin this process.

	Disagree				Agree
The wedding ceremony was smooth and wonderful	1	2	3	4	5
I was humiliated and embarrassed	1	2	3	4	5
The wedding day revolved around me	1	2	3	4	5
Our parents behaved and got along	1	2	3	4	5
I had no doubts about getting married	1	2	3	4	5
My spouse had no doubts about getting married	1	2	3	4	5
Events started on time	1	2	3	4	5
I looked and felt glorious	1	2	3	4	5
Other people honored and respected me	1	2	3	4	5
Everything, for the most part, went according to plan	1	2	3	4	5
The wedding and reception were a lot of fun	1	2	3	4	5
Our families were happy for us	1	2	3	4	5
No one did anything stupid	1	2	3	4	5
The wedding honored Jesus Christ above all things	1	2	3	4	5
I was exhausted after the wedding	1	2	3	4	5
The wedding brought great glory to God	1	2	3	4	5

I need to repent and seek forgiveness for my attitudes or actions during the wedding day   1 2 3 4 5

I believe that my spouse needs to repent and seek forgiveness for his or her attitudes or actions during the wedding day   1 2 3 4 5

I am harboring bitterness toward others from the wedding day, and I need to forgive them   1 2 3 4 5

Please list any other significant events from your wedding day that seem relevant.

The Wedding Night and Honeymoon

I cannot tell you how many interesting stories I have heard from people concerning their honeymoons. Some of these stories left me in stitches from laughter. Others left me in tears because of the brutal heartache and pain they portrayed. I know a couple who spent their honeymoon night trapped inside an airport terminal because of a snowstorm; they were miserable and angry. Another couple decided to go camping for their honeymoon. Their vehicle broke down thirty minutes after sundown, eleven miles from the nearest town. They spent the night in their vehicle and described the whole event as "Awesome!"

I met with a couple recently who had just returned from their honeymoon three days earlier than they planned. On the wedding night, when they started touching each other sexually, the wife became so terrified that she jumped out of bed, ran into the bathroom, and locked the door. Despite all the husband's efforts to talk her out of the bathroom, she refused to come out. Despite all her best intentions to serve her husband, she was not able to overcome the fears that had gripped her heart. She fell asleep on the bathroom tile. He fell asleep leaning against the outside of the bathroom door. The days thereafter did not bring much healing or improvement, so they decided to come home early and get help.

Countless times, I have heard couples talk about the sweetness of their wedding night. I have heard men and women describe it as everything they imagined it would be. The dinner, music, time alone, laughter, sexual delight, and so many other positive newlywed experiences helped to make the evening quite magical to them.

All the couples who I just mentioned are married to this day, and God has been very good to them. Whether your wedding night and honeymoon were delightful or painful, God still loves you and remains faithful to you and your marriage.

Please take some time to appraise your wedding night and honeymoon, and thank God for His faithfulness.

	Disagree				Agree
The wedding night was romantic	1	2	3	4	5
The wedding night was fun and relaxing	1	2	3	4	5
We had sex on our wedding night	1	2	3	4	5
Sexual intercourse was pleasurable	1	2	3	4	5
My spouse was really thrilled to be married to me	1	2	3	4	5
I was really thrilled to be married to my spouse	1	2	3	4	5
My spouse felt like I did about being married	1	2	3	4	5
There was guilt and shame over past sins	1	2	3	4	5
No one cried on the wedding night	1	2	3	4	5
We prayed together	1	2	3	4	5
My spouse was patient with me	1	2	3	4	5
We read and spoke of Scripture together	1	2	3	4	5
We enjoyed each other's company	1	2	3	4	5
Our time on our honeymoon was restful	1	2	3	4	5
We each did things we enjoyed	1	2	3	4	5
We argued a lot on our honeymoon	1	2	3	4	5

I need to repent and seek my spouse's forgiveness for my attitudes or actions during the wedding and honeymoon   1 2 3 4 5

I believe that my spouse needs to repent and seek my forgiveness for attitudes or actions during the wedding and honeymoon 1 2 3 4 5

I am harboring bitterness toward others from the wedding night or honeymoon, and I need to forgive them   1 2 3 4 5

Please identify other experiences from the wedding night or honeymoon that seem significant to you.

The Days to Follow

Most men and women question whether or not they should have married their spouse at some point in their marriage. A few of them regret their decision within hours or days of the wedding. A sense of panic overtakes them, and they begin doubting everything.

For many couples, however, these doubts do not creep in until later, and their return from the honeymoon is everything they expect it to be. There are no regrets. Their first days in their new home are full of exciting newness and adventure. Their time together is joyful, pleasant, and full of rest.

Please share your appraisal of the days that followed your return to "real life."

	Disagree				Agree
There were no big problems returning home	1	2	3	4	5
It has been exciting to start a new life together	1	2	3	4	5
We were grateful and joyful	1	2	3	4	5
There has not been any suffering	1	2	3	4	5
We have prayed together	1	2	3	4	5
We have read and spoken of Scripture together	1	2	3	4	5
My spouse has been kind and considerate	1	2	3	4	5
I have no regrets about getting married	1	2	3	4	5
My spouse has no regrets about getting married	1	2	3	4	5
I need to repent and seek my spouse's forgiveness for my attitudes or actions in recent days	1	2	3	4	5
I believe that my spouse needs to repent and seek my forgiveness for his or her attitudes or actions in recent days	1	2	3	4	5
I am harboring bitterness toward others from the days that followed our honeymoon, and I need to forgive them	1	2	3	4	5

Please share any other significant events or experiences that have happened since your return from your honeymoon:

Building Your House on the Rock

The world will offer you a great many resources for building your marriage and home. It will thrust into your hands a great many tools for dealing with questions, troubles, and conflict in your early years together.

Jesus Christ provides the surest, sweetest, and most powerful resources for putting your marriage on solid ground and helping it grow. Namely, He provides Himself. And He provides Himself to you through His Spirit, His Word, and His church.

If you abide in Me, and My words abide in you, ask whatever you wish, and it will be done for you. (John 15:7)

Why do you call Me, "Lord, Lord," and do not do what I say? Everyone who comes to Me and hears My words and acts on them, I will show you whom he is like: he is like a man building a house, who dug deep and laid a foundation on the rock; and when a flood occurred, the torrent burst against that house and could not shake it, because it had been well built. But the one who has heard and has not acted accordingly, is like a man who built a house on the ground without any foundation; and the torrent burst against it and immediately it collapsed, and the ruin of that house was great. (Luke 6:46–49)

If you want to build your home and marriage on solid ground, then you must take these statements from Jesus seriously. Just like every other aspect of human life, marriage should be built on Jesus and His Word.

God has designed marriage to function well His way. A life, marriage, or family can rest on solid ground only when its members are *abiding in the Word of God*—that is, when we believe, obey, and enjoy all that He has spoken. For Jesus to be our Lord, we must come to Him by faith, trusting in who He is and what He promises. The Holy Spirit gives us the ability to hear, understand, and act on the words of Jesus Christ, and we must exercise that ability day after day in marriage.

Whether the early weeks of marriage have been pleasurable, painful, or some mix of both, it will be important for you to understand that Jesus and His Word provide an abundance of comfort, wisdom, and power. While books and other people can help you understand and apply His Word rightly, they cannot add to its truth and power. Nor can they lessen its truth and power. Walking alongside other people is essential, but doing so must be founded on God and His Word. All the winds and rains of earthly life cannot tear down what has been founded on Him.

Your personal ideas and agendas for your home, however, will not last. They are not meant to last. If you are moving forward in your marriage based on your own strength and wisdom, then you are walking on shaky and fragile ground. If you are trying to resolve your problems and handle your pain based on personal grit and bright ideas, then your marriage will probably—at some point in the future—fracture and crumble.

Abiding in Jesus Christ through His Spirit and His Word

I am not saying that reading the Bible and memorizing lots of Bible verses will make your marriage flourish and flow with joy. Just doing the intellectual work is not what I mean by abiding in the Word of God. Demons and unbelievers can hear, memorize, and regurgitate Scripture without ever experiencing its transforming power. The exercise of careful Bible study is absolutely necessary. It is not, however, enough.

What I am saying is that fruitful life on earth depends on our constant abiding in Jesus Christ, and we abide in Him when His Spirit and Word abide in us. So when I say we must abide in Him, I am also saying we must abide in His Spirit and Word, because they all work together in harmony.

The Spirit of God gives us eyes to see, ears to hear, and humble hearts to receive the Scripture in a way that causes growth and prompts action (see Luke 6:47).

Unbelieving people cannot truly understand and obey the Word of God from the heart, because they do not have the Holy Spirit living inside them. By the grace of God, we can understand and obey—the

Word of God can abide in us because the Spirit abides in us. The Spirit of God and Word of God work together.

So when I say that we must abide in the Word of God, I am saying that we must be filled with His Spirit and constantly feeding on the Word of God so that it will take deep and lasting root in our souls. Colossians 3:16 says, "Let the word of Christ richly dwell within you." The Word of God is the raw material that His Spirit uses to bring hope, healing, and transformation to our souls. It is our spiritual food. God uses His Word to nourish and transform us.

1. Have you been feeding on the Word of God and trusting His promises? Share specific ways that you learn and memorize the Word of God.

2. Are you beginning to see how much you depend on the Word of God for wisdom and strength? How does Scripture guide the way that you live and shape the way that you see the world?

The Story of Eddie and Aisha

Several years ago, Eddie and Aisha needed and sought counsel for their marriage. They had been married for one month at the time.

The buildup to their wedding had been intense. Apparently Eddie's mother was not fond of Aisha. She had voiced her opinion, a few weeks before the wedding, that Eddie "could have done better." If that wasn't enough, she added, "That little girl doesn't know the first thing about taking care of my son." Aisha was hurt and incensed. Eddie was surprised and confused. Neither knew what to do. Keeping his mother on the periphery of their lives became Aisha's goal from that point onward. Pretending that nothing had happened, Eddie believed, was the best approach.

Although Eddie's parents were still married, his dad was extremely quiet and withdrawn. It took their engagement period to expose just how attached his mother had become to Eddie over the years—and just how resistant she was to letting him go. Though she would never admit it, Aisha was a threat to her self-centered relationship with her son. Though a professing Christian, she had never come to understand and embrace God's will for her son's marriage (see Matt. 19:6).

In the days leading up the ceremony, Aisha had started seeing Eddie's mom as a serious threat to their marriage. Once they had wed and were safely away on their honeymoon, she voiced her desire and view that his mom should be removed from their life entirely. "There is no way we can have a happy marriage," Aisha asserted, "with her in the picture."

Eddie felt trapped in the middle. He agonized over the dilemma. "Do I honor my wife's wishes, or do I honor my father and mother?"

Aisha made it clear: "If Eddie really loves me, then he will pick me over his mother."

Eddie felt that it was an unfair and selfish ultimatum. A cloud of pain, bitterness, and dejection descended onto their home, and they didn't know how to dispel it. Only days into their marriage, they felt the foundation of their marriage crumbling beneath them.

What Every Marriage Foundation Needs

It became evident in our initial conversations that Eddie and Aisha did not know how Christ and His Word were supposed to shape their approach to daily life. They didn't realize how important the Word of God would be in helping them to address his mother, their fears, and their opposing opinions. Like all of us, they struggled to bring the living truth of Scripture into the painful realities of each day in order to gain fresh wisdom for the moment. The Word of God did not seem near and rich to them; it seemed distant and frail. It was a great book with wonderful, lofty truths that were meant for people who lived a long time ago and faced questions unlike their own.

Eddie craved ease, comfort, and acceptance in his relationships. Keeping everyone happy with him, not rocking the boat, pretending that nothing was wrong, and even praying for conflict to blow over— these were a few of Eddie's instinctive reactions. He didn't go to the Word of Christ for comfort and direction.

Eddie had never realized that the Bible was full of people who struggled in just the same ways. Moses, Elijah, David, and Peter battled fear, rejection, and conflict. Whole psalms had been composed to provide comfort and strength to the anxious heart.

The fears and habits that Eddie carried were the same kinds of fears and habits that God addresses throughout His Word. His tendencies to avoid conflict, to submit to his mother's subtle demands, and to resent his wife's sinfulness were not outside the scope of God's Word but were carefully woven into the story.

Aisha reacted to adversity in her way. She tended to circle the wagons, defend her turf, defeat the threat, and preserve what belonged to her at all costs—these were a few of her preferred methods. But they are also the preferred methods of people throughout the Bible. God knew all about the frustrations and worries that Aisha carried. He knew what to do with them. When God called Aisha to "be submissive to [her] own husband" (1 Peter 3:1) and adorn herself with "a gentle and quiet spirit" (v. 4), He knew what He was asking. He knew it would require a deep hope in Him and a willingness for Aisha to face her fears by learning to trust her heavenly Father completely (see vv. 5–6).

In all their hours of debate before and after their wedding day, Eddie and Aisha had not opened the Scriptures together a single time. They had not sought the face of God together in prayer. They had not started asking God for His opinion and for His grace to face their challenges. This needed to change.

3. Do you quickly go to God's Word for aid? Or is it a last resort? Please explain your answers.

4. When do you tend to read your Bible? What have been some of your most fruitful times reading Scripture? Please explain.

Reading and Listening to the Word

If Eddie and Aisha wanted to know what God wanted for them and from them in marriage, then they needed to start reading His Word on a consistent, attentive, and responsive basis.

The same truth applies to each of us. None of us grow in appreciation and understanding of Scripture if we don't actually read it. We must carefully and constantly listen to God speaking if we are to know Him personally and understand what He thinks, desires, and counsels (see Luke 6:47).

Likewise, our souls cannot be healthy and strong without feeding on the Word of God. Deuteronomy 8:3 clearly states, "Man does not live by bread alone, but man lives by everything that proceeds out of the mouth of the LORD." God provides the nourishment and strength our souls need through our reading of His Word.

If you have ever seen pictures of men, women, and children on the brink of starvation, then the images are probably seared into your mind. The skin pulled tightly to the bones, the hollow eyes, and all the other features of gross malnourishment are striking and sobering. Bodies require food and water in order to survive. A lack of proper nourishment leads to weakness, sickness, and eventual death.

When we refuse to feed on God's Word and drink on His promises, we actually starve our souls of the resources necessary for their health and vitality. Our souls require food just as our bodies require food. We cannot survive without the nutrition of God's Word.

So imagine this for a moment: If you could see a physical picture of your soul, what do you think it would look like? Would your spiritual body be refreshed and strong? Would it be well nourished on the Word of God? Or would you look like a victim of starvation—frail, fragile, and dying?

Meditating on the Word

After listening to the Word of our God, we must take His Word to heart. If Eddie and Aisha wanted to understand and remember the Word of God in their daily lives, then they needed to dwell on it.

It is the same for us. After eating the Word, we need to digest it well. Psalm 1:1–2 says,

> How blessed is the man who does not walk in the counsel of the
> wicked,

Nor stand in the path of sinners,
Nor sit in the seat of scoffers!
But his delight is in the law of the LORD,
And in His law *he meditates day and night.*

Now imagine eating a bowl of food every morning, then vomiting into the kitchen sink. What value and growth could this meal really offer? The food hasn't been digested, so it cannot help the body. When we read the Word of God, put it down, and carry on with our day without a second thought—consumed with our own thoughts, desires, and frustrations—then we are eating His Word only to vomit it back. We cannot simply skim the surface of Scripture if we want it to nourish our hearts. We should absorb and digest it through sober reflection and thoughtfulness.

Talking to God about His Word

After listening to God speak through His Word and thinking about His words, we can talk to Him about what He says. Sincere and humble response to the Word of God is a vital aspect of prayer. Men and women throughout the story line of Scripture have modeled this kind of personal relating to God (see Ps. 119:17–18).

If we talk to God a great deal without reading and listening to His Word, then our conversation with God is not conversation at all, but a series of monologues centered on our personal thoughts and opinions. He becomes the silent party—not because He is silent, but because we have chosen to leave Him outside the interaction. It is a one-way conversation based mostly on our ideas, not God's. Meaningful and fruitful prayer begins with humble and active listening to the Word of God. When we speak to Him in return, with our thoughts shaped by His thoughts, we are more likely to engage with the Lord in a wise and sensible conversation.

5. What do you enjoy about prayer?

6. To what degree are your conversations with God shaped by His Word?

7. When do you tend to pray? What kinds of experiences and circumstances drive you to your knees?

Communing in the Word

Eating and digesting the spiritual food of Scripture can be enjoyed as a family meal. We all need help making sense of God's Word and seeing it rightly. We need encouragement from others to keep studying and considering God's Word, and we can benefit greatly from men and women who have been studying and learning His Word for years before us.

Soon after my first meeting with Eddie and Aisha, I encouraged them to find a healthy community group in their church—a group that gathered around the Word and dealt with personal struggles in an honest, open, and gracious way. They also acquired a written resource to help them with basic Bible study methods. These were two simple means of aiding their knowledge and understanding of the Scripture in the context of community.

Trusting and Obeying the Word

Many of us, like Eddie and Aisha, begin marriage on the wrong footing because we believe that our personal insights and methods are trustworthy and good. We believe they will make our marriages work. Perhaps, deep inside, we think that God's insight and methods are irrelevant or outdated. Perhaps we simply don't like His thoughts and refuse them altogether. Either way, we cannot call Jesus our Lord and then reject His Word for our lives. When we reject His Word, then we, by default, will lean and stand on our own understanding.

After hearing the Word of Christ, we must act on it. Jesus says in Luke 6:47–48, "Everyone who comes to Me and hears My words *and acts on them*, I will show you whom he is like: he is like a man building a house, who dug deep and laid a foundation on the rock."

God wants us to stand on firmer ground. He wants our footing to rest on His promises, not on our personal agendas. He is with us and for us (see Isa. 41:10). He will never leave us or forsake us (see Deut. 31:6–8; Heb. 13:5). He is in control, and His way is good (see Matt. 6:25–26; Rom. 8:28–30). What He wants for our lives is better than what we want for our lives.

Though Eddie and Aisha would not be able to understand all the implications of these promises for their marriage by the end of their first month, they could begin to trust the God who had made these promises to them. Aisha could battle her frustrations and fears by realizing that God was with them and was in control. Christ had already told her how to be a wife under difficult circumstances (see Eph. 5:18–24; Titus 2:3–5; 1 Peter 3:1–6). She could trust Him and His way. He never promised that it would be easy, but He promised to be a near and strong Helper. So she could rest. She was free to encourage her husband, share her thoughts in a humble way, and repent of the sinful anger that was driving her words. God would take care of her in everything else.

In a similar way, Eddie could face his insecurities and worries about his mother through a growing trust in Jesus Christ. He was free to love his wife just as Christ loved the church—even in neglect of his mother's wishes—and to know that his Lord would help and deliver him at the proper time. He could gently and lovingly put his mother in the proper place in his life. And if his mother became angry, sulky, or disapproving, Eddie could again trust God with these outcomes and accept them as good pieces of the Lord's perfect plan that were within the Lord's strength to handle.

Just as importantly, Eddie could begin praying with Aisha, receiving her concerns and helping her to deal with his mother in a gracious, Christ-honoring manner. Because his sins were forgiven in Jesus Christ, he could repent of his self-centered fear, seek his wife's forgiveness for his apathetic attitude, and be bold in his love for his wife. Because he was God's child, Eddie could speak the truth in love to his wife without fearing her response and could ask her to believe the gospel right alongside him. According to the gospel, his mother did not belong in the middle of their marriage. According to the gospel, his mother did not need to be destroyed. She needed their steadfast love, their gracious words, and a clearer picture of where she would fit in their lives from their wedding day onward.

In the early days of your marriage, more likely than not, your understanding of the gospel may be put to the test. God will probably ask you to believe a great number of His promises. He will probably ask you to obey Christ even when it hurts.

8. Where in your marriage might God be calling you to obey "even when it hurts right now"?

9. What realizations about your marriage and spouse make you the most thankful right now?

10. Please share what you have learned since the wedding day about being a husband or wife.

14

Reality

For not one of us lives for himself, and not one dies for himself;
for if we live, we live for the Lord, or if we die, we die for the Lord;
therefore whether we live or die, we are the Lord's. (Rom. 14:7–8)

Now, approximately three months into your marriage, reality may be starting to settle in—that is, you are probably beginning to see, hear, and taste what married life truly entails hour by hour and day by day. Married life is less and less something you have to imagine and more and more something you experience and can describe firsthand.

This is good. It is always better to live in reality than in fantasy. And the reality you are coming to realize may be better or worse than what you imagined.

A Story of Disillusionment

They met through mutual friends shortly after graduating from college. Geoff noticed Tatiana's physical beauty right away. Almost everything that he wanted in a girl, Tatiana possessed. Beauty, intelligence, a love for sports, and a great sense of humor—it was all there. She was also a follower of Christ and was involved in the same church.

His relationships with girls in the past had been frustrating and hurtful. Talking to Tatiana was easy and fun. He hadn't thought very deeply about marriage until he saw her. The fact that she was so interested in him was flattering—even intoxicating.

Tatiana had been thinking about marriage since she was nine years old, and she was equally thrilled by the attentiveness and adoration that Geoff expressed toward her. Her dad was "a total bum," in her words. Family life growing up had been full of strife and pain. Her parents had divorced when she was ten. She was ready for a man who was serious about life and marriage, serious about God, and able to create the family life that she knew was right in God's sight—the family life she had always wanted. Geoff, she felt, was perfect. He seemed hard-working, moral, and strong. He knew and talked about the Bible. He prayed. Wherever he could take her in life, she believed, would be far better than everywhere she had been.

Both Geoff and Tatiana saw many appealing things in each other. They were physically attracted to each other. They shared an interest in spiritual things. They enjoyed similar foods. Both of them loved the outdoors and regular exercise. They were educated. They wanted children. Each could see faithfulness, maturity, diligence, and commitment to righteousness in the other.

They started dating. Five months later, at the beginning of a new year, they were engaged. Their plan was to marry in late summer. So they did.

In the weeks and months that followed their wedding, Geoff and Tatiana began to see each other with more clarity. The hard-to-notice parts of their characters and styles started being exposed. Little quirks and qualities, which were previously hidden, came into full view. They experienced each other in ways they hadn't before. *Shocked, hurt, angry,* and *disillusioned* were all words that they used to describe what they began feeling during the first year. There was pleasure, happiness, and encouragement too, but mostly disappointment and frustration.

Geoff and Tatiana were sinners, really big sinners, just like everyone else. And this critical reality had escaped their notice before marriage. At least, the implications of this reality had escaped their notice. They would commit sin every day, whether in heart affection or in outward action. They would be sinned against every day. They would be hurt, in some form, every day. Neither one of them grasped the reality of this before marriage. They didn't realize how constantly their sinfulness would collide, or how constantly repentance, forgiveness, and meditation on the gospel would need to happen in their hearts and home.

Marriage did not exist in order to give them the love, acceptance, approval, and family life they had always dreamed to possess. This reality had escaped their notice, too.

God intended to use their marriage to reflect His glory and bring about His purposes in their lives—whatever that would mean. They had assumed it meant something far different than the reality that they now knew. God had a vision for their marriage that they had not imagined. He gave them a reality of marriage that they hadn't conceived. Even though they wanted a "good Christian marriage," they wanted it their way and for their reasons. They wanted it more for their ease and comfort than for God's glory and their growth toward holiness.

For example, Geoff craved the appreciation of people, and especially his wife. What he received from her was a lack of appreciation. If she became angry with him, he would shut down, avoid her, or get defensive.

Whenever he failed as a husband, he tried to make quick amends, cover up, or just move on. Though he wanted to be a spiritual leader in public, he tended to be apathetic and passive as a spiritual leader in the privacy of their home. Initiating prayer or meaningful conversation with Tatiana was intimidating. So he steered clear of it. Sex was his preferred way of being close.

In fact, Geoff liked to look at pornography from time to time. He felt really ashamed and guilty about it, but he would inevitably go back. He confessed to the Lord time and time again, but he still felt the claws of sexual temptation digging into his back.

When Tatiana finally caught him looking at lewd images on the computer, each of their fears, hurts, frustrations, and disappointments came to a head. She felt betrayed. He felt hopeless and beaten down. He had expected his wife to be his biggest fan, not his biggest critic. She had expected him to be her hero, not another source of pain.

Tatiana, unbeknownst to Geoff before marriage, was very quick tempered. Though "her father warned him," he blew it off. She wanted things done the right way, especially in her home. When displeased,

Tatiana would either "blow up" or "freeze him out." Affection and sexual intimacy were totally out of the question if she was upset. The way that he cleaned or failed to clean, the amount of television he watched, his lack of leadership, and many other qualities were constant sources of irritation and resentment for Tatiana. She had expected Geoff to be someone she could rely on. He was supposed to rescue her from the home of her childhood in order to create the home she wanted as a woman. Instead, in her words, "Geoff is not much of a man at all."

They kept plugging away at church. They attended Sunday services and a weekly Bible study, and they spent time around believing friends. Though both of them were growing in marital misery and angst, they learned to "play the game."

God used a perceptive, godly, and loving couple in their weekly Bible study to throw the curtains back and help them to face what was going on in their hearts and home. After one of their weekly meetings, the other couple pulled Geoff and Tatiana aside and offered them help. They accepted. In fact, their second year of marriage would bring greater pain than the first, but with far more spiritual fruit.

The older, godly couple invited Geoff and Tatiana to begin meeting with them on a regular basis. Geoff and Tatiana agreed, so the four of them began meeting every week or two and studying through the book of Exodus.

What God accomplished for Geoff and Tatiana through the riches of His Word forever altered the trajectory of their marriage. They began to experience the depth of God's love for them—a love that redeems and transforms them, a love that never fades away, and a love that never promises an easy, pain-free life on earth. They realized that they needed to start embracing the unexpected pains of their redemption. God intended to use their marriage as one means to conform them to His image, for His reasons and in His way.

The Truth We Must All Embrace

Redemption can hurt! The process of being freed from our slavery to sin and death can be painful. The promises of the gospel are sweet, but the context in which we hear, learn, and believe them can be bitter. First Peter 1:6–7 says,

> In this you greatly rejoice, even though now for a little while, if necessary, you have been distressed by various trials, so that the proof of your faith, being more precious than gold which is perishable, even though tested by fire, may be found to result in praise and glory and honor at the revelation of Jesus Christ.

The genuineness of our faith is proven and grown inside the furnace of daily life. Marriage often provides a great deal of heat and fuel for this furnace.

If the gospel is to work itself into our hearts and shape the way we live before God and one another, then we must cheerfully accept, as part of the gospel message, the unexpected pains of redemption.

A Sweet and Costly Deliverance

It may be worthwhile for you to take the next hour and read through the first fifteen chapters of Exodus. It will provide the structure for the rest of this chapter.

The narrative of Exodus begins where Genesis leaves off, with the mention of Israel (Jacob) and his sons in Egypt. It mentions the death of Joseph. The story jumps forward three hundred years when it references a new king arising over Egypt.

This new Pharaoh decided to deal shrewdly with the people of Israel by forcing them into slavery. The Egyptians began to "afflict them with hard labor" and "compelled the sons of Israel to labor rigorously; and they made their lives bitter with hard labor . . . all their labors which they rigorously imposed on them" (Ex. 1:11, 13–14). In a fear-driven attempt to control the growth of God's people, Pharaoh ordered his own people to cast every newborn boy from the nation of Israel into the Nile River. These were brutal and vicious days for the people of God.

Moses was born around this time. His mother hid him initially, then committed him to the providence of God by placing him in a basket on the Nile River. God beautifully orchestrated events so that

Moses was adopted into the household of Pharaoh. In the royal household, he was cared for and educated.

When he was forty years old, Moses "went out to his brethren and looked on their hard labors" (2:11). To defend a fellow Hebrew, he killed an Egyptian. When Pharaoh heard about it, he sought Moses' life. So Moses fled to Midian.

In the land of Midian, Moses married Zipporah and lived as a shepherd for another forty years. When he was around eighty years of age, the Lord appeared to him in the midst of a burning bush and announced his plan of redemption for his people. The Lord commissioned Moses to face Pharaoh and called him to lead the children of Israel out from bondage in order to worship the Lord, their covenant-keeping God, at Mt. Horeb. Despite a number of fears and concerns that Moses raised, God promised to accompany him, give him words to speak, and deliver Israel with much power, plunder, and joy (see Ex. 4).

Moses somewhat reluctantly obeyed. When Moses and Aaron brought the good news of salvation to the people of God in Egypt, the people were genuinely thrilled. "So the people believed; and when they heard that the LORD was concerned about the sons of Israel and that He had seen their affliction, then they bowed low and worshiped" (Ex. 4:31).

A message of salvation tends to bring this kind of response. If enslaved, we are thrilled at the idea of freedom. If condemned, we love forgiveness. The avenue from death to life, from sickness to health, and from lands of misery to lands of milk and honey is an avenue that we long to be taken down. The hope of such a road compels us to worship and thank God. We go home, pack our bags, and prepare to receive heaven by morning.

It is a rude awakening when the heavenly realities of salvation are not packaged on our doorsteps by dawn. An even ruder awakening is when the morning brings stiffer pains. The promise of salvation remains, but so does suffering. The reward is coming, but under a divine sense of time.

The initial audience between Moses and Pharaoh brought greater hardship in the hours to follow, not lesser. The children of Israel were commanded to make bricks without straw while their quota remained the same. Their labors grew more treacherous, not less. The Hebrew foremen were beaten, not released. The Egyptians dealt more severely than ever with the already oppressed people of God. It takes a Spirit-wrought faith to accept and appreciate the delay of deliverance during an escalation of immediate pains. Read the response of the people and, afterward, of Moses:

> When [the foremen of the people] left Pharaoh's presence, they met Moses and Aaron as they were waiting for them. They said to them, "May the LORD look upon you and judge you, for you have made us odious in Pharaoh's sight and in the sight of his servants, to put a sword in their hand to kill us." Then Moses returned to the LORD and said, "O Lord, why have You brought harm to this people? Why did You ever send me? Ever since I came to Pharaoh to speak in Your name, he has done harm to this people, and You have not delivered Your people at all." (Ex. 5:20–23)

In light of their pain and suffering, the promises of God had lost their luster. They wanted deliverance right away, not later. (So do we!) They expected it to come without too much cost. (So do we!) At least, they expected it to come with little to no suffering attached.

Since the circumstances had gotten worse for the Israelites, they blamed Moses. Rather than seeing him as a bearer of good news, they saw him as the author of a cruel joke.

Embarrassed and perplexed, Moses brought accusations of his own before the Lord. Yet God again shared His plan of redemption with Moses. He spoke to Moses about the glory He would soon display at Pharaoh's expense. He affirmed His faithful nature as a covenant-keeping God. He expressed His compassion for His people and repeated His promise to deliver them by His outstretched arm. Moses expressed these promises and words to the people, but they refused to listen to or find comfort in the message (see Ex. 6:9).

Wow! What an incredible turn of events! What an amazing shift of attitudes in the hearts of the people from Exodus 4:31 to 6:9—from worship to despondency! In one moment, they are rejoicing. In the next moment, they are bitter and dejected. What happened? Why the change? Why the move from happiness to depression, from gratitude to anger, from being open to the ways and will of God to being closed and hardened? Why had the gospel message, the message of their salvation, lost its beauty and delight? What had they missed?

They missed the same thing we can miss almost every day. We constantly play with the very attitudes and affections that they are displaying. The realities of life may not unfold as we imagine. The circumstances of marriage may not follow the plan that we had in our minds before marriage began. Oftentimes, the actual experience of being God's children includes a lot of pain and confusion. What are we to do?

1. Think about a few areas of your life that have not gone according to your plans. What are your ways of dealing with the disappointment?

2. What realities in your marriage are far more difficult than you expected? Share some of these.

3. Do you carry strong opinions about the way that God should orchestrate your life? Do you believe that he should care and provide for you in certain ways? Give a few examples.

The *process* of our deliverance, it would seem, is every bit as essential to God as our *arrival* is. The road of salvation provides as much testimony to the glory of God as getting there. Seizing on immediate physical spoils and presumed earthly rewards will only produce disappointment and rage by the end of the week. When Jesus Christ didn't give the people of Israel the kind of deliverance that they wanted, they delivered Him over to be crucified (see Matt. 21:9; Luke 19:37–38; John 12:12–13). So it may be worth our time to consider what God means by redemption—and why!

Here, I believe, is the pressing question for this chapter: *How is the sweetness and power of the gospel to deepen in our hearts and lives when marriage gets painful?* Life and marriage can get messy. There will be grief, mistreatment, failure, and heartache. What should we do? How can we come to believe and express every day that we "consider that the sufferings of this present time are not worthy to be compared with the glory that is to be revealed to us" (Rom. 8:18).

The Mission of God

The sweetness and power of the gospel deepens in our marriages *when we understand the mission of God in the world.* God has set in motion His plan to redeem us, display His power in us and around us, and fill the earth with His glory through us. The salvation of our souls is not first or centrally about us, but about Him. Of course, we benefit from His mission beyond imagination, but the ultimate point of our redemption is to prove and highlight His splendor and power in order to provoke awe and worship. Our marriages are not ultimate. God is ultimate. Peace and happiness do not come from getting our way in our lives—they come from God having His way in our lives.

Read how God helps us keep this in perspective.

"Say, therefore, to the sons of Israel, 'I am the LORD, and I will bring you out from under the burdens of the Egyptians, and I will deliver you from their bondage. I will also redeem you with an outstretched arm and with great judgments. Then I will take you for My people, and I will be your God; and *you shall know that I am the Lord your God*, who brought you out from under the burdens of the Egyptians.'" (Ex. 6:6–7)

"But I will harden Pharaoh's heart that I may multiply My signs and My wonders in the land of Egypt. When Pharaoh does not listen to you, then I will lay My hand on Egypt and bring out My hosts, My people the sons of Israel, from the land of Egypt by great judgments. *The Egyptians shall know that I am the LORD*, when I stretch out My hand on Egypt and bring out the sons of Israel from their midst." (Ex. 7:3–5)

"But, indeed, for this reason I have allowed you to remain, *in order to show you My power and in order to proclaim My name through all the earth.*" (Ex. 9:16)

What if God, although willing to *demonstrate His wrath and to make His power known*, endured with much patience vessels of wrath prepared for destruction? And He did so *to make known the riches of His glory upon vessels of mercy*, which He prepared beforehand for glory, even us, whom He also called, not from among Jews only, but also from among Gentiles. (Rom. 9:22–24)

God sees our afflictions and has compassion for our estate. He loves us and delivers us at the proper time. God gives, and God takes away (see Job 1:21). He gives seasons of ease and bliss as well as seasons of hardship and pain (see Eccl. 3:1–8). Under all manner of circumstances, God redeems our souls as a testimony to His grace and power.

The ultimate meaning and purpose of our lives and circumstances ends not with our individual lives but with God and His perfect plan for the whole cosmos. We are cast as beloved characters in a bigger story—His story. Like individual instruments in a mighty orchestra, we are part of a grander performance—His performance. He is primarily concerned not with our circumstantial comfort, but with sharing His glory, love, and power with us, and with growing us to be more like Him and to bear His image well.

4. When you think about "the glory of God," what do you think about? How does the idea of "God's glory" affect your marriage?

5. When you think of your life and marriage being not mainly about you, but about God, what thoughts and emotions come to your heart? Are you encouraged or discouraged? Do you feel privileged or insulted?

The Love of God

The sweetness and power of the gospel deepens in our marriages *when we understand the depth of God's love and compassion for us.*

God sees and hears His people. He knows our affliction. He sees real problems. God does not live in denial or confusion. Jesus Christ lived, died, and rose from the grave to deliver us from real problems and enemies.

This is a constant theme of the Exodus narrative. God preserved His people in Egypt, thwarting the plans of Pharaoh to exterminate them. He also prepared and provided a deliverer in Moses.

> Now it came about in the course of those many days that the king of Egypt died. And the sons of Israel sighed because of the bondage, and they cried out; and their cry for help because of their bondage rose up to God. So God heard their groaning; and God remembered His covenant with Abraham, Isaac, and Jacob. God saw the sons of Israel, and God took notice of them. (Ex. 2:23–25)

He said also, "I am the God of your father, the God of Abraham, the God of Isaac, and the God of Jacob." Then Moses hid his face, for he was afraid to look at God. The LORD said, "I have surely seen the affliction of My people who are in Egypt, and have given heed to their cry because of their taskmasters, for I am aware of their sufferings." (Ex. 3:6–7)

Now, behold, the cry of the sons of Israel has come to Me; furthermore, I have seen the oppression with which the Egyptians are oppressing them. (Ex. 3:9)

God allows His people to suffer, sustains them in suffering, and then, under His perfect sense of time, delivers them from suffering. The truth that God loves us does not mean He will preserve us from painful circumstances. Rather, it means that He preserves us amidst painful circumstances.

The apostle Paul made this beautifully clear:

Who will separate us from the love of Christ? Will tribulation, or distress, or persecution, or famine, or nakedness, or peril, or sword? Just as it is written,

"For Your sake we are being put to death all day long;
We were considered as sheep to be slaughtered."

But in all these things we overwhelmingly conquer through Him who loved us. (Rom. 8:35–37)

If His love continues and strengthens us through "persecution," "famine," and "sword," then how much more sufficient is His love to sustain us throughout the joys and pains of marriage?

Marriage had brought some pain to Geoff and Tatiana, but they could always trust in the intentions and care of their loving Father. He was with them. He was for them. His love had been proven to them time and time again, especially in the giving of His Son for their salvation.

They had taken for granted the depth of God's love for them. They had assumed that God's love would keep them from suffering. They had forgotten just how many reasons Jesus had given them to be joyful, content, and full of gratitude each day.

We tend to forget, too. We need constant reminders. At those moments when marriage gets hard and confusing, we are more likely to question the love of God and His plan for our lives. The gospel reminds us of how constantly and faithfully God pours His love on our souls (see 1 John 3:1).

Our Condition Apart from Grace

The sweetness and power of the gospel deepens in our marriages *when we understand our idolatrous and helpless condition apart from God's redeeming grace.*

The Egyptians weren't the only sinners in Egypt. While Egypt was the oppressing nation, they were not the only idolatrous nation. Even though Israel was enslaved and afflicted beneath Egypt, they were first and more seriously enslaved to sin and trapped beneath the justice and wrath of God. They were innocent of the crimes being committed by the Egyptians. They were not, however, innocent in regard to their sinful condition before God. They were helplessly at the mercy of God, not merely for their physical destiny but also for their spiritual destiny.

Worse yet, they were completely ignorant of their estate. They were deceived. They saw the wretchedness of those who afflicted them, but not their own wretchedness. They believed that they deserved deliverance when they actually deserved wrath.

In many ways, the children of Israel in Egypt were representative of the human condition apart from saving grace. They represent every one of us before God intervened through Jesus Christ on our behalf.

When God sent His Son into the world to save our souls, we weren't even aware that we had a problem. The healthy don't seek a physician (see Matt. 9:12). They don't see a need for one. The deadliest feature of our sin is the blindness it gives us to its existence. We were too helpless to notice just how helpless we were.

But Romans 5:6 tells us the fantastic news: "For while we were still helpless, at the right time Christ died for the ungodly." Jesus provided a way of salvation that we didn't think we needed.

So after God unleashed nine plagues on the land and people of Egypt, while sparing His own people along the way, He prepared the hearts of His people for the final plague: death. He instituted Passover (see Ex. 12).

On the tenth of the month, the people of God were to select a one-year-old, male, unblemished lamb. On the fourteenth of the month, during Passover, they were to sacrifice it. If the people of God were to be redeemed, then God had to provide atonement for their sins. Blood had to be shed on their behalf.

Busyness or anger or suffering in our lives tempts us to forget that we deserve far worse than we have received. We deserve hell on earth and hell thereafter. If we are recipients of grace, then we must never see ourselves as victims of a raw deal in life.

While we are tired, afflicted, or oppressed, we are also richly blessed. While life is challenging, circumstances are difficult, and our frame is weak, God keeps laboring for our good. Our sins have been put on Jesus Christ, and the Father's wrath has been poured out on Him. The righteousness of Jesus Christ has been put on us, and the Father's love and blessing has been poured out on us.

Passover foreshadowed the cross, where the perfect Lamb of God was slain to make atonement so that sinners could be declared righteous and could go free.

This is vital for us to realize in our marriages. No matter how sinful our spouses may be, we are sinners too. If we are honest and attentive, then our sinfulness should be clearer and more wretched to our souls than any sin that we see in our mates. There is no greater danger to my life and marriage, I should believe, than myself.[1] No one does more destruction to my soul than I do.

And God has provided a way of salvation in Jesus Christ. He has atoned for our sins in Jesus Christ. Even though we deserve death, we

---

1. Paul Tripp develops this idea in *What Did You Expect?: Redeeming the Realities of Marriage* (Wheaton, IL: Crossway, 2015).

have been given life instead. The reality of the gospel should make the reality of our marriages far more worthwhile. And the reality of our marriages should make the reality of the gospel sweeter and more precious than ever before.

6. Do you see your sinfulness more clearly and constantly than your mate's sinfulness? Or do you see your mate's sinfulness more clearly and more often than your own? Please explain.

7. Whose sinfulness grieves you more: your own or your spouse's? Please explain your answer.

8. Why do you need the grace of God?

9. Does His grace make you more patient and gracious toward your spouse? Since you have been forgiven so much, why is it sometimes difficult for you to forgive others—especially your mate?

Fixing Our Eyes on Jesus Christ

The sweetness and power of the gospel deepens in our marriages *when we see and fix on Jesus Christ above all things.*

The deliverance that God offered His people along the Exodus journey was deliverance to Him. He was the prize. No matter what trial or success they faced, He wanted their hearts and minds fixed on Him. "I am the LORD, and I will bring you out from under the burdens of the Egyptians, and I will deliver you from their bondage. I will also redeem you with an outstretched arm and with great judgments. Then I will take you for My people, and I will be your God; and you shall know that I am the LORD your God, who brought you out from under the burdens of the Egyptians" (Ex. 6:6–7).

It is no different today. God wants to be in the middle of our minds and lives. We are His people. He is our God. He wants us focused on Him. The gospel grows in delight and power in our lives when we become more fixated on Jesus Christ and less fixated on ourselves. "But we all, with unveiled face, beholding as in a mirror the glory of the Lord, are being transformed into the same image from glory to glory, just as from the Lord, the Spirit" (2 Cor. 3:18). The approach to human transformation that Paul suggested is quite foreign to human intuition. None of us look intently into a mirror in order to see someone other than ourselves. When we stand in front of a mirror, we hope to see an image of ourselves. Mirrors help us see and evaluate our physical appearance in order to judge our appearance against the standards of our day. If necessary, the mirror helps us adjust and fix our appearance in order to conform it to the preferred image of our day. This is how physical transformation happens.

Well, according to Paul, this is not how spiritual transformation happens. When we come to the mirror of God's Word, we come to see Jesus Christ. We come to behold Him, worship Him, and enjoy the beauty of His image. And when we do, the Spirit of God conforms us to the very image that we are beholding. When humble, Spirit-filled people see Christ, they become more like Christ.

If we are to face the realities of marriage with joy and thanksgiving, then we must learn to see and cherish Jesus Christ in our marriages. We must look more often and deeply at Him, not at ourselves. We must gaze into His Word in order to behold His glory rather than gazing into our marriages in order to behold our glory, or even the glory of our beloved mates. Confessing and repenting of our sinfulness will always be essential to our life in Christ, but it will be secondary to seeing and praising His beauty and grace.

Geoff and Tatiana spent plenty of time and energy looking at their marriage. They spent a lot of time and energy looking at each other. They thought often about themselves and how to fix themselves. God wanted them to fix their eyes instead on Jesus Christ. He used disappointment, confusion, and sin to drive their attention toward Him. This was the only way that true and lasting change would happen.

10. Do you look to yourself, your spouse, or Christ for your deepest joy and hope? Why?

11. How can you look to yourself less and to Christ more? How can you encourage your mate in this as well?

Taking the Point to Heart

The reality you are coming to see in your marriage may be better or worse than you imagined. Perhaps you approached marriage as some kind of God-given promised land, only to find it more like a wilderness. Maybe you expected it to be a wilderness, only to find that it overflows with milk and honey. Either way, our God provides wisdom and power for dealing with reality.

The Exodus narrative is one example of such wisdom. This story, by the grace of God, can help us to tackle the painful realities of our marriages with humble resolve and joy. It can help us to embrace the unexpected pains of our redemption. It can help us to fix our eyes on Jesus Christ. And, when we do, the Spirit will conform us to His image, giving us more of Christ and, therefore, more of what marriage has been created to provide.

15

Life Ahead, in Community

*Speaking the truth in love, we are to grow up in all aspects into Him
who is the head, even Christ, from whom the whole body, being
fitted and held together by what every joint supplies, according to
the proper working of each individual part, causes the growth of the
body for the building up of itself in love. (Eph. 4:15–16)*

I could say a great many things on the following pages in some kind
of effort to prepare you for your years ahead as husband and wife.
I don't think I need to say them now. The Lord, the Scripture, faithful
friends, and your spouse will help you to learn what is necessary for
the journey.

Of course, you have to listen. If you are humble before God, His
Word, and the counsel of Christ-loving people, then I believe you will
learn everything needed for fruitful marriage and vibrant life in Christ.
I believe the Scripture promises this in James 1:25: "One who looks
intently at the perfect law, the law of liberty, and abides by it, not having
become a forgetful hearer but an effectual doer, this man will be blessed
in what he does."

Whenever we humble ourselves before the Lord and His Word,
our hearts transform and bear fruit. The Spirit takes the raw material of
God's Word and uses it to feed and grow our souls. First Peter 2:1–3 says,

Therefore, putting aside all malice and all deceit and hypocrisy and
envy and all slander, like newborn babies, long for the pure milk of

the word, so that by it you may grow in respect to salvation, if you have tasted the kindness of the Lord.

God has promised to support and help us when we are broken and submitted beneath His Word. "'For My hand made all these things, thus all these things came into being,' declares the LORD. 'But to this one I will look, to him who is humble and contrite of spirit, and who trembles at My word'" (Isa. 66:2). The God who created all things by His Word offers His supernatural help to us through His Word. We receive this grace from God by having reverence for His Word.

In addition, whenever we humble ourselves before God's people, our hearts grow and bear fruit. The Spirit takes the raw material of Christian fellowship and uses it to expose, teach, and refine us. Hebrews 10:24–25 instructs us to "consider how to stimulate one another to love and good deeds, not forsaking our own assembling together, as is the habit of some, but encouraging one another; and all the more as you see the day drawing near." God intends for the body of Christ to provide an environment in which sinful people can be challenged, convicted, encouraged, and built up together by His grace.

Maintaining a healthy trajectory of marriage during the years ahead will require your daily dependence on the infinite grace of God as a husband and wife, and especially those graces He supplies to you through His body, the church. The saving grace of God brings many graces along with it. The body of Christ should be considered one of these many graces. The life, death, and resurrection of Jesus Christ has gained our entrance into an eternal family—a body of people being conformed to His image and sharing and enjoying His glory together. Your marriage needs to be a part of this family. It needs the body of Christ for its safety, daily health, and strengthening.

A Communal People

Although social in nature, human beings tend to resist truthful, honest community—especially those who have something to hide. People who practice evil hate exposure. Read how John stated it:

> This is the judgment, that the Light has come into the world, and
> men loved the darkness rather than the Light, for their deeds were
> evil. For everyone who does evil hates the Light, and does not come
> to the Light for fear that his deeds will be exposed. (John 3:19–20)

Jesus Christ is a threat to the world, because people loathe being seen
and known in their spiritual ugliness. We all possess some inkling of
just how corrupted we look apart from Jesus Christ. It is always tempting to keep this hidden.

One of the first steps that our Lord takes when redeeming our sinful
hearts is to bring us into the light. He throws the curtains back. As He
did with Adam and Eve, God strips away our self-made fig leaves and
stands us before Him naked. Then, by His grace in Jesus Christ, He
washes us and clothes us in new garments that only He can provide. He
clothes us in Jesus Christ. No longer do we hide from God in shame. No
longer do we hide from people in shame. Though we should never be
proud of our sin or comfortable as sinners in the presence of a holy God,
we can stand before Him with the confidence that the covering He has
supplied in Jesus Christ is not only sufficient but pleasing in His sight.

Part of what it means to walk in the light is to live in the open
air of Christian fellowship. Other people should see us in action and
know about our struggles. In the days and months ahead, I believe, your
church community should get to know you and your marriage well.
The Lord provides a community of redeemed people who can know
us, pray for us, and counsel us (see James 5:16).

1. How are you involved, individually and as a couple, in the
   church—the body of Christ?

2. Who *really* knows you—the good, bad, ugly, and lovely?

Community Helps Us to Grow

A true Christian community (in which the Father's will prevails through His Word, Jesus Christ is cherished and exalted, and the Holy Spirit rules the hearts of people, even though those people are a work in progress) can help us to grow in our understanding and application of the gospel. Only through fellowship with God and one another do we really learn to experience and enjoy the gospel. Living in community with other human beings forces us to apply the gospel every hour. It will force us to deal with our own pride and the pride of others in a humble, gracious manner.

Consider what Paul said to the church at Philippi:

> I urge Euodia and I urge Syntyche to live in harmony in the Lord. Indeed, true companion, I ask you also to help these women who have shared my struggle in the cause of the gospel, together with Clement also and the rest of my fellow workers, whose names are in the book of life. (Phil. 4:2–3)

These are fascinating words. All these people were sharing with Paul in the cause of the gospel and yet still learning how to live out the gospel within their relational circumstances. Euodia and Syntyche were at odds. They needed help, just like we do. The leaders of the church were somehow involved and needed encouragement applying the gospel to bring peace and unity in their church community.

The congregation of believers at Philippi provided the right environment for exposing the sin of people's hearts and their need for God's grace to bring reconciliation and change. Without living in community, they might never have seen the pride and selfishness of their souls. They would not have seen how dependent they were on God in order to love as He loves. Daily interactions with one another heightened their awareness of sin and increased their need for God's help.

It is no different for followers of Christ today. No one can truly know themselves while walking through life alone. No one grows alone. Sanctification cannot and will not happen apart from the body of Christ. God has designed it this way.

Ephesians 4:15–16 says,

> But speaking the truth in love, we are to grow up in all aspects into Him who is the head, even Christ, from whom the whole body, being fitted and held together by what every joint supplies, according to the proper working of each individual part, causes the growth of the body for the building up of itself in love.

We learn together. We become more like Jesus Christ together. We learn to love as Jesus loves in the presence of people.

At the same time, no one person alone truly reflects the image of God. God exists as Father, Son, and Holy Spirit. From eternity, He exists in holy fellowship. We cannot bear His image well without living in fellowship with others.

God has placed us into a holy community centered on Himself—on His loving, other-oriented nature. The good news of our salvation makes far more sense in the company of others, because the very purpose of our salvation is to bring us back into fellowship with an other-oriented God (see 2 Cor. 5:18–19; 1 John 1:3–4). We have been baptized into one body (see 1 Cor. 12:12–13). We have been saved to live more oriented toward others in love. Living in such a way requires us to spend our lives among people.

Community Depends on the Gospel

Of course, once people begin to gather in one place at one time, an entire host of problems will also begin to emerge. Though the gospel grows and shines forth in the midst of human relationships, so does our sinfulness and uniqueness. Even if we are gathering together as new creations in Christ and are grafted by the Spirit of God into one body, we will occasionally expose the worst of our hearts and the worst of others' hearts over the course of time.

Only the grace of God can face this problem. James 3:17 says, "But the wisdom from above is first pure, then *peaceable*, gentle, reasonable, full of mercy and good fruits." While the gospel compels us into community, the community itself cannot survive without a constant supply of God's mercy and power.

The authors of Scripture understood that true fellowship could not be achieved without a growing understanding of the gospel. First John 1:3–4 says,

> What we have seen and heard we proclaim to you also, so that you too may have fellowship with us; and indeed our fellowship is with the Father, and with His Son Jesus Christ. These things we write, so that our joy may be complete.

Hearing, believing, and acting on the truth of the gospel, John argues, is essential to the birth and health of Christian community. Fellowship based on anything other than the body and blood of Jesus Christ will always be temporal, self-serving, and false.

3. To what degree do you and your mate live in a biblical community? In what ways are you active in a church family?

4. Do other people really know you and your marriage? When troubles arise in your marriage, to what extent do other people see and become aware of it?

5. Share a few ways that you avoid Christian fellowship and hide from the light. In what ways do you put pressure on your mate to keep your marriage struggles a secret?

6. In what ways can you as a couple contribute to biblical community?

The Ministry of Reconciliation

Though the body of Christ is certainly a blessing and help to our souls, it does not exist to serve our personal interests. God does not give His church to be a spiritual buffet for our souls to binge on. He has grafted us into the body of Christ so that each of us will serve as an individual member for the health of the whole. We are divinely gifted body parts that are knit together by the Spirit of God to embody and express the very presence of Christ on earth (see Eph. 4:14–16). The same can be said of marriage. We have been joined to our mates—not as a parasite to a host but as a Spirit-filled minister of the gospel to someone who continually needs the gospel. Together we reflect and enjoy the glory of God's grace. We accomplish this, in part, by serving as ministers of reconciliation in our marriages and churches.

> For the love of Christ controls us, having concluded this, that one died for all, therefore all died; and He died for all, so that they who live might no longer live for themselves, but for Him who died and rose again on their behalf. Therefore from now on we recognize no one according to the flesh; even though we have known Christ according to the flesh, yet now we know Him in this way no longer. Therefore if anyone is in Christ, he is a new creature; the old things passed away; behold, new things have come. Now all these things are from God, who reconciled us to Himself through Christ and gave us the ministry of reconciliation, namely, that God was in Christ reconciling the world to Himself, not counting their trespasses against them, and He has committed to us the word of reconciliation. Therefore, we are ambassadors for Christ, as though God were making an appeal through us; we beg you on behalf of Christ, be reconciled to God. He made Him who knew no sin to be sin on our behalf, so that we might become the righteousness of God in Him. (2 Cor. 5:14–21)

On the day we received Christ as Lord and Savior, we also received the ministry of reconciliation to which Paul speaks. God gave it to us as a precious, lifelong assignment. We no longer represent ourselves but live in this world to represent Jesus Christ. As citizens from another country, representing a King and kingdom of another world, we are called to offer terms of peace to a foreign people. The terms of peace are given through the gospel. At the same time, we are called to represent Christ in the lives of fellow believers, just as political ambassadors represent the interests of fellow citizens in a foreign land.

Ambassadors at Home

Consider the role of a political ambassador. There are two significant functions that ambassadors assume in their places of service. First, ambassadors live in a foreign land in order to represent the interests of their king/government and country in that foreign land. Ambassadors are concerned with bringing and promoting peace between their king and the subjects of another realm.

As ambassadors for Christ, we are called to assume this role. We are called to be evangelists. We are called to introduce people to Jesus Christ. We are called to represent the interests of our King among a people of another realm.

Ambassadors, however, serve another function in their places of service. They also care for the interests of subjects from their homeland who are currently residing inside the borders of a foreign country. Ambassadors also represent the interests of their king in the lives of their fellow citizens. They are to care for their fellow citizens and to help them to love and represent their king and homeland well.

As ambassadors for Christ, we are called to assume this role as well. We are ministers of reconciliation among the citizens of our homeland (our fellow believers) who currently live as aliens in this world. We are also ambassadors for Christ in the lives of our God-given mates.

Many of us, usually, do not view our spouses and fellow believers as ripe fields of gospel ministry. Once they profess faith in Christ, we tend to assume that they don't need any additional help seeing, believing, and living out the gospel. This can be a grave mistake in marriage. In fact, we often expect our mates to know and express the love of God without much trouble at all. We expect them, generally, to serve us well and not require too much service of their own. They should be strong, we assume, and be available to care for us the way that God instructs in His Word.

A Whole New Motivation in Life

According to 2 Corinthians 5:14, the love of Christ should now control us in life. The depth and delight of His love should motivate all that we think, feel, and do.

Paul explained why the love of Christ controls us: "One died for all, therefore all died." The death of Jesus Christ in our place, and all its implications, seizes the steering wheel of our souls. When Christ died, we died in Him. When He was raised, we were raised in Him. He surrendered His life for our salvation, and such sacrifice, by the grace of God, is very compelling. Paul knew of no other affection in human life more motivating than Christ's steadfast love—especially that love that He expressed on Calvary.

Napoleon Bonaparte made a fascinating observation about Christ and the motivation of His followers. He claimed, from his experience of human nature, that Jesus Christ is no mere man. The impact that Jesus Christ had on the souls of people, from his point of view, had transcended time and space. It was misguided, Napoleon thought, to compare Him to all the other great men of history. "Alexander, Caesar, Charlemagne, and I myself have founded great empires; but upon what did these creations of our genius depend? Upon force. Jesus Alone founded His empire upon love, and to this very day millions would die for Him."[1]

Napoleon realized that people honored and obeyed him as a leader because they would be killed if they didn't. They were motivated by his army, not his love. The same rule applied to every emperor before him. Their empires were built and sustained by force. Of course, their empires didn't last. Once these rulers were distant, displaced, or dead, people weren't motivated to serve them any longer. Napoleon

1. Quoted in Henry Parry Liddon, "Lecture III: Our Lord's Work in the World a Witness to His Divinity," in *The Divinity of Our Lord and Saviour Jesus Christ: Eight Lectures Preached before the University of Oxford, in the Year 1866* (London: Rivingtons, 1867), 222–23. In a footnote on page 224, Liddon notes that this quote is "freely translated" from French sources.

understood this and marveled at how the followers of Christ, centuries after Jesus' time on earth, being so deeply stirred by His love, were willing to give their lives for His kingdom and renown.

A growing grasp *of* the love of Christ will always produce a growing love *for* Christ. Rightly understood, it will control everything that we think, feel, and do.

We can learn from 2 Corinthians 5:15 just how Christ's love comes to control us. It happens when the Spirit of God helps us to embrace the truth and glory of a very particular message: "having concluded this, that one died for all, therefore all died" (v. 14). We become more controlled by the love of Christ by beholding and understanding the love of Christ. Seeing, marveling at, and absorbing the gospel each day surrenders us to its control. The Spirit helps in this. When the Spirit helps us to see and worship Jesus Christ, His love controls us.

The reason Jesus died for us was so that we would live for Him— and be really excited about it. We are not our own masters; Jesus is our master. We no longer seek first our own kingdom and will, but His kingdom and will. Our treasures are in heaven, not on earth.

The application to marriage, I believe, seems very clear. I am not to see marriage as a divine invention to serve my own cravings. It does not exist for the glory of my name. It exists to honor Christ.

Loving and serving our spouses should become our primary commitment in marriage. Since Christ poured out His life for us, we can pour out our lives for the eternal good of our mates. We are bond servants of Christ and ministers of the gospel.

For example, if my wife struggles with fears and anxieties about death, then I can listen to my wife's concerns (as often as they arise), pray for her peace and comfort in the Lord (daily), and speak to her (on an ongoing basis) not about the improbability of her death in the near future, because she is so young and healthy, but about God's love for her and His promises to care for her and preserve her soul through eternity. Even if her anxieties create discomfort in my own life and distractions from things I would rather be doing, being an ambassador for Christ in her life means I should see her struggles as an opportunity to minister the gospel to her soul and encourage her faith in the Lord.

We Recognize No One According to the Flesh

Not only does the gospel help us see ourselves in a new light, but it also helps us see others in a new light. The gospel transforms the way we see everyone—especially our spouses. "We recognize no one according to the flesh" (2 Cor. 5:16). This means that we no longer view our mates according to external appearance or human standards. We view them according to what God is doing in and through them. Our view of Christ is not based on His physical appearance and worldly achievements. Our view of our mates should not be based on their physical appearance and worldly achievements, either.

Please take a few moments to consider several questions about this idea.

7. In what ways are you prone to see and esteem your spouse based on his or her accomplishments in the world—such as his or her income, education, athletic ability, fashion, social status, and so on?

8. Do you relate to your spouse based on how he or she benefits your kingdom and glory, or according to how he or she serves Christ's kingdom and glory?

9. Do you define your spouse by his or her sins, or through the covering that he or she wears in Jesus Christ? Do you judge your spouse's performance, or do you delight in the way that God displays His infinite grace through your spouse?

10. How can you better appreciate the inward person of your mate? How is he or she growing to look more like Christ? How can you encourage your mate in this?

In the years I have spent counseling, I have seen men and women plunge themselves into misery and divorce because they spent the years of their marriages regarding each other according to the flesh. I have seen husbands and wives constantly judging each other by their physical appearance, career success, and quirky habits.

People feel drawn to measure other people by external appearance. I don't think any of us have to work at viewing our spouses according to the flesh. It just happens naturally.

We can silently measure the quality of our mates' performance against our personal preferences and tastes, only to find our spouses less than appealing over time. This should not surprise us. When we evaluate one another according to outward forms and to patterns of the world, only disappointment can result in the long run. Frustration and bitterness simply cannot be avoided.

God has something far better in mind for us. He wants us to look at people through a different lens. Paul says in verse 17, "If anyone is in Christ, he is a new creature; the old things passed away; behold, new things have come." Every redeemed child of God is a new creation in Christ. New things have come. Old things have passed away. And this transaction has happened in the inner person, not the outer person. This is a big reason why we are not to view and treat the children of God according to first glances or outward appearance. God is doing something spectacular in the hearts of His people. We must ask Him to help us see and appreciate His work, and the *full and complete* glory of His work will not be fully revealed until Jesus returns (see Rom. 8:18; Col. 3:4).

Marriage in the Meantime

How can we embrace our identity as ministers of the gospel toward other believers, especially in our homes and marriages?

Realize that all believers, including our spouses, need continual help in order to believe, follow, and enjoy Jesus Christ. People need help following Jesus. They need help with becoming less ruled by sin and more ruled by the Spirit of God. We tend to expect our brothers and sisters in Christ to live loving, joyful, peaceful, and thankful lives without any aid. Wrongly do we assume that people, especially our spouses, don't need ongoing assistance believing the gospel and living straightforward lives in its truth. The substance of our marriages changes drastically when we start rising every morning committed to helping our mates to trust, follow, and enjoy Jesus Christ.

Realize how constantly and deeply we need help in order to believe, follow, and enjoy Jesus Christ. Not only do other people need help trusting and obeying Christ, but we do too. We need to embrace other people messing with our lives. We need to confess sin and live in the light so that people can pray for us and counsel us. We need to delight in other sinners exposing our sinfulness. We need to delight in godly people digging around in our lives (see Ps. 141:5). Our mates are uniquely and strategically placed, probably better than anyone else on earth, to bring the corrective and comforting words of the gospel into our lives. We must make this easy for them, not difficult. Our mates should feel free to address the troubles of our lives without fear of our response.

Accept that other people, even our spouses, are sinners. When fellow believers fall into sin, act selfishly, or perhaps cause pain in my life, it is amazing how quickly I become shocked and surprised . . . then I become angry and disgusted . . . then I become condemning and accusing . . . then I become withdrawn from them or eager to make *them* stop being such an awful sinner. Perhaps I put all kinds of conditions on my fellowship with them: "I will love you and have fellowship with you if you stop being such a big sinner."

So when others treat us poorly or fail to care for us the way we think they should, we feel justified withdrawing from them, avoiding them, and becoming bitter. The idea of moving toward them in love and service, at this point, seems absolutely ludicrous. Why on earth would we move toward people who hurt us? Why would we expend energy and time on people who are so difficult for us to handle? I expect people to love me, not mistreat me. I shouldn't have to love people who don't love me well.

We need Jesus Christ to help us change these expectations. The ministry of reconciliation presumes regular dealings with sin and sinners. The very word *reconciliation* implies that someone is broken or estranged or wandering or in trouble. Embracing an identity as a minister of the gospel in marriage means that we joyfully embrace the sinfulness of our mates and their need for grace.

Accept that helping our spouses and other believers to trust and fol-low Jesus in their daily lives could be very costly to us. Gospel ministry can be very costly (see Luke 9:23–24, 57–62). Truly knowing and loving people does not usually happen quickly or easily. Helping people to trust and follow the Lord Jesus Christ takes time, energy, and constant prayer. It requires us to learn to swallow our pride. It can hurt our reputation and image. It could be emotionally agoniz-ing. People may reject our efforts or scorn our words.

Perhaps we refuse to speak the truth in love to one another because we are afraid to upset someone, lose someone's approval, or look silly. We refuse to speak the truth in love because we don't have the time to really deal with doing so or with the fallout. Our counsel to others could become a series of "do this" and "do that," or "stop this" and "stop that," without really praying and talking through how the life, death, and resurrection of Jesus Christ applies to our lives.

Perhaps we leave the actual ministry of reconciliation to other people—specialists in dealing with people's troubles, like counsel-ors and pastors—so that we can get on with activities that are more important to us.

Again, we need the Spirit of God to help us change these ways of viewing and treating marriage and the church. You are part of the church. You are called to gospel ministry. There are no human beings who are better positioned in the life of your mate in order to minister grace to him or her than you are.

Convince ourselves that enjoying and ministering the gospel with the people closest to us is a wonderful and eternal activity. When our spouses and fellow believers are struggling, we easily call these "dis-tractions from ministry." Why don't we just call it ministry, too? Why don't these kinds of moments get thrown into "ministry of the gospel"? Sadly, "distraction from ministry" is usually a code phrase for "anything that I don't want to deal with right now."

The spouse who God gives to each of us in marriage will provide the most constant, precious, and important field of gospel ministry we may ever know on earth. Our spouses need help, just as we need help. They need to understand just how deeply the Father loves them, just as we do. May the Lord strengthen our hearts to serve Him well in this field!

11. When your mate is struggling in his or her walk with Jesus Christ, and perhaps sinning against you along the way, do you move toward him or her in order to be a minister of reconciliation? Or do you fight back, defend yourself, and avoid him or her altogether? Please explain.

12. In what ways do you regard your spouse according to the flesh? What are your ways of judging him or her by external appearance or performance?

13. What do you think it would mean to see your spouse as a new creation in Jesus Christ and in the process of becoming like Jesus Christ? How could this influence the manner in which you interact with your mate every day?

Final Words

If you and your spouse have finished this book, then let me say thank you and congratulations! Of course, the key to your marriage will not be this book or the fact that you finished it. The key will be abiding in Jesus Christ and His Word with the power and grace that His Spirit supplies. It may be helpful for you and your mate to continue meeting with older men and women in your church. It may be helpful to revisit a few of the chapters you have covered in this book. Definitely don't try to run the course of marriage on your own. God has given Himself, His Word, and His church to strengthen and guide you along the way.

May He be sweeter and more precious to your souls every day! May His Word dwell in you richly and bear fruit! May the love of the Lord Jesus and the power of the Spirit and the glory of the Father rest on your precious home and marriage!

Appendix

Proposed Household Budget

Using your current income and expenses, as well as your projected income and expenses once you are married, please complete the following household budget. If you have a better tool or strategy for budget planning, then please feel free to use it instead. This document exists only to be a helpful guide in developing your budget.

A. Projected Gross Monthly Income

Once you are married, what will be your expected monthly income before any tax, gift, or insurance payments are made?

Husband's Employment	$_____
Wife's Employment	$_____
Shared Assets (properties, funds, investments, etc.)	$_____
Miscellaneous Income	$_____
Total A:	$_____

B. Monthly Giving, Taxes, Insurance, and Retirement

Items within this category may not be taken directly out of your monthly paychecks, but are often based on your gross monthly income. You may even project nothing for several of these items because you do not intend to put any monies into these categories at this time.

Giving (church, charities, missions, etc.)	$_____
Taxes (FICA, Medicare, self-employment, etc.)	$_____
Retirement (pension, 401K, 403B, Roth funds, etc.)	$_____

Health Insurance	$_____
Disability Insurance	$_____
Life Insurance	$_____
Child Support	$_____
TOTAL B:	$_____

C. Projected Net Monthly Income (A-B)

TOTAL C:	$_____

D. Projected Monthly Expenses

Please estimate the amount you intend to spend in each of the categories below. Even though several of the items may be occasional costs or yearly expenses (such as car registration), try to estimate what each item will cost if spread across every month. For example, a $60 car registration fee once a year will mean a monthly cost of $5.

1. Housing

Mortgage (principle + interest) or Rent	$_____
Property Taxes	$_____
Homeowner's or Renter's Insurance	$_____
Homeowner Association Dues	$_____
Utilities (electricity, water, sewage, etc.)	$_____
Cable, Phone, and Internet Service	$_____
Anticipated Maintenance (repairs, etc.)	$_____
Miscellaneous	$_____
TOTAL HOUSING:	$_____

2. Food, Clothing, and Household Supplies

Food	$_____
Clothing	$_____
Household Cleaning Supplies	$_____
Laundry Products	$_____
Cosmetics, Shampoo, etc.	$_____
Miscellaneous	$_____
TOTAL FOOD, CLOTHING, & HOUSEHOLD SUPPLIES:	$_____

It's never too early to work on your marriage.

GOD HAS DESIGNED MARRIAGE to be a relationship of deep unity and strength. Any husband and wife, no matter how happy, benefit when they intentionally pursue greater harmony together.

In this study for couples, biblical counselor Wayne A. Mack shows us how to meet marital challenges with growing success. Gathering a wealth of biblical insight and practical information on marital roles, communication, finances, sex, child rearing, and family worship, Mack provides a profoundly useful resource that gets to the heart of what matters.

More Counseling Resources from P&R

  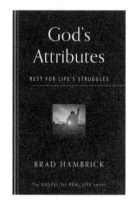

"The gospel isn't just an ethereal idea. It's not a philosophy, and it's not static. It moves and shapes and transforms the lives of those who by God's grace alone put their faith in Jesus' life, death, and resurrection. I am grateful for [the Association of Biblical Counselors]'s work of letting the gospel bear its weight on these real life sorrows and pains."

> —**Matt Chandler**, Lead Teaching Pastor, The Village Church, Flower Mound, Texas

Also in the Gospel for Real Life series:

Abuse, John Henderson

Borderline Personality, Cathy Wiseman

Burnout, Brad Hambrick

Cutting, Jeremy Lelek

Depression, Margaret Ashmore

Post-Traumatic Stress Disorder, Jeremy Lelek

Self-Centered Spouse, Brad Hambrick

Sexual Abuse, Robert W. Kelleman

Vulnerability, Brad Hambrick

3. Medical Expenses *(estimated per month)*

Deductible	$_____
Co-pays	$_____
Medication	$_____
Miscellaneous	$_____
TOTAL MEDICAL EXPENSES:	$_____

4. Transportation *(estimated per month)*

	Car 1	Car 2
Loan Payment	$_____	$_____
Insurance	$_____	$_____
Gas	$_____	$_____
Inspection & Registration	$_____	$_____
Maintenance & Repairs	$_____	$_____
Miscellaneous	$_____	$_____
Bus, Train, or Cab Fares	$_____	
TOTAL TRANSPORTATION:	$_____	

5. Savings & Debts

Allocated to Savings	$_____
Allocated to Debt (credit card fees, school loans, etc.)	$_____
TOTAL SAVINGS & DEBTS:	$_____

6. Education

College Tuition	$_____
Private School Tuition	$_____
Tutoring	$_____
Books	$_____
Miscellaneous	$_____
TOTAL EDUCATION:	$_____

7. Recreation

Eating Out	$_____
Movies/Entertainment	$_____
Travel	$_____

Fitness Club Memberships	$_____
Sport Leagues, Equipment, etc.	$_____
Newspapers, Magazine Subscriptions, Books	$_____
Babysitting	$_____
Miscellaneous	$_____
TOTAL RECREATION:	$_____

8. Special Celebrations

Birthdays	$_____
Christmas	$_____
Other Holidays	$_____
TOTAL SPECIAL CELEBRATIONS:	$_____

GRAND TOTAL D:	$_____

SUMMARY:

Projected Gross Monthly Income (A)	$_____
Monthly Giving, Taxes, Insurance, and Retirement (B)	$_____
Projected Net Monthly Income (C = A-B)	$_____
Projected Monthly Expenses (D)	$_____

E. Projected Balance at Month End (E = C-D) $_____

The goal of a healthy budget is to end the month with a balance of $0 (line E). If you have a surplus of $50 at the end of the month, then you can commit that $50 to savings, or additional giving, or some other end. If you have a shortage of $50, then you will want to decide where to cut back in order to balance the monthly budget. Please don't feel obligated to keep your budget at this level of detail or in this way. Again, this document serves to help you get a clearer sense of income and expenses so that you do not walk into marriage on foolish or ignorant financial ground.